Table of Contents

PART ONE: A DESCRIPTION OF COMPLIANCE PLANNING

PART TWO: BUSINESS RESEARCH AND ANALYSIS

PART THREE: LEGAL RESEARCH

PART FOUR: CREATING AND USING THE COMPLIANCE PLAN

Introduction

At some point, most businesses will be on the defending side of an action brought by a current or former employee. Employee complaints range from grievances to lawsuits claiming wrongful termination. Even the smallest business may find itself the subject of an employee suit.

This book attempts to provide guidance to human resource professionals and business owners about ways to protect their business from complaints brought by employees. One of the primary ways to do this is to develop and implement a compliance plan. Step-by-step guidance on formulating a compliance plan, along with suggestions designed to help businesses avoid or lessen liability throughout the employment process are contained within the chapters. This book is also meant to increase awareness of the particular federal statutes that apply to employers, and offers suggestions for complying with these statutes.

There are also sections on writing job descriptions, hiring policies and practices, discipline and termination, employer liability, union issues, workers' compensation and unemployment benefits.

The companion computer disk provides in electronic format copies of all of the checklists and forms contained within the text. These materials are intended to help the reader develop a compliance plan for their business while referencing the text.

Patricia Grzywacz, Esq.
Editorial Director
Oakstone Legal & Business Publishing

About the Author

Kevin B. Johnson is a practicing attorney with his office located in Wichita, Kansas. His practice is limited to business representation, which includes handling employment matters of all types. He also serves as a *pro tem* hearing officer for the Kansas Human Rights Commission, hearing employment discrimination cases. He speaks often on employment law issues at continuing education seminars and teaches university courses in business law.

Mr. Johnson is a 1981 graduate of Washburn University School of Law, Topeka, Kansas. He graduated from Wichita State University in 1978, earning a bachelor of arts with honors. He is admitted to the bar in Kansas, the 10th U.S. Circuit Court of Appeals, and the United States Supreme Court.

How To Use This Book

Description of Book

This book provides the information necessary for any firm to prepare and implement an employment law compliance plan. A compliance plan is an effective method for a firm to identify its areas of risk through business and legal research. This information is then used to prepare a plan to avoid and reduce the identified risks, which results in fewer problems overall and in a significant reduction in claims against the firm. Compliance planning works. It has been used effectively by Department of Defense contractors, Medicare providers, and many other firms for a number of years. In 1998, the U.S. Supreme Court decided *Faragher v. City of Boca Raton*, 524 U.S. 775, 118 S.Ct. 2275, 141 L.Ed.2d 662 (1998), in which the Court ruled against an employee who had filed a sexual harassment claim against her employer. The employer won this lawsuit because it had in place a compliance plan designed to protect its employees and itself from sexual harassment. The plan worked. The Faragher Defense, as it has come to be known, is a clear signal that an Employment Law Compliance Plan can be any employer's best defense against employee claims.

How the Book is Organized

The book has four parts, each identified and described below:

> *Part One: A Description of Compliance Planning*
> Two chapters that describe compliance planning in detail and give an overview of the steps involved in preparing a compliance plan.

> *Part Two: Business Research and Analysis*
> Three chapters which give specific instructions on what research and analysis to conduct, as well as how it should be conducted.

> *Part Three: Legal Research*
> Ten chapters that are really a book within a book. All important issues in employment law are described in text supported by case law. The major federal statutes are included with an explanation of what each statute requires, to whom it applies, and how to deal with the requirements of each statute. Discussion of state employment laws and public policy are also included.

Part Four: Creating and Using the Compliance Plan
Six chapters which explain how the compliance plan is put together, implemented within the firm, and what to do once it has been implemented.

How to Use this Book

This book has been written for use by attorneys, business consultants, compliance officers, human resource professionals, and employers who need a compliance plan. It is designed to be a "how-to" book on compliance planning without requiring that the reader be a lawyer.

A good understanding of what compliance planning is and what is involved in preparing a compliance plan is the message of Part One. This section should answer the question, "What is compliance planning and why should we use it in our firm?"

Part Two describes how to perform the firm's self-analysis. It also describes how to research and analyze competitors, the market place, and the firm's industry for industry-wide standards, but the self-analysis is the most important section in Part Two. This section should answer the questions, "What do we analyze and what are we looking for?" and, "What do we do with all this information?"

Part Three is, basically, an employment law handbook. Non-lawyers may find it useful as a source for doing much of their legal research (how to conduct legal research is explained in Part One). Lawyers should find it useful as a source for beginning and mapping out additional research. It is also a reference for use once the compliance plan is in place and operating.

Part Four describes how to actually put the firm's compliance plan together. It explains how to take the information obtained from business and legal research and make it into a compliance plan. These chapters also describe how to implement the plan and how to monitor its effectiveness. It also discusses how to identify the need to make changes and how to make and implement the necessary changes. The final chapter offers suggestions for handling various problems that can arise within the entire process.

Cost

This book gives a great deal of information on how to prepare an effective compliance plan on a wide range of budgets. Compliance planning can be done within the budget requirements of any firm, from a one-employee office to the largest firms. Any company who desires to have their own compliance plan can have one. This book is very conscious of small budgets and is written for the smaller business every bit as much as for the larger business.

CHAPTER 1
Compliance Planning: An Overview

CONTENTS

1.1 The Need for Compliance Planning

1.1(a) Definition

Compliance planning is the process of preparing, adopting, and implementing a program to help a firm come into, and remain in compliance with, the laws and regulations applicable to that firm. The compliance program may be broad-based to cover a number of issues, or it may be targeted for a specific issue of importance to the firm (such as the employer-employee relationship).

1.1(b) Description

The theme of compliance planning is that a business which understands its legal risks can plan ahead to deal with those risks. As a result, some risks can be eliminated and some risks can be reduced, often significantly. Planning to identify and reduce risk is nothing new to business, but fully exploiting the idea of legal compliance planning is too often overlooked. Instead, a common method for handling legal matters is to conduct business as normal until a legal problem is identified. The matter is then turned over to a lawyer and the lawyer handles it, giving the business advice on what it should do to resolve the problem. While this method "works," it is far from the best way of dealing with legal issues. It is like deciding to drive from New York to San Francisco. A driver can simply get into their car and begin driving. Knowing they must go west, they follow the interstate signs that take them in that direction. When gasoline is needed, they look for a service station. When hungry or tired, they look for a restaurant or a hotel. If they have car trouble, they rely on their mobile phone to call a garage, or perhaps they wait for a state trooper to stop and give assistance. This is a "plan" that will get a person across the country. However, a professional driver will not begin any trip without having first planned their route, determined when and where they will purchase fuel, food, or lodging, as well as how and where they can obtain repairs or other services that might become necessary. While there is always the potential for the unexpected, the professional will complete the trip much more efficiently than a casual driver. Even if something unexpected does occur, having become prepared for the trip enables the professional to better handle the situation.

Like planning a cross-country trip, legal compliance planning can be done by a business on its own or with the help of others (a lawyer or a business consultant). This is true for any type of business planning. Regardless of how it is accomplished, a firm that uses legal compliance planning is accepting the fact that legal problems are always possible, but that it is also possible to be ready to avoid them or to at least lessen their impact. It is like running through a forest. Even if you have run along the same path a hundred times, there is never a guarantee that your old, familiar forest path can be taken for granted. You must look ahead to avoid the fallen branch, or to jump over the hole that was not there last time, or to cope with the changed course of a stream. Planning is looking ahead. Companies plan ahead to help ensure that their products and services will find a market. Instead of taking for granted the tradition of calling the lawyer when something comes up, a business should plan ahead to know where the problems will be waiting. Then, by using this plan, the problems can either be avoided completely or diminished. Even unpleasant surprises can become less of a surprise.

Consider also the issue of profit.

Any business must make a profit if it is to continue in existence. (Even a nonprofit organization that is tax-exempt pursuant to the Internal Revenue Code must make more money than is required to pay its operational expenses. If it fails to have such "excess" income, it cannot fulfill its nonprofit purposes. Likewise, each part of all local, state, and federal governments must have enough funding to meet their respective objectives and missions.) The two primary factors that contribute to profit are income and controlling expenses. Both income and the controlling of expenses are issues realized only through planning.

When planning for income, the firm must consider a number of factors. Whether it provides products, services, or both, a business must know how to deliver the necessary quality at the necessary price and within the necessary time-frame to its customers. Acquiring and using this knowledge successfully requires effort. It is not possible to simply rely on "instinct" or to handle things only as they arise, at least not if the firm plans on having a future. (Even people with a true, natural talent for business work hard to develop and maintain that talent.) It takes investigation and research to determine what customers really want, what prices they are willing to pay, what range of quality they will accept, which marketing methods will work, how to compete with competitors, and how to successfully deal with every other issue involved in getting income. The information obtained from this investigation and research must then be organized in some fashion so it can be analyzed and used. Some information is relatively easy to obtain and use, while other information is difficult to process. One person, depending on their qualifications and the issues involved, may be able to handle much of this process on their own. It may, instead, be advisable to use the experience and talent of others within the company or to hire outside consultants. The one constant that applies to any company throughout this process, however, is the necessity to plan ahead.

The other part of the equation for making profit- controlling expenses- must also be planned for if expenses are to be less than income. If it has been determined that a particular product will generate a specific amount of income during a specific period of time (for example, $10,000 during the month of August), it is necessary to make sure the expenses of selling this product during August will not only be less than $10,000, but will be below the amount necessary to realize the planned for profit. As with planning for income, it takes investigation and research to determine the sources and amounts of cost associated with an activity. Once this information is obtained, decisions must be made and plans implemented to keep the costs at acceptable levels. Which costs can be cut? Should certain costs be increased? How will the change in costs of a particular activity affect quality, price, and sales? Is there a better way to spend our money?

It takes planning to determine all the questions to ask, how to answer them, how to use the answers, and how to set and achieve goals. The need for such business planning is readily accepted as basic knowledge required from anyone in business, as well as from students in their first undergraduate business course. The need for legal compliance planning should also be considered as basic knowledge.

1.2 The Elements of Compliance Planning

(This section describes generally the issues that are discussed in detail in Chapter 2.)

1.2(a) Key Elements of Compliance Planning

Statement of Purpose: Any compliance planning is undertaken to reduce legal risk. This, therefore, is not what would be stated as the purpose of a firm's compliance program. Instead, the firm should decide what issues it specifically intends to address with the compliance program. This statement should be brief and it must be clearly written. The chief importance of the statement of purpose is to remind those in the firm what they are trying to accomplish with the compliance program. Questions will inevitably arise over some issue or about which of available options should be pursued. There will also be times when there will be disagreement. A clear, meaningful statement of purpose can be quite helpful in reminding everyone of the central purpose of the compliance program. It may not settle all arguments, but it can at least define the relevant subject areas the argument should address.

The statement of purpose also informs others who are not a part of the firm (i.e., stockholders, attorneys, judges, and juries) what the firm means to accomplish with the particular compliance program. It can almost serve as an opening argument in the firm's defense.

Compliance Officer: Somebody must be officially designated as the person with the authority and responsibility to oversee the compliance program. The compliance officer must first be intimate with all parts of the compliance program. They must understand the requirements of the statutes and regulations that apply to the company and they must develop a relationship with those outside the company who can help explain these regulations as needed. Whenever anyone within the company has a question about the compliance program, it is the compliance officer who must provide the answer.

The compliance officer is also the person in charge of the education and training of company personnel with regard to the compliance program. Monitoring and ensuring compliance with the program, as well as determining any need to make modifications to the program, are part of this officer's duties. Finally, when an investigation, an audit, or when a claim or any type of trouble arises which is of the type contemplated by the compliance program, the compliance officer is the person in the company who takes charge of the company's response.

Depending on the size of the business, the duties of compliance officer may be fulfilled by someone whose "real" job in the business is something else or it may be a person hired specifically to handle these responsibilities. The duties of this position may even be divided between various people, as long as they have a coordinated method of working together on these issues.

Analysis of the Firm: With regard to the purposes of the compliance program, what is the firm's position within its industry, its community, and its own history? For employment law compliance planning, this portion of the program would include (among other things) a description of the firm's work force, its rate of employee turn-over, how compensation is determined, the types of grievances and claims that are made, and so on. This information would then be compared to what is known of the competition, and how it all compares to industry standards. The point is to present as accurate an analysis as possible, including both good and bad (being careful not to emphasize either good or bad out of proportion). This analysis is one portion of the compliance program that must be reevaluated on a regular basis, as it is a crucial part used in setting the policies and procedures that will become a part of the compliance program. This section is similar to the information a doctor obtains from a patient's history and from the doctor's own examination of the patient. It is all used to determine the proper treatment and maintenance plan. As the patient's condition changes over time, the course of treatment must also change.

Summary of Applicable Laws and Regulations: This section describes the nature of the laws and regulations that apply to the firm. It is not necessary, nor even advisable, to reprint the text of the applicable laws and regulations. Instead, a listing and brief description of the general purposes of the various laws and regulations would be sufficient. (However, if your attorney recommends that the full text or that a detailed description of a particular law or regulation be included in your program, follow your attorney's advice.) The purpose of this section is to identify for the business and its personnel which laws and regulations must be followed and, therefore, must be addressed by the policies and procedures of the compliance program.

Risk Assessment: An analysis of the firm's situation and of the laws and regulations applicable to the firm will reveal the areas of greatest and of least risk for the firm. The purpose of this section is not to eliminate issues from being included in compliance planning, but to become knowledgeable about your business' strengths and weaknesses. The information in this section is used to determine how to maintain strengths, and how to take action to change a weakness into an area of strength. Successful risk assessment requires honesty, as it is not much different than looking into a mirror in order to see what is really there, not just which angle is best.

The firm must determine which activities it will assess for risk. Some of the activities may be generally stated and some may be given in detail, all dependent on the sensitivity of the issue to the firm. Some scale must then be used to grade the risk of each activity. It is probably better to have a relatively simple scale, such as a "high – medium – low" risk designation, as this is often a workable scale. The firm could use a risk scale with any number of levels for risk designation it prefers, but such a scale tends to become unmanageable and impractical. Keep it simple.

Policies and Procedures: This section describes how the firm will get into and remain in compliance with the law. Existing policies and procedures that are relevant to the purpose of the compliance program would be included, as well as changed and new policies and. The most important things about this section are that the policies and procedures must be very clear, they must be relevant, and they must be practical. In other words, the policies and procedures included in this section must work.

Enforcement: What happens when it is discovered that someone is violating the compliance program? Answering this question is the purpose of this section. The answer may be as simple as giving a reminder of the applicable policy or procedure. Or, some sort of discipline may be required, which could include termination of employment. The nature of some violations may also require that a report be made to the entity the supervises the professional license of the person involved. Whatever is appropriate and necessary for enforcing the compliance program must be done. The compliance officer is responsible for enforcing compliance (or for recommending to a committee or to a board what action should be taken), and this officer cannot waiver in this responsibility. *How well the company lives up to the terms of its own compliance program is one of the criteria for evaluating its program.* If exceptions are made, if certain activities are reclassified so as not to call for required consequences, or if things are simply overlooked, the compliance program serves no purpose. On the other hand, the actions to be taken for enforcement of a compliance program do not need to be a list of specific remedies. It could be quite proper to state, "action will be taken as appropriate." The important issue in enforcement is not to establish a police state, but to have a method for enforcing the compliance program consistently and reasonably.

Training and Education: The only way to be sure that anyone knows anything about the compliance program is to train and educate people. Every person who is hired should be trained in the compliance program as part of their orientation procedure. Each person should also be required to attend an in-house seminar on a regular basis (at least once a year) at which they will be reminded of the requirements of the compliance program. This regular review can also include testing, designed to demonstrate the effectiveness of the training program. Everyone must know what is expected under the compliance program, in order to avoid an exercise in futility.

Auditing Compliance: Every company should audit themselves on a regular basis to determine how well they are complying with their compliance program. This should be an honest and objective audit. If possible, an outside consultant may be used to conduct parts or all of the audit.

The fact that regular audits will be conducted should be stated in the compliance program. While it may not be necessary to describe the precise audit procedure to be used, describing the types of things that an audit will include can be helpful. Such things as interviews with personnel, reviews of records, interviews of customers and other stakeholders, and a comparison of actual practices to those described in the compliance program are examples of typical methods for gathering information to be used in the audit.

Once information has been gathered, it must be analyzed. A determination must be made about whether the company is following its compliance program, whether the compliance program is working, and whether changes are needed. When the analysis is complete, recommendations must be made for any changes or other action to be taken. The recommendations should then be acted upon.

1.2(b) The Research Necessary for Compliance Planning

Two types of research are necessary: 1) Legal research, to determine which laws and regulations must specifically be a part of the compliance program; and, 2) Business research, to determine how things are actually being done in your own company and how this compares with your competition and with industry standards.

Legal Research: While legal research is best when conducted by an attorney, it is not necessary to be an attorney to research the law. Most employment law is set out in state and federal statutes. These statutes are written, debated, voted on, and enacted by state legislatures (state statutes) and by the U.S. Congress (federal statutes). The members of the various state legislatures and of Congress are not all lawyers. In fact, some legislatures are mostly non-lawyers and include business people, teachers, farmers, doctors, accountants, and anyone who was successful in being elected. Therefore, if the principal source of employment law is largely written and enacted by people who are not lawyers, people who are not lawyers should be capable of reading and understanding this law.

The goal of legal research in preparing and maintaining an employment law compliance program is to know what laws and regulations apply to your company. This research could, of course, be turned over to an attorney and the legal opinion received can become the basis for this section of the compliance plan. This research could also be conducted by the owner of the business, by someone in the company besides an owner, or by a non-lawyer business consultant. However, it is advisable to have the results of legal research conducted by a non-lawyer reviewed by a lawyer in order to have a legal opinion on the matter. The company sends a signal to the world (which includes opposing attorneys and judges) by the way it prepares its compliance planning. The world might conclude that the company is "somewhat serious" about its legal research merely because it has conducted legal research, but that it is not "serious" about the issue if it does not have a licensed, legal expert (an attorney) participating in the legal research.

Legal research without an attorney can be conducted in several ways:

- Refer to a publication written by an attorney (such as this book). Part III of this book contains a detailed description of state and federal employment law. It is included in this book for the purpose of assisting in the preparation of a compliance program.

- Professional newsletters prepared by a legal publisher for both attorneys and non-attorneys can be especially useful. Such newsletters contain a number of articles discussing various issues all within the same area of the law, such as employment law. Newsletters are generally released monthly, bi-monthly, or quarterly. Whichever schedule is followed, a newsletter is certain to be a good source of timely information.

- Legal websites can be excellent sources of information for legal research. However, be careful to determine the qualifications of the author of any site you study. While it is not so important who sponsors the site, the author should be an attorney or a judge. Some of the best websites for legal research are sponsored and prepared by legal publishers, law schools, law firms, and government agencies.

- Trade publications often contain articles addressing legal issues of particular interest to subscribers.

- Business magazines and newspapers can be a good source for all types of information, including legal issues. However, even when written by an attorney, articles in these types of publications tend to be summaries of a legal issue that is currently newsworthy. Useful information can be found in these articles, but they are not generally written as a source for legal research. Instead, they are news articles. However, a new development in a legal issue can be learned from these articles, which then allows for actual legal research to begin on that issue.

■   Be aware of anecdotes from others, even from trusted business associates. Legal research is done with *written* materials, not from an oral tradition.

However legal research is to be accomplished, remember that it is research of the law. It will be necessary to read statutes and cases. Books and newsletters will contain these statutes and cases, along with the citations of each to enable anyone to read the actual statute or the actual case. Finding, reading and evaluating differing opinions about how a law should be interpreted is also a part of legal research. Some legal issues have no room for argument (i.e., under Title VII of the Civil Rights Act of 1964, race can never be a legitimate basis for any employment decision). Many legal issues, however, do have plenty of room for argument. Even if a particular law is well understood and has a strong consensus in how it should be interpreted, its application to a specific set of facts may cause legitimate argument. In addition, one should never forget that the American legal system is an adversarial system. It is the nature of our legal system that differing opinions are expected with regard to many legal issues. Care must be taken to be thorough when conducting legal research.

Business Research: The business research necessary for compliance planning is to enable a company to know itself with regard to its own identity and history, its competition, and the industry or field of business in which it operates. It is not broad-based research, however. It is, instead, research that is focused by the statement of purpose in the firm's compliance program. For employment law compliance planning, the issues to be researched by the firm might include:

I.   The Firm's Identity and History

   A. Current employment policies and procedures, including written and unwritten.

   B. Whether and how written job descriptions are used.

   C. What it is like to work for this company.

   D. The types and nature of employee grievances, complaints and claims.

   E. Any particular problems involving employees.

F. What employees are happiest or proudest of in this company.

G. What positions are most difficult to fill and why.

H. What positions are the easiest to fill and why.

I. Why do employees leave?

J. Why do people apply for positions with this company?

K. How are qualifications for positions in this firm set?

L. How are hiring, promotion, changes in responsibility, discipline, termination, and other employment decisions made?

M. What employment laws apply to this company?

II. Comparison of the Firm to Competition

A. With regard to the above issues, one by one, how does this company compare to the practices and characteristics of its closest competition?

B. Since this information may not be readily available from the competition, a certain amount of observation and other research must be undertaken to make conclusions about the competition.

C. Take a position on whether this company or the competition has a better way of handling the relevant issues. If issues are handled in a similar manner, is it really the best method for doing things?

D. If differences in how relevant issues are handled are found, are there one or more reasons for distinguishing why these differences are the result of truly different circumstances between this company and the competition?

E. Do different employment laws apply to the competition than to this company (this can be an actual issue, depending on number of employees, whether or not government contracts are involved, whether or not the competition is located in a different state, or whether your company or the competition is engaged in other activities that have other applicable regulations).

III. Comparison of the Firm to Industry Standards

   A. Determine any applicable industry standards. Verify that these are actually current standards (can they be derived from a formal code of ethics adopted by an industry association or other organization; are they formal, written standards from such an organization; are they mandates from a government agency which has regulatory authority over the industry, etc.).

   B. Determine how this company's practices compare to industry standards.

   C. Determine how the competition's practices (if different than this company's) compare to industry standards.

   D. What is the reason(s) for any deviation by this company and/or the competition from industry standards?

   E. Are there potential consequences (whether formal or informal) for any deviation from industry standards? Consider such consequences from a governing body, a regulatory agency, from the rest of the industry, from competition, from employees, from customers, from the community, and from others who deal with this company.

   F. Take a position on whether this company or the competition has a better way of handling the relevant issues in comparison to industry standards. If issues are handled in a similar manner, is it really the best method for doing things?

   G. If differences in how relevant issues are handled are found, are there one or more reasons for distinguishing why these differences are the result of truly different circumstances between this company and the basis for the industry standards?

IV. Other Factors

   A. Are there additional factors that affect employment decisions of this firm?

      1. The use of employment contracts;

      2. Involvement of labor unions;

      3. Community issues;

      4. The economy (locally, regionally, nationally, or internationally);

      5. Current events (local, regional, national, or international);

B. Are there factors within the company that affect employment decisions?

   1. Change in business planning;

   2. Change in ownership;

   3. Change in the marketplace;

   4. The nature of the firm's business;

   5. The firm's own ethics and philosophy (whether formal or informal);

   6. The firm's financial situation.

As with legal research, business research must be as thorough as possible, but it must be focused within the relevant subject matter.

1.2(c) Whether to Hire Outside Help to Prepare a Compliance Program

Any firm should be involved in the preparation of their own compliance program. A firm may choose to handle the entire process itself, or it may work with consultants (including attorneys), but it should not simply turn the matter over to consultants. Compliance planning is a personal process. While much of the structure and some of the features of compliance planning may be similar from firm to firm, the detail and the elements that make a compliance program successful are unique to each firm. This detail, this uniqueness that will make the program work, can only be achieved if the firm is actively involved.

It is possible for an employer to prepare and implement a compliance program entirely in-house. Whether small, medium, or large, a business may decide to handle their compliance planning entirely on their own. A decision to do this is not necessarily good or bad. The key is to do it properly and to devote the necessary resources to the project. It is a big mistake to make this decision solely because it saves the cost of hiring a consultant. Instead, consider the following factors:

■ There must be someone in the company who is willing to take the time necessary to be in charge of creating the compliance program.

■ Whoever is selected (appointed, volunteered, etc.) to handle the compliance planning within the firm will have significantly less time to devote to other responsibilities, at least until the compliance plan is implemented.

- The company must have access to the resources necessary to know how to create the compliance program.

- It is necessary to objectively evaluate information gathered about the company. This can be more difficult than it seems, as it often requires admitting to weaknesses that may be hard to accept. It also requires that all information be considered for what it is, not that any of it be re-cast into a better form. It requires the ability to look into a mirror and see the blemishes along with the beauty, as well as not minimizing or exaggerating what is seen.

- Every business has knowledge of itself and of customers that is confidential and that must remain so. It often seems that the best way to preserve confidentiality is to reveal nothing to anyone except for in-house personnel. There is legitimacy in this position; however, professional consultants always operate under a legal duty to preserve their client's confidential information. This is a duty that is enforceable in court against the consultant in the unlikely event it is violated. Furthermore, there is no guarantee that company personnel will always preserve the confidential nature of information they have. In fact, there is likely to be less recourse against an employee for the unauthorized release of confidential information than against a professional consultant.

- In-house personnel are more likely than anyone else to fully understand and appreciate the firm's history, goals, position in the marketplace, community relations, and other intimate factors about the firm. A consultant can obtain this information, but there is a difference between being a part of the organization and being an "outsider" hired to come in and do something for the organization.

- The compliance planning process can be intrusive. This may be easier to put up with from an "insider" than from an "outsider."

- A consultant will charge a fee for their services. The amount of this fee varies depending on who the consultant is, how much of the process they will be handling, the length of time they will be involved, the size of the firm, the nature of the firm's business (i.e., whether it is highly regulated, routinely engaged in complex transactions, or a high-risk business, etc.), and other factors which the consultant will identify. Consultant's fees can become expensive, although they are usually well earned.

- Not using a consultant, or a limited use of a consultant, may save consultant's fees, but it is not necessarily a total elimination of cost (even though it may be a better option to control cash flow). Without a consultant the process usually takes longer, errors may be made that would not have been made, and a certain amount of frustration may be experienced.

- Whatever the size of your company, any consultant hired will be working closely with one or more persons in your company. Consider who these people are likely to be, consider the personal dynamics of your company, consider whether a consultant can successfully work with these people and within the "personality" of your company. Some firms simply work better with consultants than others.

An evaluation of the above factors should be helpful in deciding whether to hire a consultant and in determining the amount of involvement the consultant should have in the compliance planning process. As stated at the beginning of this section, the firm must expect to be involved in the creation of its compliance program, regardless of how much use is made of consultants. Never hire a consultant who claims to be able to do everything with only minimal involvement by the company.

Although many companies will be able to successfully create their own employment law compliance program, it is recommended that an attorney be hired to review your analysis of applicable legal issues. This is simply buying a little insurance.

1.2(d) Estimating Costs

The best thing for a particular business is worthless if it is unaffordable. Whether something is unaffordable depends on the situation of the business in question. Fortunately, there are options in implementing a compliance planning program that allow any business to afford their own program. This section will identify the types of costs that will be part of the total cost of creating and implementing a compliance program (although not every cost identified in this section must be incurred by every business; it all depends on each firm's situation and budget). Costs of compliance planning include both actual expenses and the amount of time personnel or other resources will not be available for other duties or projects. In order to have the proper resources necessary to create and implement an effective compliance program, it is necessary to identify: a) the resources that will be needed; b) how much or how many of these resources will be needed; and, c) when these resources will be needed.

The types of resources and costs that can be a part of compliance planning include:

Compliance Planning Publications: Written materials describing compliance planning and how it is done (such as this book). Whether a firm plans to do their own compliance program or to rely heavily on consultants, the firm should begin by educating itself about compliance planning. This information is available from a number of sources, including trade associations, government agencies, business magazines, trade journals, books and the Internet.

Seminars: There may be seminars, classes, or other meetings about compliance planning that a firm may find beneficial. While not a necessary part of preparing a compliance program, seminars can be an excellent source of information and contacts regarding the process.

The Time of the Firm's Owners, Managers, and/or Administrators: While not an additional cash expense, the decisionmaker(s) of the firm must budget their time for various meetings, including: deciding whether to proceed with compliance planning; creating and implementing the compliance program; receiving reports and other information about the program during its creation and implementation; and, other activities as necessary to make sure everything is handled properly.

Compliance Officer: Someone must be appointed or hired as the project manager for the creation and implementation of the compliance program. Whether this is an additional cash expense or the assignment of duties to someone already on the payroll is up to the firm. Even if consultants are hired to handle everything, there must be somebody from the firm designated as the project manager to oversee the work of the consultants and to be the liaison between the consultants, management, and others who may be involved.

Office Support Staff: The time of employees of the firm may be required to gather information, prepare reports or other documents and papers, and to conduct their normal activities but for the purpose of creating and implementing the compliance program. Unless overtime pay results or the need to hire temporary help arises, this is not ordinarily an additional cash expense, but a different allocation of current employees' time.

Materials Expense: This would include the use of office supplies, photocopying, printing, binding, computer time, use of phone lines, long distance charges, and so on. Depending on the size of the firm this expense may not be too significant, but it is an expense to budget.

Consultant's Fees and Expenses: The amount of these costs is entirely dependent on how much use is made of consultants. It also depends on who the consultants are and how they determine their fees and expenses. Whether to incur these expenses is solely up to the firm. If the decision is made to hire one or more consultants, hire them as carefully as you would for any other project. Determine, as much as possible, how much the consultant will cost before agreeing to hire one. At the very least, the firm must clearly understand (and have in writing) how the consultant determines his or her fees and expenses, as well as how these are billed and to be paid.

Attorneys' Fees: The amount of these fees is entirely dependent on how much use is made of an attorney. An attorney may be hired as the consultant to create and implement the compliance program, or to give legal opinions about the program as it is being prepared and implemented, or simply to review specific portions of the program (such as the portions concerned with the law and legal matters). An attorney is a consultant, so the above paragraph would also apply to the cost of using an attorney. However, it is recommended that even the smallest firm with the simplest compliance program hire an attorney to review the program. Having a written legal opinion (as well as complying with recommendations in the opinion) can be very helpful in establishing the credibility of the compliance program with a court.

Training of Personnel: Company personnel, whether one person or thousands, is a crucial part of compliance planning. A firm can control this expense by the method adopted for carrying out this training, although the firm should be careful not to choose an ineffective method just to save money. The types of expenses involved in training include: use of facilities, preparation of materials to be used in the training, any cost for the use of consultants or others to conduct the training, and the payment of wages of company personnel for attending the training (if they are employees who are covered by the Fair Labor Standards Act of 1938 -minimum wage and hour laws- and their training takes place at any time other than their usual hours of work).

Ongoing Review of the Compliance Program: This includes the salary paid (or allocated) for the firm's compliance officer (whether someone hired for the purpose or a current employee who is given this responsibility), any additional consultant's and attorney's fees, any seminar and/or publication fees, and ongoing training of new and current personnel in the compliance program.

Miscellaneous: There are always cash expenses in every project that are not anticipated or that do not easily fit in another account. A firm should be able to estimate the amount of such miscellaneous expenses by examining the rest of their budget. Miscellaneous expenses should not exceed 2% to 5% of the total amount budgeted for creating and implementing the compliance program. If it is any higher, the budgeting process may need to be re-examined.

Overhead Allocation: While this is not a cash expense, it is a common expense item added by many firms to their products, services and other activities. Overhead allocation is definitely an expense for budgeting purposes, but it is unwise to base the compliance planning decision solely on the addition of this item to the budget.

1.2(e) Implementing and Maintaining a Compliance Plan Over Time

A compliance program is implemented once it has been prepared. The purposes, policies and procedures of the program must be successfully communicated to all company personnel. This includes owners who are involved in operations, as well as all personnel from top to bottom of the firm's hierarchy. Different methods of informing and training the different personnel in the company may be used, but the firm must determine (as a part of the creation of the program) what methods are most likely to be successful with all personnel.

Monitoring a compliance program is necessary to verify that it is as effective as possible. The specific goals of monitoring the program are: a) to make sure the compliance program is actually in place and is actually being used and followed; and, b) to make sure the compliance program is effectively addressing areas of risk. The actual steps to be included in the process of monitoring the compliance program should include:

- Constant monitoring of laws and regulations that affect the organization.

- Review of the actual compliance program.

- Periodic audits of company records to ensure they are in compliance.

- Periodic audits of company procedures as they are actually being followed.

- Solicitation of comments and recommendations from personnel regarding the effectiveness of the compliance program.

- Evaluation of the effectiveness of procedures within the compliance program for dealing with known or anticipated risk, as well as with any unusual problems that arise.

The findings from the above steps must be put in writing. These written findings can then form the basis for feed back to appropriate personnel. This feedback is necessary to enable those involved to learn their effectiveness with the compliance program. As necessary, these written findings will also form the basis for justifying any discipline or termination of personnel. Equally important, the written findings from monitoring the compliance program will serve as a series of benchmarks that can be compared over time to establish a pattern of compliance for the organization. This allows the organization to compare its progress to itself, as well as to competition and to industry standards.

Another key element of monitoring the compliance program is to prepare written recommendations based on the findings. These recommendations will form the basis for any and all modifications to be made to the compliance program.

1.3 Summary

Compliance planning is a system prepared and adopted by a company (of any size or type) to help it come into and remain in compliance with the laws and regulations applicable to the company. Employment law compliance planning is a compliance program specifically designed to identify risk to the employer, to determine how to best handle this risk, and to adopt and implement procedures that deal with this risk. Compliance planning is preventive maintenance. The idea is to determine likely problems before they occur and to take steps to eliminate, avoid, or to at least diminish the consequences of the problems.

Compliance planning works. Companies who have government contracts with the U.S. Department of Defense have been committed to compliance planning for a number of years because it significantly lessens their potential for liability from issues of contract performance, government regulation, and employment issues. Likewise, the health care industry has become committed to compliance planning in order to significantly lessen their liability from violation of Medicare and Medicaid regulations. All companies benefit from tax planning in order to reduce the risk of audits and violations of the Internal Revenue Code, as well as of state tax regulations. Individuals benefit from estate planning in order to pass their property to their heirs with a minimum of tax liability. Business benefits from marketing research and planning in order to lessen the risk of failure when it produces, advertises, and attempts to sell products and services. The passengers and crew of an airliner benefit because their flight plan has been thoroughly analyzed and planned to reduce risk and is also monitored throughout the flight to ensure risk remains under control. Those on board the *S.S. Titanic* had the benefit of a well-planned course across the Atlantic Ocean, but they suffered greatly when their ship's progress and compliance with this plan was not properly monitored. Ford Motor Company did extensive research and planning before it introduced the Edsel, but their planning was flawed. A project based on poor research and planning, as well as on poor monitoring of results, was the Susan B. Anthony Dollar Coin. As well as compliance planning works, a poor plan will not work and may even be worse than no plan.

CHAPTER 1: COMPLIANCE PLANNING, AN OVERVIEW

An effective compliance program results in several definite benefits to the company, including:

a) Personnel are more knowledgeable about any legal and regulatory requirements that apply to their company;

b) Personnel have a better understanding of the reasons for the paperwork and procedures they must use (even if they never learn to like or to even agree with such things);

c) Effectiveness of communication within the company increases;

d) Quality of record keeping increases;

e) The likelihood of successfully completing any audit or examination by a government agency, accreditation organization, or other entity increases; and,

f) In general, the risk of liability from noncompliance with the law, or negligence.

Compliance planning is not, however, a cure for all problems. While a good compliance program will definitely accomplish the above listed things, it will not make unqualified or incompetent personnel better. Other characteristics a compliance plan does not have include:

1) The same compliance plan will not work for all companies. While there are features common to many compliance programs, each program should be custom made.

2) Features of a compliance program such as length, number of issues addressed, number of procedures described, and overall format do not correspond to the effectiveness of the program. A good compliance program may be simple or complex, depending on the needs of the company. The true test of effectiveness is whether the compliance program aids the company in its compliance with applicable laws, regulations, and other issues. It must actually reduce risk.

3) A good compliance program, by itself, guarantees nothing. A commitment to the program is required for any real degree of success.

An employment law compliance program is an effective tool for coming into and remaining in compliance with the laws and regulations that apply to an employer. Compliance planning can reduce the risk of exposure to civil and criminal penalties, as well as to sanctions that may be imposed for violations of the law. While a compliance program will not cure every problem, it is a very effective system for confronting and handling problems that may be faced by employers. This point has been verified by the U.S. Supreme Court in two significant employment law cases decided in 1998. In each case, the employer was charged with sexual harassment, but each employer

17

had in place a plan for handling sexual harassment. These plans had been developed as specialized compliance programs to identify sexual harassment, the types of conduct that could amount to sexual harassment, and how to report complaints of harassment. Specific procedures where set up by each employer to deal with reports of harassment (which included investigation and appropriate action). In one case the employer did not follow its compliance program exactly and was found liable for damages, but not to the extent they would have been liable had they had no program in place. The other employer successfully defended itself on the basis of its compliance program. The Supreme Court stated in one of these decisions:

> ". . . a defending employer may raise an affirmative defense to liability or damages, subject to proof by a preponderance of the evidence ... The defense comprises two necessary elements: (a) that the employer exercised reasonable care to prevent and correct promptly any sexually harassing behavior [in other words, the employer has and uses an effective compliance program], and (b) that the plaintiff employee unreasonably failed to take advantage of any preventive or corrective opportunities provided by the employer or to avoid harm otherwise.

> ...

> If the victim could have avoided harm, then no liability should be found against an employer who has taken reasonable care, and if damages could reasonably have been mitigated, then no award against a liable employer should reward a plaintiff for what her own efforts could have avoided."

Faragher v. City of Boca Raton, 524 U.S. 775, 118 S.Ct. 2275, 141 L.Ed.2d 662 (1998). See also *Burlington Industries, Inc. v. Ellerth*, 524 U.S. 742, 118 S.Ct. 2257, 141 L.Ed.2d 633 (1998).

Therefore, an effective compliance program that is actually used fulfills an employer's affirmative obligation to prevent violations and gives credit to employers who make reasonable efforts to discharge their duty, and, no liability should be found against an employer who has taken reasonable care if the result would have been the avoidance of harm to the employee, and, even if an employer is found to have some liability, the award of damages against that employer will be reduced to the degree that harm is not suffered by the employee or would not have been suffered had the employee, him or herself, complied with the program. Employment law compliance planning works.

CHAPTER 2
Compliance Planning Details

CONTENTS

2.1 Structure of the Compliance Plan

Section 1.2(a) in Chapter 1 of this book lists and describes the Key Elements of Compliance Planning in a narrative format. This section sets out the structure of the employment law compliance plan in an outline format. However, the information in this section is taken directly from Section 1.2(a) of Chapter 1.

Employment Law Compliance Plan:

I. STATEMENT OF PURPOSE

    A. Describes what the firm intends to accomplish with its compliance plan. The particular issues addressed in the plan are identified.

    B. The firm must include a statement of its commitment to its compliance plan.

        1. The firm's mission statement or general philosophy, as it relates to this issue, can be included here.

        2. The firm's code of ethics, or a code of professional or industry ethics applicable to the firm, can also be included here.

II. COMPLIANCE OFFICER

    A. An individual or a committee of personnel in the firm must be appointed and given the responsibility of overseeing, operating and monitoring the compliance program. This entity will report directly to the firm's chief executive officer, owner, board of directors, managing partner or other governing body.

        1. The compliance officer, whether an individual or a committee, should be physically located at the firm and should also be an employee or owner. An on-site insider is the best choice.

        2. Depending on the size and budget of the firm, the compliance officer can be someone hired specifically for this position, or it can be one or more people who handle this responsibility along with their other responsibilities.

III. ANALYSIS OF THE FIRM – A SELF-ANALYSIS

A. Compliance planning always begins with determining exactly where a firm stands at the time of the analysis.

    1. What are the characteristics of the firm's work force?

    2. What is it like to be employed by the firm?

    3. How does the firm's status on employment issues compare to its competition and to industry standards?

    4. What is the firm's history with regard to employment issues? What trends exist?

B. The self-analysis must be accurate and include the good with the bad. However, neither good nor bad points should be emphasized out of proportion or out of context. The goal is a thorough, objective analysis.

IV. EMPLOYMENT LAWS THAT APPLY TO THE FIRM

A. Determine which state employment statutes, as well as which state employment administrative rules and regulations apply to the firm and its employees.

B. Determine which federal employment statutes, as well as which administrative rules and regulations apply to the firm and its employees.

C. Determine which employment related "public policies" apply to the firm. Public policy is a source of law on many issues, including employment law. Unfortunately, public policy issues are sometimes difficult to accurately define, although they are based on statutes and applicable case law. Public policy is the way a firm should do things, even when there are no laws directly requiring things to be done that way.

V. RISK ASSESSMENT

A. By applying the applicable employment laws to a firm's current situation (as determined from its self-analysis), a firm can determine its strengths and weaknesses in employment law issues.

B. Areas of strength should be maintained. Procedures and policies that help create strengths may be adapted to improve areas of weakness.

C. Areas of weakness should be analyzed to determine the causes.

    1. These are areas of risk which should be assessed or graded on some scale (i.e., high risk, medium risk, low risk).

D. By knowing its areas of low to high risk, a firm can determine where and how to focus efforts for improvement. It also knows where trouble is most likely to occur, which is helpful in working to prevent trouble from occurring or from worsening.

VI. POLICIES AND PROCEDURES

A. How the firm will come into compliance with employment law and how it will stay in compliance with employment law.

    1. Likely to include existing employment policies and procedures.

    2. Also likely to include modified or new policies and procedures.

VII. ENFORCEMENT

A. Policies and procedures that are adopted must actually be used and followed.

B. How well a firm lives up to the terms of its own compliance program is one of the criteria for evaluating its program.

C. Courts often conclude that a company which does not follow its own policies and procedures is in a worse position than a company with no policies and procedures.

(In other words, a judge might say, "I can understand why that other firm fell apart, they didn't know what they were doing. But you had analyzed your situation, you knew the rules, and you had procedures in place. You knew what you were doing, yet you ignored your own knowledge. It's no wonder you fell apart. Judgment of Biblical proportions is entered against the firm!")

VIII. TRAINING AND EDUCATION

A. The only way to be sure that anyone knows about the compliance program is to train and educate people.

    1. Every newly hired employee must be trained in their part of the compliance program as part of their orientation process.

    2. Current employees must receive training on a regular basis, such as annually.

    3. Owners of the firm, executives, administrators and managers must also be trained on a regular basis, such as annually.

    4. Independent contractors and other non-employees who work with the firm must be trained in their part of the compliance program.

B. All personnel in the firm must know what is expected under the compliance program.

IX. AUDITING COMPLIANCE

A. A firm must audit themselves on a regular basis.

B. Information gathered from the audit must be analyzed.

    1. Determine how well the firm is following its own compliance program.

    2. Determine whether the compliance program is working.

    3. Determine whether any modifications to the compliance program should be made, as well as the nature of any necessary modifications.

C. Recommendations based on the results of the audit should be made to the firm.

    1. The firm must determine what action to take, then it must take the action.

2.2 Specific Steps in Preparing the Compliance Plan

2.2(a) Statement of Purpose

This statement should describe the overall objective to be accomplished by the compliance plan, as well as the main goals of the plan.

The most practical purpose of this statement is to create a document that serves both as a guide and a reminder of the main purpose and goals of the compliance program. This guide and reminder can then be used while the program is being prepared and implemented. It is easy to lose sight of the compliance program's purpose as it is being created. It can become tempting to take short-cuts or to become side-tracked. There may be times of confusion and frustration during the development of an effective compliance program. Every so often it will be necessary to ask, "now, why are we doing this?" The statement of purpose should be able to answer this and similar questions. A good statement will serve as the right tool for focusing all efforts during the creation and implementation of the compliance plan.

Ideally, the statement of purpose is written by the person who will become the firm's compliance officer. However, the decision of who to appoint to this position is not likely to have been made this early in the process. Therefore, the person in the firm who is most familiar with the firm's operations, problems, known risks, and with the concerns of the firm's owners and stakeholders becomes the next choice. If there is not one person who has all this knowledge, someone should be appointed to determine these issues – or to at least have access to the best sources for this knowledge – who will then become the person to write the statement of purpose. Another option is to appoint a committee for this purpose. If this option is selected, the committee should be as small as possible. It should also be composed of people who have knowledge of the firm's operations and who have access to needed information. One person should be appointed as the clearly designated leader of the committee. The leader's main job is to keep things moving. The leader must also have the necessary authority to settle and resolve disputes that may arise, as well as to make decisions in the event the committee is unable to reach a consensus. (Always keep in mind the profound affliction that is a potential threat to anything assigned to a committee, *Death by Committee*.)

A professional consultant may also be hired to prepare the statement of purpose (as well as to develop the entire compliance plan). If this is done, it is important to appoint someone as the liaison between the consultant and the firm. It is also important to allow the consultant complete access to necessary materials. A good consultant will know exactly what he or she needs and will go over these matters with the firm before accepting the job.

Upon completion of the statement of purpose, it should be formally approved by the same procedure used by the firm to formally approve anything binding on the firm. This signals the firm's commitment to the statement and to the compliance plan.

2.2(a)(1) Contents of the Statement of Purpose

Each firm must prepare its own statement of purpose for its employment law compliance plan. One size does not fit all; however, there are general points that should be common to any statement of purpose. These include:

(1) The firm's philosophy about its relationship with its employees. This philosophy can incorporate the firm's general mission statement to show this issue is a part of the firm's overall purpose for existing;

(2) Whether as separate statements or incorporated into the firm's philosophy or other portions of this statement, the following points must be made:

   (a) The firm is committed to ethical and legal business practices (the firm's code of ethics may be included at this point, or it may be included as an attachment);

   (b) The firm is committed to refusing to participate in any unethical or illegal activities, either directly or indirectly;

   (c) The firm is committed to complying with all applicable employment laws, rules, and regulations;

   (d) The firm is committed to using internal standards and procedures that are consistent with its employment philosophy and in complying with employment law;

(3) The general and specific goals to be fulfilled by the employment law compliance plan. This section should be very straight-forward and not written as if it is to be inscribed in an eternal book of noble ideals. Some of these goals may change over time. The statement of purpose is meant to be a working document useful in day-to-day operations. Any lay person should be able to read and understand what the firm is attempting to accomplish with the plan.

Form 2.1
Compliance Plan Statement of Purpose

Prairie Shark Ltd.* is a legal consulting firm. Our mission is to provide exactly the information needed by our clients, exactly when our clients need this information. This is only possible with competent and committed personnel; thus, our priority is to attract and keep only the best professionals. We have, therefore, developed this Compliance Program in order to ensure the best possible environment for our personnel to build their careers. As the first part of our Compliance Program, this firm is committed to these principles:

(a)   The standards required of the Code of Professional Responsibility for Attorneys and for all legal professionals and personnel;

(b)   A refusal to participate in any unethical or illegal activities, either directly or indirectly;

(c)   Full compliance with all applicable employment laws, rules, and regulations; and,

(d)   The use of internal standards and procedures that are consistent with these principles.

The mission of our firm, as well as the careers of our personnel, will best be fulfilled by practices and procedures that accomplish the following:

❑   Knowing what the law expects from this firm as an employer;

❑   Having and using effective, written job descriptions for all positions;

❑   Having a hiring process that focuses on the abilities of applicants;

❑   Having an evaluation process that measures performance;

❑   Avoiding unlawful discrimination, including successful anti-harassment policies;

❑   Avoiding disputes over compensation and benefit issues; and,

❑   Avoiding problems that can arise when an employee resigns, is terminated, or leaves the firm for any reason.

We are a legal consulting firm and we want to focus on taking care of our clients. This Compliance Plan will allow us to ensure the environment we need to fulfill our mission. It will also allow our personnel to know that this environment truly is important and will be maintained properly.

Approved by:_____   Date:_____

*While this is the actual name and description of a corporation owned by the author, all other information presented in this form is fictitious and is included only for purposes of illustrating contents of this type of form.

2.2(b) The Schedule and Budget for the Compliance Plan

Since time and resources will be necessary for the creation and implementation of the compliance plan, a schedule and a budget should be prepared. This can be done by the same person, committee, or consultant who prepared the statement of purpose. While the schedule and the budget need to be prepared at the beginning of the compliance planning process, they can be prepared at the same time as the statement of purpose, or after the statement has been prepared and approved.

Preparing the Schedule:

One of the real values of a written schedule is that it sets deadlines. It seems to be a fact of life that nothing much is accomplished unless there is a deadline to meet. Deadlines also serve as milestones for measuring progress of the project.

The actual format used for the schedule should be the same as for other schedules used by the firm. There is no real reason to devise new schedule formats or procedures, or to do anything that will make this process complicated. As much as possible, use what is familiar and what has already been proven effective. Whatever scheduling format is used, however, the schedule should: a) describe the various tasks to be accomplished, b) state who has primary responsibility for making sure the task is successfully completed on time, and, c) state the date by which each task is to be completed.

Preparing the Budget:

Budgets are, of course, necessary to make sure sufficient resources are made available to meet the needs of the firm. In order to have the proper resources necessary to create and implement an effective compliance program, identify, a) the resources that will be needed, b) how much or how many of these resources will be needed, and, c) when these resources will be needed.

Preparation of the budget at the same time as the schedule generally works out well, as the demands of one typically coincide with the requirements of the other. When both the schedule and the budget are completed, they should be approved by the same process used to approve the schedules and budgets of other projects.

2.2(c) Compliance Officer Job Description

At some point, the firm must decide who will be in charge of the compliance program. Even if most of the responsibility is to be handled by a consultant, someone in the firm must be designated as the contact person for the consultant. This same person must also become the in-house expert on the firm's compliance program.

The firm has options in appointing a compliance officer:

1) A full time compliance officer can be hired. This person will have no other responsibility within the firm except those responsibilities related to being in charge of the compliance program.

2) A part time compliance officer can be appointed or hired. This could include someone hired as the compliance officer, but the position is a part time job and there would be no other responsibilities. It could also be a person hired, or already with the firm, who has other responsibilities in addition to being the compliance officer.

3) A compliance committee can be appointed. Like any committee, this is a group composed of people who will have the responsibility for being in charge of the compliance plan. Members of such a committee could include firm personnel only, or firm personnel and one or more consultants.

4) A professional consultant can be hired to handle these responsibilities. While this can work, it will still be necessary to designate someone in the firm as the liaison with the consultant.

The factors used by the firm in selecting one of the above options are most likely to involve the firm's budget, the size of its work force, the nature of the employment laws applicable to the firm, the number and type of employment problems the firm has had, and any other factor important to the firm. Any of these four options can be successful. It all depends on the firm being able to determine what *it* needs.

However the role of compliance officer is to be filled, the following checklist contains the elements that should be made a part of this person's (or committee's) job description:

Checklist 2.1
Key Elements in the Job Description
Of the Compliance Officer

❑ Reports to the chief executive officer, owner, managing partner, or board of directors, or to whatever governing body the firm has in place.

❑ Chief responsibility for all aspects of the compliance program, including but not limited to:

❑ Creation and implementation of the compliance program;

❑ Monitoring and auditing the firm's policies and procedures to ensure compliance. Identifying areas where improvements can be made;

❑ Reviewing, updating and modifying the compliance program and related policies on a continuing basis;

❑ Ensuring that training of personnel is conducted on a regular basis and that training is effective;

❑ Responding to questions or comments from personnel about the compliance program;

❑ Responding to reports of suspected violations of law, regulation or policy. This includes advising management whether a report of a violation to an outside authority is appropriate, as well as whether the firm should conduct an internal investigation of the matter;

❑ Recommending to management the appropriate corrective or disciplinary action in any given situation. Then, ensuring that management acts timely on these recommendations;

❑ Recommending to management revisions of any policies or procedures in order to avoid future problems. Then, ensuring that management acts timely on these recommendations;

❑ Reporting regularly to management to advise on the overall status and effectiveness of the compliance program.

2.2(d) The Firm's Self-Analysis

This issue is discussed in detail in Chapter 3.

2.2(e) Determining Which Employment Laws Apply to the Firm

The chapters included in Part Three of this book will assist an employer in determining the relevant legal issues to cover, as well as how to determine which employment laws apply to the firm. Also, the discussion of Legal Research in Section 1.2(b) of Chapter 1 provides information on conducting your own legal research. This section will focus on specific instructions and strategies for conducting research into employment law, as well as how to read the law.

Legal research always begins by asking questions. Whether the question is general and very broad, or specific and precise, legal research is conducted to find answers. Therefore, begin with a question, or simply with the need to understand something. Then, set out to find the answer.

Answers to legal questions are found in a variety of places. The authoritative answers (which are the answers used in court to resolve lawsuits, and by attorneys when advising clients) are found by reading statutes and cases. Federal employment statutes are contained in the United States Code, primarily in Title 29 (Labor Statutes), and in Title 42 (Civil Rights Statutes). However, there are federal statutes that affect employers and employees in other titles as well.

State employment statutes are found in the statutes of each state. State statutes are only enforceable by the courts of the state that enacted them, while federal statutes are enforceable throughout the United States.

Copies of the United States Code are available at law libraries located in all mid-size to large cities, in the libraries of all law schools, and on the Internet at a variety of locations (go to your preferred search engine and enter a search for "United States Code"). State statutes for the state you are in are available at many public libraries, in all law libraries, in the libraries of all law schools, and on the Internet through the home page of the web site maintained by each state.

The interpretation of statutes, the way in which statutes are applied to actual situations, and the courts' explanations of the law are found by reading case law. Case law is the body of legal opinions of appellate and supreme courts (both state and federal). This body of law is published in books known as "reporters," which are compiled in sets of hundreds of volumes each. Case law is also available over the Internet through subscription services, as well as through several free sites. (The number of cases available through free Internet sites, however, is substantially smaller than the number available through subscription services.)

Federal employment statutes, as well as case law which analyzes and explains the issues contained in these statutes, are both included in this book.

2.2(e)(1) How to Read the Law

Whether reading a statute, a case, or a book explaining legal principles and issues, the most important thing is to pay attention to what you are reading. Statutes do not make suggestions or recommendations, they are statements of the law. They mean what they say and it is crucial to read statutes objectively in order to understand what they mean. Cases also mean what they say, but they are not as straightforward as statutes. Cases describe the facts of the particular case, and the arguments given by each party in the case. Then the court deciding the case explains their analysis of the law and how the law is to be applied to that case. It is possible at times to pull meaningful excerpts from case opinions and to rely on them effectively. Usually, however, it is necessary to read the entire case to get a proper understanding of how and why the law is applied by the court as it is in that case. It takes practice to learn how to read case law effectively.

Law books, whether written for lawyers or nonlawyers, are often the best source for information about a particular legal subject. These books are generally devoted to one area of the law, or even to a limited set of issues within one area of the law. The author explains the applicable legal principles and discusses relevant statutes and case law as part of the explanation. The result is a very good source for learning about the law. However, such books, regardless of how well-written and regardless of who wrote them, are not acceptable in court as an authoritative reference to any legal issue. (Some law books are acceptable as being *learned treatises*, but these are generally not marketed to nonlawyers and are relatively few in number.) Use these books, which includes this book, as a good source of knowledge for the area of law they cover. The information in these books can be relied upon (although be sure the publication date of the edition you are reading is fairly current). Be sure to read for thorough understanding, whether or not you like what you are reading. In fact, it may be best to take a conservative approach to analyzing the information. This means be slow to accept any information you really like and be slow to doubt any information you do not like. Continue reading and learning to be sure a true understanding of the issues is gained.

The actual "rules" for interpreting the meaning of the law are often an issue in lawsuits. It is very common for lawyers to disagree on the meaning of a statute or of the opinions in case law on a particular issue. Therefore, the appellate courts have had to address legal interpretation, or construction, a number of times. The basic rules are:

> "A fundamental rule of statutory construction is that the intent of the legislature governs when that intent can be ascertained from the statute. When a statute is plain and unambiguous . . . give effect to the intention of the legislature rather than determine what the law should or should not be . . . [I]nterpretation must be reasonable and sensible to effect legislative design and intent." *State v. Lewis*, 953 P.2d 1016 (Kan. 1998)

And,

"When construing a statutory provision, legislative intent is the polestar that guides our inquiry and thus when the language of the statute is clear and unambiguous and conveys a clear and definite meaning . . . the statute must be given its plain and obvious meaning. Further, courts . . . are without power to construe an unambiguous statute in a way which would extend, modify, or limit its express terms or its reasonable and obvious implications." *McLaughlin v. State*, 721 So.2d 1170 (Fla. 1998)

While these cases specifically address how to interpret statutes, these same rules are applied when reading rules, regulations, ordinances, and case law. The presumption is *always* that the law being read is clear and unambiguous. Only if a judge can be convinced that the law is unclear and ambiguous will its meaning beyond the clear interpretation of its words be sought. It is not easy to convince a judge of this. Therefore, read the law carefully and give the words their literal and ordinary meanings, which is their meaning as contained in any American-English dictionary (remember, U.S. laws, whether state or federal, are written in American-English, even though many of our legal principles originated in England). Also U.S. law is written using American-English grammar, punctuation, and spelling.

Checklist 2.2
How to Read the Law

❑ The presumption is always that the wording of any statute, rule, regulation, ordinance or case law is clear and unambiguous.

❑ Interpret the words and phrases used in the law by their ordinary meanings.

❑ American law is written using American-English grammar, punctuation, spelling, and definitions.

❑ The purpose of reading the law is to determine what the law is currently. The purpose is not to determine what the law should or should not be (that is the function of the legislature and of Congress, not the courts).

❑ Statutes, rules, regulations and ordinances are statements of the law.

❑ Case law is a collection of various court opinions that interpret statutes, that explain what law applies to a given situation (as well as how the law is to be applied), and that explain the status of the law as of the date of the case.

❑ Law books written by lawyers on legal subjects can be a valuable source of information on the law, both for lawyers and for nonlawyers.

❑ Reading the law is done for understanding. It takes time and care to read the law successfully. It also requires an objective and honest approach to be sure a true understanding is acquired.

2.2(e)(2) Strategies for Researching Employment Law

The Easiest, Most Effective Method:

Ask your lawyer your question and state that you want a written opinion in response. While less work for you, it will cost more money than the following strategies.

Basic, Useful Research:

Begin with a question. This could be anything from, "What do I need to know and where do I start?" to, "What is a reasonable accommodation for this particular employee, pursuant to the Americans with Disabilities Act?"

Start the search for answers to your question by looking for a book, article, newsletter or web site that gives information about the subject matter of your question. This type of source is excellent for providing general and specific information. The knowledge gained from these sources will help focus your initial question (it may even answer part or all of your question), so you will be able to go further with your research.

The next type of resource to research will be law books and journal articles written by attorneys and judges specifically for attorneys and judges. Every law school publishes a law journal which contains thorough discussions of the topics included. In addition, state bar associations publish journal articles, as do several organizations for attorneys (such as the American Bar Association and the American Trial Lawyers Association). These are all excellent sources of information. Law books for attorneys include single topic books, single issue books, and legal encyclopedias. Two excellent legal encyclopedias that are available through any law school library and through most public law libraries are *American Jurisprudence 2d*, and *Corpus Juris Secundum*. Each is organized as any encyclopedia, alphabetically by subject, and each has thorough articles on many legal issues. They also contain numerous statutory and case law citations, which allows for easy research in the statute and case law books.

The final place to conduct research through this strategy is to read statutes and the case law.

Professional Research (how lawyers conduct legal research):

All research starts with questions that must be answered. A lawyer's experience and knowledge is his or her guide for determining the precise questions, as well as where to actually begin research.

Actual research often begins with single subject books and in legal encyclopedias, particularly when the lawyer is starting with more general questions, especially if the book gives "how-to" type information. Lawyers love how-to books.

For employment questions, however, the real research begins in the statute books. This is where the law is contained. After reading the applicable statutes, the next step is to research each statute in the case law. It is always necessary to know how the statute has been and is being treated by the courts. Case law is studied until the issue is thoroughly understood. This means the favorable, unfavorable and indifferent opinions about the issue are known and can be applied to the facts of the case at hand. With this information, a legal opinion or argument for court can be prepared.

Using This Book as a Source for Legal Research:

This is a "how-to" book for employment law compliance planning. The intent is for this book to be useful for lawyers, business consultants and nonlawyers. It explains how to prepare an employment law compliance program. The information, checklists and forms should be useful to any lawyer or nonlawyer who intends to create and implement this type of compliance plan for a client or themselves. The discussion of employment statutes and case law in Part Three is intended to be, at the very least, a description and analysis of current employment law in the United States. While a citation of this book may not be appropriate for use in court or in a legal brief, it does contain a great deal of information and answers that will be useful in day to day practice, for both lawyers and nonlawyers. This book is also useful as a resource for beginning additional research intended to be relied upon in court or in briefs.

Checklist 2.3
Conducting Legal Research

❑   Start with a question or with a desire to learn something.

❑   The general approach is then to start with general information and focus toward specific information that answers your precise question.

❑   "How-to" books and books on employment law, or on specific employment issues (such as disability, discrimination, worker's compensation, etc.), are very good resources for obtaining general, and sometimes specific, information.

❑   The primary source of employment law is state and federal employment statutes. These statutes must be read, either in the actual statute books, or in an employment law book that includes and discusses the relevant statutes.

❑   Case law is researched to determine how the statutes are to be interpreted and applied to given fact situations. Case law will always include favorable and unfavorable information, which must all be understood in order to really know how to answer your question.

❑   For all legal issues, keep in mind that your research is likely to be challenged. The legal system is adversarial in nature and there is always an opponent, or a potential opponent. Your opponent will conduct their own research for the purpose of supporting their position and attacking yours. Therefore, conduct your research carefully and objectively. If your conclusions are correct, you will win.

2.2(f) Risk Assessment

When a firm has completed its self-analysis and has determined which employment laws apply, it is ready for risk assessment. This is the application of relevant law, which sets the standards to be followed, to the actual situation facing the firm. By comparing current reality to the relevant standards, a firm will be able to determine where it exceeds, meets or fails to meet the standards. Risk is low when standards are met or exceeded, and high when standards are not met. Areas of high risk are where trouble is most likely to develop, or already exists. Once it knows its areas of high risk, the firm can make plans to resolve the problems and to reduce or eliminate the risk. Areas of low risk can be looked at to determine how the firm succeeds in keeping its risk in those areas low. Some or all of the methods that work for those areas may also prove successful if applied to high risk areas. This whole process of risk assessment forms the basis for the policies and procedures to be included in the compliance plan.

Checklist 2.4
How to Conduct Risk Assessment

❑ Identify the areas or activities to be analyzed. These can be general, specific, or a combination of both. The guiding principle is what is most useful to the firm. (See Form 2.2 for examples of such activities.)

❑ From the firm's self-analysis, determine the current status of each activity identified. How is it currently handled? What procedure is followed? What problems have already developed? What is the reality of the situation?

❑ For each activity, determine the applicable legal standard.

❑ For each activity, determine whether the firm's actual status on the issue meets or does not meet the relevant legal standard.

❑ Create a system for evaluating how well the firm meets or does not meet the applicable legal standards. This becomes the risk assessment grade. It is generally best to use a simple grading system, such as: Low Risk — when the standard is substantially met; Medium Risk — when the standard is generally met, but there are occasionally problems; and, High Risk — when the standard is not met. However, each firm should adopt the system that would be most useful to that particular firm.

❑ Finally, use the completed risk assessment when preparing policies and procedures for the compliance plan.

Form 2.2
Risk Assessment

Name of Employer_____ Date_____

ACTIVITY	LEGAL STANDARD	FIRM'S STATUS	CURRENT RISK
job descriptions for each position	highly recommended	not used for all positions	high
review of job descriptions	do on a regular basis	done annually	low
job descriptions used during hiring process	highly recommended	this is done	low
job descriptions used during performance evaluations	highly recommended	not done consistently	high
Anti-harassment policy	required by Title VII	does not have	high
wages for non-exempt employees	$5.15 hour minimum	in compliance	low
overtime requirement for non-exempt employees	time and a half over an average of 40 hours per week per pay period	in compliance	low
discrimination in employment decisions	employment decisions cannot be based on race, sex, color, religion, national origin, age, or disability	appears not to be a problem	moderate
employee grievance procedure	not required, but recommended	does not have	high
written policy for use of firm computers and other electronic equipment	highly recommended	have an incomplete policy	moderate to high

(continued on next page)

(Page 2 - Form 2.2)

ACTIVITY	LEGAL STANDARD	FIRM'S STATUS	CURRENT RISK
written policy for use of firm phone lines, including e-mail and Internet use	highly recommended	have an informal policy, but nothing written	high
employee files	must have for all employees	do not have for all employees	high
access to employee files	must be controlled and confidential	not controlled consistently	high
information in employee files	determined by state and federal law (see info from analysis of the laws that apply to firm)	mostly in compliance	high
employee absence requests, when they must be honored	determined by state and federal law (see info from analysis of the laws that apply to firm)	in compliance, but nothing is in writing to serve as a guide for this issue	moderate
employee absence request, when firm has discretion for honoring	determined by state and federal law (see info from analysis of the laws that apply to firm)	in compliance, but nothing is in writing to serve as a guide for this issue	moderate
accommodation of employee disabilities	determined by the Americans with Disabilities Act	in compliance, but this is an ongoing issue	moderate to high
withholding of money from employee's pay	can only be done as allowed by law	can only be done as allowed by law in compliance	low
termination policy	should be based on performance related issues, but can generally be based on any reason not in violation of the law	in compliance, but this is an ongoing issue	moderate

(NOTE: The previous form is presented solely as an illustration of an effective method for assessing risk by activity. A given firm's actual list of activities may contain many more activities than those listed above, or the same activities in more detail, or fewer activities, depending on the circumstances of the firm. In addition, a firm may find it beneficial to create a number of different risk assessment forms, each addressing the details of specific issues, such as the hiring process, conducting employee evaluations, absence policies, termination procedures, etc. Chapter 17 of this book addresses the issue of risk assessment in greater detail and includes a large number of suggested activities to evaluate.)

2.2(g) Creating the Policies and Procedures for the Compliance Plan

[Chapter 17 addresses this issue in detail.]

The policies and procedures created for the compliance plan will be designed and used to control risk in employment issues, thus allowing the firm to be in compliance with applicable employment law. This must be the guiding principle behind every decision concerning what policies and procedures to adopt. A word of warning; it is not necessary or even possible for a business to adopt policies controlling every conceivable issue. In fact, too many policies will result in a very stiff and unproductive environment. It is therefore necessary to find a balance between too many and too few policies. The goal is compliance with the law, but company personnel also have to be able to do their work and be productive.

The creation of policies and procedures for the compliance plan begins after the risk assessment has been completed. From that assessment, the firm can determine where it needs to put the most attention and in what order. The risk assessment also allows the firm to know where its strengths lay, and gain an understanding of what it does to create those strengths. The methods that successfully create strengths might then be used to eliminate any weaknesses.

Whatever policies are ultimately created and used in the firm's compliance plan, it is important to know how to set those policies and how to write them. Everything that goes into the policies and the compliance plan is based on the firm's efforts and research to this point. The following checklist describes how to select and write the actual policies:

Checklist 2.5
Creating and Writing Compliance Plan Policies

❑   Before beginning, have a clear idea what each policy is to accomplish. Determine the specific goal of each policy and include only the information necessary to fulfill that goal.

❑   Each policy must be the creation of the firm, although it may be written by the compliance officer, compliance committee, an attorney or a consultant. Taking suggestions and recommendations from employees may also be part of the process, but it is the firm that must actually decide what policies will be created and how each policy will be written. Since the firm is always held accountable for its policies, it must be the one who accepts full responsibility.

❑   Write each policy in the most clear and precise language possible.

❑   Write in standard American English. Do not use slang or idioms, as they are too often misunderstood.

❑   Do not use initials, abbreviations, jargon, symbols or other specialized elements of language unless you define these things when first used. It may be helpful to include a glossary for defining any such terms.

❑   Policies that are too wordy, that contain grammar and punctuation errors, or that are not well-written well may be misunderstood or interpreted differently than intended.

❑   Do not write policies with overly simple language, as if you were writing for children. Instead, write intelligently for your audience, which is firm personnel.

❑   Do not use a font style or size that is difficult to read. Use black ink on white paper. Create a table of contents and maybe even an index. Use headings and section or paragraph titles. Highlight titles and section headings, but be sparse with the use of highlighted language in the body of each policy. Too much highlighting of text tends to destroy the intended impact of highlighted language. The key is to create a document that can be easily read and quickly searched for specific information.

(continued on next page)

(Page 2 - Checklist 2.5)

❑   Do not misstate any state or federal law quoted, referred to, paraphrased, or summarized.

❑   Do not create any policy that you do not intend to follow or enforce consistently.

❑   Have each policy reviewed once it has been written. The reviewers should include the compliance officer (unless this is the person who wrote the policy), an owner or manager, one or more of the personnel who will be using the policy on a regular basis, and your attorney or consultant. Consider any comments you receive by those who review the policy. Do the comments suggest modifications? Should the policy be re-written? Or, is it okay as is? Decide whether or not to follow any recommendations, or which conflicting recommendations to follow.

2.3 Specific Steps in Implementing the Compliance Plan

[These steps are discussed in further detail in Chapter 19.]

Implementing a compliance plan consists of: a) notifying all company personnel that a compliance plan is being implemented as of a specific date, b) training all personnel in their part of the compliance plan, and c) following through with the policies and procedures contained in the plan.

Notifying personnel that the compliance plan will begin as of a certain date should be done in the same way that information is distributed to company personnel. Selecting the effective date for beginning the compliance program is a decision to be made by management, on the recommendation of the compliance officer. However, this date should be after training has been completed.

Training personnel is crucial to the success of a compliance program. The truth of this statement may seem obvious, but it cannot be overstated. The best compliance plan ever created for the best personnel ever to work for any company is not necessarily a winning combination. Personnel must first know of the existence of a compliance program; then they must know what the company is to be in compliance with, as well as the policies and procedures that will be used to be in compliance; and finally, they must know their roles in the program. This information and knowledge is learned only through training.

The person in charge of training is the compliance officer. Whether or not this person actually designs the training programs used, or conducts the training, this is the person with responsibility for getting it done successfully. The compliance officer must arrange for instructors, a place for the training, a training schedule, the goals to be accomplished through training, and anything and everything necessary.

Participation in training should be a condition of employment with the firm. Training in the firm's compliance program should first occur during the orientation process for all new personnel. A copy of the written compliance program (or the portion applicable to the particular employee or position) should be given to each person as they begin their employment. Retraining must also occur on a regular basis for all personnel. Testing should be included in the training program. The testing may be a written test to review the employee's knowledge of the program, or drills for responding to specific situations. It could include having each employee take turns being a part of the instructional staff at training sessions, or any combination of these or other methods. If anyone fails to participate in training, or if anyone demonstrates through testing that they are not learning sufficiently from the training, they should be warned that participation in training is a condition of employment. If necessary, an employee who fails or refuses to participate and learn may be terminated.

Just as the specifics of a compliance program will vary from firm to firm, the specifics of training programs will also vary. The compliance officer must determine the most effective method for ensuring personnel know and understand their own compliance program. One format for a training program is described in the following checklist:

Checklist 2.6
Training Format for Compliance Program

❑ Compliance officer trains the firm's supervisors and managers.

❑ Supervisors and managers train the personnel over whom they have authority.

❑ All new employees receive training as part of their orientation process.

❑ Independent contractors and others who are not employees, but who will be working with the firm, are trained or advised of any aspects of the compliance program that apply to them. This can be done by the compliance officer or by the person within the firm to whom the independent contractor reports.

❑ Training for current personnel should take place on an annual basis, with those personnel in high-risk areas of the firm (as determined from the risk assessment) receiving training as often as necessary.

❑ Use the firm's own facilities for training, if at all possible.

❑ Schedule enough time to accomplish the training. Depending on the personnel, the size of the firm, and the complexity of the compliance program, as little as an hour may be required or an entire day may be necessary. Make every attempt to accomplish the training for any given employee in less than one day. Attention spans will be taxed and the training session will become counter-productive if it is too long.

❑ Schedule training on a day or at a time when those in attendance will not have other responsibilities. If training is on a day not normally scheduled for work, non-exempt employees will have to be paid for the time spent in training.

❑ Schedule each training session to include personnel who work together.

❑ The goal of training is not to be able to check "training" off the list of things to do, nor is the goal to be able to show how much time was devoted to training. Instead, the goal of training is to ensure personnel are receiving necessary education about the compliance program.

(continued on next page)

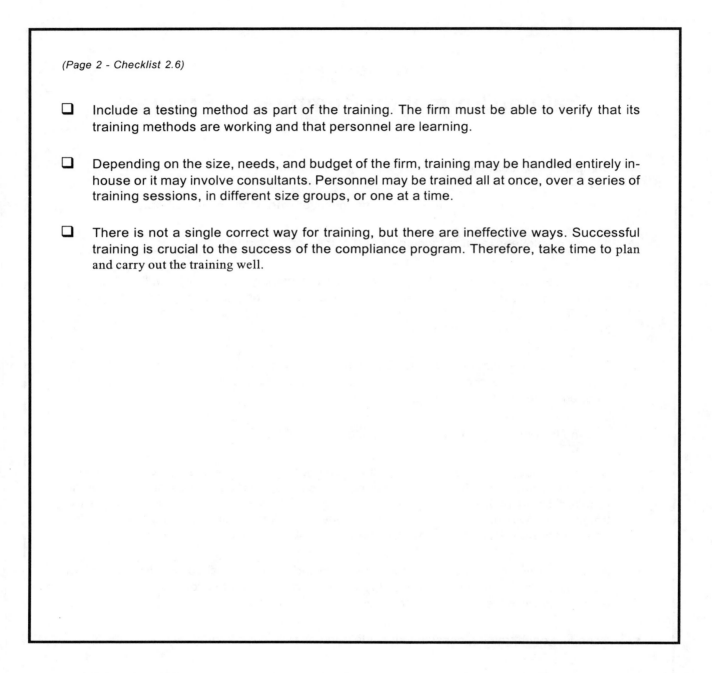

(Page 2 - Checklist 2.6)

❑ Include a testing method as part of the training. The firm must be able to verify that its training methods are working and that personnel are learning.

❑ Depending on the size, needs, and budget of the firm, training may be handled entirely in-house or it may involve consultants. Personnel may be trained all at once, over a series of training sessions, in different size groups, or one at a time.

❑ There is not a single correct way for training, but there are ineffective ways. Successful training is crucial to the success of the compliance program. Therefore, take time to plan and carry out the training well.

Special training sessions may need to be held on occasion. This type of training may only be necessary for specific personnel or individuals and it usually arises after something unusual has happened or when the compliance officer determines there is a special need. The following checklist gives examples of these special needs.

Checklist 2.7
When Special Training Sessions
May Be Required

❑   Employment law applicable to the firm changes.

❑   Changes are made to the compliance program.

❑   Circumstances affecting the firm have changed or are changing.

❑   A supervisor or manager believes a special session would be helpful for their personnel.

❑   The compliance officer believes a special session is necessary.

❑   It has been demonstrated through actual situations that personnel are not acting or responding to events pursuant to the compliance program.

2.4 Specific Steps in Evaluating the Plan's Effectiveness

Monitoring a compliance program is necessary in order to evaluate its effectiveness. This is necessary for two reasons:

(1) To ensure the compliance program is actually in place and is being used and followed; and,

(2) To ensure the compliance program is properly addressing areas of risk.

The compliance officer has responsibility for monitoring and validating the compliance program. The use of professional consultants, including the firm's attorney, should be considered periodically. While an in-house evaluation is usually very effective, a review conducted by an "outsider" has value as they are not perceived as being burdened by personal affiliation and loyalties to the firm and its personnel. Every firm should consider having an evaluation conducted every third year (for example) by an outside consultant.

Before starting the monitoring process, a monitoring protocol should be established. The process for monitoring and validating the compliance program should include the factors in the following checklist.

Checklist 2.8
Factors to be Included in a Monitoring Protocol

❑   A description of the objectives to be accomplished through the monitoring process (i.e., to verify compliance with the program, to measure effectiveness of the program, and to determine the need for any modifications).

❑   A description of the steps to be taken during the monitoring process.

❑   A description of the schedule and procedures to be followed for the monitoring process.

❑   Identification of who will conduct the various steps in the process.

❑   An explanation of how written findings or conclusions from the monitoring process will be compiled.

❑   Identification of who will analyze the conclusions and prepare any recommendations.

❑   Explanation of who will review the recommendations and how decisions regarding the recommendations will be made.

Once a protocol is established, the actual steps of the monitoring process can be carried out. Some of these steps may be ongoing and not restricted to a specific period of monitoring. Other steps may take place at specific intervals of time or after certain events have occurred. Regardless of how a firm decides to monitor its compliance program, the following general steps must be included in every monitoring process.

Checklist 2.9
General Steps to Include in
Every Monitoring Process

❑ Constantly monitoring employment laws and regulations that affect the firm. This can be effectively done by subscribing to and reading employment law newsletters, journal articles about employment law, and by staying in contact with the company attorney. This step allows the compliance officer to become aware of any changes that should be addressed by the compliance program.

❑ Pay attention to events in the news. Local, regional, national, and international events can all affect any business. If something occurs that will impact the business, a determination must be made about whether the compliance program should be modified as a result.

❑ Re-read the entire compliance program. It is easy over a relatively brief period of time to forget portions of the compliance program. The compliance officer must make sure his or her knowledge of the entire compliance program is always complete.

❑ Review company employment records. Randomly check employee files. Written records are the easiest thing for an agency or anyone to examine and find problems with. Do not let sloppy record keeping practices be the source of liability.

❑ Monitor compliance policies and procedures as they are actually being followed. This can be done by observation, by interview, and by looking for results that should be occurring (fewer complaints or problems, a decrease in absenteeism, lower turn-over rates, the full use of job descriptions, an increase in morale). This type of monitoring cannot be done from an office. The compliance officer must observe what is happening. Personnel at all levels should be observed and interviewed, both formally and informally. In addition, independent contractors, customers, suppliers, and others who deal with the firm should be interviewed.

❑ Solicit comments and recommendations from all personnel regarding the effectiveness | of the compliance program. These can be made anonymously, but should be in writing. However, if someone wants to make oral comments, listen.

❑ Evaluate the effectiveness of procedures within the compliance program for dealing with problems or unusual situations. Did personnel know what to do? Was it necessary to take different or additional actions than those described in the compliance program to deal with the situation? Did it take an unacceptable amount of time to handle the matter? Was the result from following the compliance program as anticipated during the planning stage?

The findings from the above steps should be in writing. (The form of the writing may be most effective as a memo from the compliance officer to the governing body of the firm.) These written findings can then form the basis for feedback to appropriate personnel. This feedback is necessary to enable those involved to learn the effectiveness of their participation in the compliance program. As necessary, these written findings will also form the basis for justifying discipline or termination of personnel. Equally important, the written findings from steps taken to monitor the compliance program will serve as a series of benchmarks that can be compared over time to establish a pattern of compliance for the organization. This allows the organization to compare its progress over time, as well as to its competition and to industry standards.

Another key element of monitoring the compliance program is to prepare written recommendations. Should any part of the program be modified? If so, how? What parts of the program should remain unchanged? Should the responsibilities of specific individuals be changed?

If audited by a government agency, that agency will want to review the firm's methods for monitoring and validating compliance with its own program. Monitoring procedures, as well as written findings and recommendations prepared as part of this process, will be important elements in a government audit or investigation. If it appears that the monitoring process exists in name only, or is otherwise ineffective, the severity of any penalties assessed by the agency are likely to be affected. Likewise, if a monitoring program is determined to be appropriate and likely to truly assess its value and ability to find and handle risk, the firm will have fewer problems with the government and complaining employees (or former employees) in general. A compliance program that is ineffective is worse than no compliance program at all.

2.5 Specific Steps in Modifying the Compliance Plan

[Chapter 20 discusses this issue in detail.]

The decision to update or modify the compliance program should be the natural consequence of having an effective monitoring and validation process. The recommendations made during the monitoring process should form the basis for any and all modifications to the compliance program. However, a decision will have to be made about whether or not to follow a recommendation for change. The compliance officer has this responsibility, but may seek the opinions of others (such as the company attorney or consultant) in making a decision.

Once the decision is made to modify the compliance program, do so without delay. Make the necessary changes and train all affected personnel in these changes. Also, make a written record of: a) the change to the compliance program, b) the reason for the change, and c) how the change will be made known to personnel. This record is necessary to show outside auditors that steps are actively taken to address problems as they are discovered.

After the change has been in place and personnel have been trained regarding the change, the compliance officer must determine whether or not the change has had the desired result. This is done by following the monitoring and validation process and studying the results. If the change is effective, great. If not, determine how to correct the continuing problem and do so. Then, have a new training session for the new change, followed by an analysis of the effectiveness of the change.

It is important to carefully analyze any recommendation for change, as too many changes to address the same or even similar issues can have an adverse affect on the morale of personnel toward the compliance program. Change that is not effective is a waste of resources.

2.6 Integration of Compliance Planning with the Firm's Other Business Planning

If at all possible, do not reinvent the wheel. Many businesses already do types of business planning that are essentially forms of compliance planning. Tax planning, for example, is perhaps the most common type of compliance planning. Other forms of compliance planning already in use by business include:

- Efforts to match products and services to the likes and expectations of customers.

- Evaluation of a manufacturing process to make sure it stays within budget requirements.

- Audits to ensure financial records are consistent with generally accepted accounting practices.

- Quality control.

- Monitoring contract performance to ensure compliance with contract terms.

- Determining whether sales personnel are meeting established sales quotas.

- Observing whether or not agendas are followed at meetings.

Many additional examples could be given. The point is that businesses of any size, from a firm with one part-time employee to a firm with thousands of employees, is already using many of the procedures required for compliance planning. By recognizing how it is already involved in compliance planning in non-legal issues, a firm will discover that they already have much of the necessary skill and ability to begin compliance planning for legal issues. To integrate what a firm already has into employment law compliance planning, consider the following checklist.

Checklist 2.10
How To Integrate Business Planning
And Compliance Planning

❏ A person in charge of compliance type business planning might be considered for the position of compliance officer.

❏ Using existing methods of business research to determine what the competition is up to, as well as the status of any applicable industry standards, may also be useful for determining the status of various employment issues with other firms.

❏ Existing methods for internal analysis of various procedures may be useful for conducting the employment law self-analysis.

❏ Personnel who are skilled at business research methods may have useful techniques that can be adapted to legal research.

❏ Skills and methods that are successful in determining what customers want may also be successful in determining what employees want, think, or believe.

❏ Competent budgeting and scheduling experience will serve the firm well when preparing the budget and schedule for creation and implementation of the compliance plan.

❏ Existing methods for creating and implementing policies of any type may be useful for creating and implementing policies for use in the compliance program.

❏ A successful talent for measuring actual performance of anything against the relevant standard will work well for monitoring and evaluating a compliance plan.

❏ An understanding of when and how to make changes in existing policy is a talent that will be beneficial to knowing when and how to make modifications to a compliance program.

❏ The ability of a firm to look ahead and to plan for the future is the basic ability needed to create and use an employment law compliance plan. Any business that stays open has this ability.

Any business will already possess at least some of the talent and abilities necessary for successful compliance planning. Employment law compliance planning is really nothing more than adapting business research and planning methods to the issues of employment law. Compliance planning is a business recognizing its current status, determining what standards it must comply with, developing successful methods for complying with those standards, and carrying out those methods for compliance. The measure of success in compliance planning, as in all business planning, is how well the firm complies with the relevant standards while remaining as productive and profitable as possible.

CHAPTER 3
The Employer's Self-Analysis

CONTENTS

The information presented in this chapter will allow an employer to assess and understand its own employment issues, both current and past. From this information it is possible to make predictions about the future. It is a process similar to a physician taking a patient's medical history and then conducting an examination to accurately measure the health of the patient. Section 3.1 describes how to determine an employer's current situation. Section 3.2 describes how to identify and describe trends and patterns relevant to the employer's practices and procedures. Section 3.3 measures how an employer looks at its future.

3.1 Determining Current Status

These are the steps for an employer to take to determine its current status:

1) Determine where responsibility lays for employment issues in the company.

2) Determine the size and nature of the work force.

3) Determine where the work force is located.

4) Determine which state and federal employment laws currently apply to the employer.

5) Describe whether and how written job descriptions are used.

6) Identify all written employment policies.

7) Identify all unwritten and informal employment policies.

8) Identify how wages, salaries, benefits and other compensation are determined.

9) Identify how employment records, information, and statistics are maintained.

10) Identify and describe all pending claims, complaints or grievances by employees.

The following sections describe how to determine the above list of needed information and include checklists and forms. The checklists and forms are not intended to be definitive versions, but examples that can be used as presented or adapted as necessary to meet a particular employer's needs. An owner or other primary decisionmaker(s) should be involved in the investigations based on the checklists and forms that follow. The same person(s) should also analyze the information obtained and make the appropriate decisions until someone is specifically designated to fill the compliance officer position.

3.1(a) Where Responsibility for Employment Issues Rests

Who is in charge of employment issues? Is there one person, one department, or several persons located around the company who share this responsibility? The employer needs to know who actually makes decisions and who actually handles what. If this source of authority lies where it is supposed to, it will be used to coordinate information and inquiries necessary to prepare the compliance program (at least until a compliance officer is designated - which may be the person with this authority). However, if some or all of this authority does not lie where it should, the decision must be made to formalize where the authority is, or to get it back where it should be. Either decision may require changes in personnel, changes in the responsibilities of personnel, and the will to enforce such changes.

Checklist 3.1
Who Is In Charge?

❑ Who generally has the final say — although not necessarily the ultimate hierarchical authority— in employment decisions?

❑ Whose signature on any document relating to an employment matter generally indicates to others in the firm that specific action is or is not to be taken?

❑ To whom do people usually go when they want to find out what is really happening with any employment matter?

❑ Are the person or persons identified by the first three questions the appropriate person(s)? If not, why not?

❑ Are the person or persons identified by the first three questions appropriate for this responsibility, whether or not they are whom they should be?

❑ Do you intend to change the authority of anyone who is or who is not exercising this authority? If so, decide how to do this and do it. If not, be sure you are fully satisfied with the way things are.

3.1(b) Size and Nature of the Work Force

How many employees are there? How many are full time, part time, permanent or temporary? How many are administrative, managerial, clerical, labor or some other type? What is the total character of the work force? Not only do these questions lead to a description of the work force, they also provide the information necessary to determine which state and federal employment statutes apply.

When determining numbers of employees, use averages of numbers during the previous twelve-month period, rather than current totals. A number of employment statutes are applicable to an employer based on the employer's average number of employees over a twelve-month period. Therefore, unless otherwise indicated, average the numbers.

Checklist 3.2
Definitions

❑ **Employee:** Any person working for the firm in any capacity for whom Forms W-4 and I-9 have been completed and for whom Form W-2 will be prepared.

❑ **Full Time Employee:** An employer has discretion in determining how to define "full time employee," but this term is generally defined as an employee who is hired into a position that requires a minimum of 36 to 40 hours work per week.

❑ **Part Time Employee:** Any employee in any position who is not classified as "full time."

❑ **Temporary Employee:** Any full time or part time employee who is hired to work for a limited duration of time (which could be several days, weeks, months or until a specific project is completed). When the term expires, the employment ends.

❑ **Permanent Employee:** Any full time or part time employee who is not hired as a temporary employee.

❑ **Trainee, Probationary Employee, Intern, Apprentice, etc:** An employee who may still be a student and who is working as part of their educational curriculum, or who is going through a training period before becoming a permanent employee. These persons are counted as employees.

❑ **Borrowed or Loaned Employee:** Any person who is an employee of another employer (usually of a staffing agency or other provider of temporary help), but who is placed under your control for a specified time period, to work on a project, or on some other basis. Unless specifically instructed to do so, do not count borrowed or loaned employees when determining numbers of employees.

❑ **Independent Contractor:** A person hired to work for an employer, but who does not become an employee. Independent contractors may be hired to perform a specific task or to work indefinitely. A true independent contractor generally sets their own rate of pay (although not necessarily), provides the equipment they will need to do their work, determines how they will accomplish their responsibilities, usually sets their own schedule, and may work for more than one employer at the same time. Independent contractors are often self-employed persons. The fee paid to an independent contractor does not normally have deductions for income taxes, social security, Medicare/Medicaid, or anything else.

(continued on next page)

(Page 2 - Checklist 3.2)

Independent contractors must be sent Form 1099 at the end of the employer's tax year as a record of how much was paid by the employer to the independent contractor during that year. Independent contractors do not complete Forms W-4 or I-9, nor are they provided with Form W-2. Unless specifically instructed to do so, do not count independent contractors when determining numbers of employees.

❑ **Freelance Worker or Contractor:** The same as an independent contractor.

❑ **Contract Laboror:** The same as an independent contractor.

❑ **Owner:** Any person who has an actual ownership interest in the business. This includes a sole proprietor, general or limited partners, shareholders of a corporation, and members of a limited liability company. Sole proprietors and general or limited partners are not generally counted as employees. However, corporate shareholders who also meet the definition of employee (as defined above) should be counted as employees. The members of a limited liability company are not generally counted as employees and should not be so counted unless you have a legal opinion that states that they should.

❑ **Administrative, Managerial, Clerical, Labor and other classifications of employees based on type of work or authority:** The employer has total discretion in creating and naming any such classifications. If employees are classified on the basis of the type of work they do, or on the basis of their authority, or on any other basis, the key is that the employer know exactly how to classify each employee. In addition, classifications must be used consistently.

❑ **Exempt Employee:** Any employee who is not covered by minimum wage and hour laws. These employees can be paid any wage and can be required to work any number of hours per week with no restriction or consequence from state or federal law. Generally, these are full time employees with administrative or managerial authority who exercise at least some discretion in how they do their job. Exempt employees may be compensated on an hourly basis or by a salary, may or may not have benefits, may work a specific schedule, or may have no formal schedule except to keep working until their work is done.

❑ **Non-Exempt Employee:** An employee who must be paid at least the minimum hourly wage required by law and who must be paid overtime (time and a half) for every hour worked over an average of 40 hours per week per pay period. Non-exempt employees are not defined by whether they are paid an hourly wage, a salary, or by whether they do or do not have a specific work schedule, they are covered by the minimum wage and hour law because of the type of work they do. Unless an employee is exempt, they are considered non-exempt.

Checklist 3.3
Counting Employees

❑   Determine the average number of part time employees.

❑   Determine the average number of full time employees.

❑   Determine the number of permanent employees.

❑   Determine the number of temporary employees.

❑   Determine the number of employees who are in a training period, a probationary period, who are interns or apprentices, or who would be classified in these categories.

❑   Determine the number of exempt employees.

❑   Determine the number of non-exempt employees.

❑   If employees are classified (i.e., administrative, clerical, labor, etc.), list the classifications used and determine the number of employees in each classification.

❑   Determine the total number of employees in the work force (NOTE: this total number is the number of bodies, not necessarily the total of each category listed above, as some employees may be counted more than once if they fall into more than one category).

Checklist 3.4
Counting Other Personnel

❑ Determine the number of borrowed or loaned employees.

❑ Determine the number of independent contractors, freelancers, and others who meet the definition for these categories.

❑ Determine the number of owners who work in the company but who are not counted as employees.

❑ Determine the total number of other personnel in the work force.

Use the information obtained from checklists 3.3 and 3.4 to complete the following form 3.1.

Form 3.1
Size And Nature of Total Work Force

Name of Employer_____ Date_____

PART ONE: EMPLOYEES

(1)   Total Number of Employees Classified as Full Time: _____

(2)   Total Number of Employees Classified as Part Time: _____

(3)   TOTAL OF EMPLOYEES (*total of Lines 1 & 2*):   _____

(4)   Total Number of Employees Classified as Permanent: _____

(5)   Total Number of Employees Classified as Temporary: _____

(6)   Total Number of Employees Classified as
       Training, Probationary, Interns, Apprentices, etc: _____

(7)   TOTAL OF EMPLOYEES (*total of Lines 4, 5, & 6,
       should equal the number in Line 3*):   _____

(8)   Total Number of Employees Classified as Exempt: _____

(9)   Total Number of Employees Classified as Non-Exempt: _____

(10)   TOTAL OF EMPLOYEES (*total of Lines 8 & 9,
       should equal the number in Lines 3 & 7*):   _____

(continued on next page)

(Page 2 - Form 3.1)

If Employer Classifies Employees (i.e., Administrative, Clerical, etc.),identify each classification used and the total number of employees in each classification, as well as the total number of employees:

(11a) _____   _____

(11b) _____   _____

(11c) _____   _____

(11d) _____   _____

(11e) _____   _____

(11)TOTAL NUMBER OF EMPLOYEES
   (*should equal the number in Lines 3, 7, & 10*):   _____

PART TWO: OTHER PERSONNEL

   (A) Total Number of Owners active in operations who
       are not defined as employees: _____

   (B) Total Number of Borrowed Employees: _____

   (C) Total Number of Independent Contractors and any
       other personnel who are not defined as Employees: _____

   (D) TOTAL NUMBER OF OTHER PERSONNEL: _____

Total Number of Work Force (the sum of Line 11 and Line D):   _____

3.1(c) Location of the Work Force

Where each member of an employer's work force is physically located is material for reasons of jurisdiction. (Jurisdiction is the authority of a court to hear a case. Generally, lawsuits are filed in the same district where the events that make up the case occurred. This location is generally where the parties are physically located, such as the county, state, or federal district where an employee does their job.) Additionally, it is necessary to know the physical work site of all employees in order to determine if the Family Medical Leave Act [29 U.S.C. 2601 *et seq.*] applies to any employees of a particular employer. Each state also has their own employment statutes. Although state employment law is often very similar to federal law and to the laws of other states, there may be differences in some issues. For example, if an employer has employees in New York, Connecticut, Massachusetts, and Illinois), that employer must comply with New York law for employees located there, with Connecticut law for employees in Connecticut, and so on. It may be necessary for such an employer to modify certain policies because of differences between the laws of these four states. The different states will also have their own laws dealing with unemployment compensation, worker's compensation, and payment of withholding and other employment taxes.

Where an employee is located means, where do they perform their job? For employees who work in a particular office, store, warehouse, factory, or other fixed site, this is a simple question to answer. For employees who work out of two or more locations, their "home base" is probably their principal work site. The location of this home base is probably the relevant location for determining the laws applicable for unemployment compensation, worker's compensation, withholding taxes, and for most other employment issues. However, employees who must travel as a requirement of their job may subject their employer to the jurisdiction of courts in any district where the employee is physically located when a cause of action or claim, arises. To help determine these issues, use the following checklist 3.5:

Checklist 3.5
Determining Where an Employee is Located

❏ An employee who works at a particular location, whether or not owned, leased, or otherwise maintained by the employer, is considered to be located at that location. The ordinances and statutes of the city, county and state where the employee is located apply to the employee, as well as to the actions and conduct of the employee and others who affect the employee.

❏ An employee who works at several locations, whether some or all of these locations are owned, leased, or otherwise maintained by the employer, is located at each location while physically there. The ordinances and statutes of the city, county, and state where the employee is located at a given time apply to the employee while there, as well as to the actions and conduct of the employee or of others who affect the employee in each such location.

❏ An employee whose job includes travel, but not including travel between the employee's home and their work site, is covered by the laws of each city, county, and state through which they pass while they are in each such location. In addition, a traveling employee is covered by the state and/or federal laws that regulate the method of transportation being used by the employee (i.e., traffic laws, interstate transportation regulations, travel on navigable rivers and streams, travel on lakes or seaways, air travel, travel along pipelines, and space travel).

❏ An employee who works in one state, or who works from a place of business maintained by the employer in a particular state, whether or not they travel out of state or live out of state, is covered by that state's laws and regulations for unemployment compensation, worker's compensation, tax and other withholdings from their paycheck, and that state's employment laws.

❏ An employee who works within a 75-mile radius of any work site maintained by their employer is considered to be located at that work site for purposes of determining the applicability of the Family Medical Leave Act [29 U.S.C. 2601 *et seq.*] to the employer and to the employee. Since this act is a federal law, it does not matter if the area within this 75 mile radius crosses state lines.

❏ An employee of a U.S. employer who travels, works or is based in any foreign location (any location not under U.S. jurisdiction) is subject to the laws of the nation where they are located, as well as applicable U.S. laws.

Use the information determined from the checklist 3.5 to complete the following form. This form will be useful in pointing out which city, county, state, and other laws or regulations will cover your employees (and you, as the employer) some or all of the time.

Form 3.2
Location of the Work Force

Name of Employer_____ Date_____

(1) List all incorporated towns and cities where employees either work or are based:

_____ _____ _____

_____ _____ _____

(2) List all counties (parishes) where employees either work or are based:

_____ _____ _____

_____ _____ _____

(3) List all states where employees either work or are based:

_____ _____ _____

_____ _____ _____

(4) List all states through which employees regularly travel or are likely to travel:

_____ _____ _____

_____ _____ _____

(continued on next page)

(Page 2 - Form 3.2)

(5) Identify which methods of transportation employees are likely to use in their job (but not while commuting to and from work):

___ Automobile	___ Bus, Taxi, Limousine
___ Train	___ Local Delivery Vehicle
___ Long Distance Delivery Vehicle	___ Construction Vehicle
___ Utility Vehicle	___ Agribusiness Vehicle
___ General Aviation	___ Commercial Aviation
___ Emergency Services Vehicle (Ground)	___ Emergency Services Vehicle (Air/Water)

___ Other (describe)_____

(6) Identify which transportation systems employees are likely to use (but not while commuting):

___ Interstate Highway System	___ U.S. Highways	___ State Highways
___ County or Local Roads	___ Navigable Waterways	___ Railways
___ Airways	___ Pipeline Systems	

___ Other (describe)_____

(7) Identify all international locations (any location not under U.S. jurisdiction) where employees travel, work or are based:

_____ _____ _____

_____ _____ _____

3.1(d) State and Federal Employment Laws that Apply to the Employer

Whether or not a particular federal employment law applies to an employer is determined by the number of employees that employer has. When counting employees to determine applicability of federal law, use the total number of employees obtained from Line 11, Form 3.1. The following checklists include key federal laws, but not all federal laws. The following laws are all discussed further in Part Three.

Checklist 3.6
Federal Employment Laws that
Apply to All Employers

❑ Child Labor Act [29 U.S.C. 212, 213]

❑ Civil Rights Statutes (prohibiting racial discrimination) [42 U.S.C. 1981 *et seq.*].

❑ Employee Polygraph Protection Act [29 U.S.C. 2001 *et seq.*].

❑ Equal Pay Act of 1963 [29 U.S.C. 206(d)].

❑ Fair Labor Standards Act of 1938 ("wage and hour law") [29 U.S.C. 201 *et seq.*].

❑ Occupational Safety and Health Act (OSHA) [29 U.S.C. 651 *et seq.*].

❑ Personal Responsibility and Work Opportunity Reconciliation Act ("deadbeat dad law") [PL. 104-193]

❑ Veteran's Reemployment Rights Act [38 U.S.C. 4301 *et seq.*].

Checklist 3.7
Federal Employment Laws that Apply to Employers with 15 or More Employees

❑   All laws listed in the previous checklist.

❑   Americans with Disabilities Act [42 U.S.C. 12101 *et seq.*]

❑   Title VII of the Civil Rights Act of 1964 [42 U.S.C. 2000e *et seq.*]

Checklist 3.8
Federal Employment Laws that Apply to Employers with 20 or More Employees

❑   All laws listed in the two previous checklists.

❑   Age Discrimination in Employment Act [29 U.S.C. 621-634]

❑   Consolidated Omnibus Budget Reconciliation Act of 1986 (COBRA) [26 U.S.C. 4980B].

Checklist 3.9
Federal Employment Laws that Apply to Employers with 50 or More Employees

❑ All laws listed in the three previous checklists.

❑ Family and Medical Leave Act [29 U.S.C. 2601 *et seq.*].

Checklist 3.10
Federal Employment Laws that Apply to Employers with 100 or More Employees

❑ All laws listed in the four previous checklists.

❑ Worker Adjustment and Retraining Notification Act [29 U.S.C. 2101 *et seq.*].

Federal employment laws apply to all employers located in any state, territory or district of the United States, whether the employer is a U.S. or foreign firm. (In addition, federal employment law applies to U.S. firms that operate and have employees in foreign nations, although if the laws of the host nation are contrary to the requirements of U.S. law *and if they apply to the U.S. employer located in that nation*, the foreign law will generally prevail.) State employment laws, however, only apply in the state which enacted the laws. For example, Pennsylvania employment law is enforceable only in Pennsylvania, not in Ohio. Refer to the information from Form 3.2 to determine which state's laws apply to your employees.

As with federal law, the applicability of state employment laws is generally determined by how many employees an employer has (from Line 11, Form 3.1). In addition, many state laws are substantially the same (if not identical) to corresponding federal law, particularly anti-discrimination laws. However, the minimum number of employees an employer must have in order to be covered by the laws of its state is often far less than the number set by federal law.

Checklist 3.11
Types of State Employment Laws Applicable To All Employers in that State

❑ Unemployment compensation.

❑ Worker's compensation (although this is sometimes based on total dollar amount of annual payroll).

❑ Child labor laws.

Checklist 3.12
Types of State Employment Laws Applicable To Employers with A Minimum Of 2 to 4 Employees in that State

❑ All laws listed in the previous checklist.

❑ Anti-discrimination and anti-harassment laws.

❑ State minimum wage and hour laws.

State and federal employment laws are not necessarily mutually exclusive. State law often covers different issues than federal law and federal law is generally more extensive than the laws of any state. However, when a state law and a federal law both cover exactly the same issue, whichever is more strict and comprehensive is generally the one that will apply to the situation. Since state laws are generally stricter in their requirements than federal law (primarily by being applicable to employers with fewer employees than required by federal law), state law will be relied upon to enforce employment issues for those employers who do not meet the federal requirements. If an employer meets both state and federal requirements, the complaining employee gets to choose whether to take their case through the applicable state court system or through the federal court system. The deciding factor is often based on which system gives the employee the better chance of winning.

While this book is helpful in determining which state and federal laws apply to a given employer, it is not a substitute for specific legal advice. Always seek the advice of a competent attorney for a legal opinion specifically covering your situation.

Form 3.3
Applicable State and Federal Employment Laws

Name of Employer_____ Date_____

(1) List by Title and Statute Number the Key State Employment Laws Which are Applicable:

_____

_____

_____

_____

_____

_____

_____

_____

_____

_____

_____

_____

_____

_____

_____

_____

(continued on next page)

(Page 2 - Form 3.3)

(2) List by Title and Statute Number the Key Federal Employment Laws Which are Applicable:

_____

_____

_____

_____

_____

_____

_____

_____

_____

_____

_____

_____

_____

_____

_____

_____

_____

_____

3.1(e) Use of Job Descriptions

Using written job descriptions is one of the most important things an employer can do for itself. A written job description does not need to fully describe every detail expected of the person in the job, nor must it fully describe the qualifications the person in the job must have, or describe all compensation and benefits for the position. All that is required of an effective job description is:

a) That it is in writing;

b) That it is prepared by the employer, preferably before looking for the person to fill the position being described;

c) That it describe the essential duties of the position, as required by the employer;

d) That it describe the essential qualifications required or preferred by the employer for any person who will hold the position; and,

e) That it be used and maintained over time.

An employee's job description is always one of the very first things requested (or demanded) by opposing counsel, as well as by an administrative hearing officer or court, when a claim has been made by an employee against the employer. Judges and lawyers consider a written job description to be the employer's own description of what is expected of the person in a particular position. It provides the standard against which the actual performance of the employee can be measured. This makes the written job description a valuable piece of evidence in any situation and it may or may not help exonerate the employer's actions toward the employee.

Every employer has a job description for every position held by an employee. Those employers who do not have current, written job descriptions are simply using informal job descriptions. An informal job description is "found" to exist by a court based on the actual practices of the employer, as well as on any conversations and correspondence concerning the employee and the position in question. Using informal job descriptions is like using "dead reckoning" for navigation. It can work, but it will not work for long, and unless you are lucky, it will be useless in a crisis (such as in employment disputes and litigation).

Preparing and using job descriptions are discussed in Part Three. The following checklists will provide information to show whether and how job descriptions are being used.

Checklist 3.13
Use of Job Descriptions by an Employer

(Ideally, the answer to each of these questions will be "yes.")

❑ Is there a written job description for every position in the firm (whether each employee has their own job description or all employees holding the same position have the same job description)?

❑ Are written job descriptions reviewed by the employer on a regular basis (at least annually)?

❑ Are modifications made to written job descriptions when necessary to reflect changes or modifications in the position?

❑ Are job descriptions used when hiring to fill the position described?

❑ Are job descriptions used when evaluating employee performance?

❑ Are job descriptions referred to when deciding whether and how to discipline or terminate an employee?

❑ Do the employee and the employer both have a copy of the same version of the job description for the employee's position?

❑ Is the employer the one who has sole discretion in writing and modifying the job description? (Answer yes even if the employee or others provide information or recommendations to be considered when writing the job description, as long as the employer always has the final say in what is included or not included.)

Checklist 3.14
Employer's Attitude Toward Use
Of Job Descriptions

(Ideally, the answer to each of these questions will be "no.")

❑   Are there some positions that do not have a written job description?

❑   Are there some employees whose responsibilities are just too varied or otherwise to difficult to put into a written job description?

❑   Are written job descriptions prepared only after a request or demand has been made for one, and that request or demand must be complied with?

❑   Has it been longer than one calendar year since a written job description has been reviewed?

❑   Are there occasions when a position will be filled without using a written job description during the hiring process for that position?

❑   Are there occasions when an employee's performance will be evaluated without either having or using a written job description for that employee's position?

❑   Are there written job descriptions for any positions that are not being used or referred to for any reason?

❑   Are you simply too busy to use written job descriptions for all positions?

❑   Is it impractical to use written job descriptions for all positions?

❑   Do informal job descriptions work as well as written job descriptions?

Form 3.4
Use of Written Job Descriptions

Name of Employer_____ Date_____

(1) List all positions in the firm, from top to bottom, that do NOT have a written job description:

_____   _____

_____   _____

_____   _____

_____   _____

(2) List all positions which have a written job description, but the job description has not been reviewed during the past 12 months*:

_____   _____

_____   _____

_____   _____

_____   _____

(3) List all positions which have a written job description that has been reviewed during the past 12 months*, but any recommended modifications from the review have not been made:

_____   _____

_____   _____

_____   _____

_____   _____

(continued on next page)

(Page 2 - Form 3.4)

(4) List all positions that have been filled within the previous 36 months** without using a written job description:

_____   _____

_____   _____

_____   _____

_____   _____

(5) List all employee performance evaluations that have been conducted within the previous 36 months** without the use of a written job description:

_____   _____

_____   _____

_____   _____

_____   _____

Employer_____ Date_____

(6) List any employee who, during the previous 36 months, has been terminated or against whom disciplinary action has been taken without referring to their written job description. This applies to employees terminated or disciplined primarily on the basis of job performance. It would not necessarily apply to employees terminated or disciplined for insubordination, criminal conduct, intoxication on the job, or other reasons that may justify immediate action regardless of job performance.

_____   _____

_____   _____

_____   _____

_____   _____

(continued on next page)

(Page 3 - Form 3.4)

(7) Describe how written job descriptions are prepared. Clearly identify the type and degree of any involvement in this process by employees, consultants, lawyers, or others besides the employer:

_____

_____

_____

_____

(8) Describe how written job descriptions are reviewed and modified. Clearly identify the type and degree of any involvement by other than the employer:

_____

_____

_____

_____

(9) Describe why positions without written job descriptions do not have written job descriptions:

_____

_____

_____

_____

* It is recommended that written job descriptions be reviewed no less than annually.
** 36 months is used as a time period here because it should include the applicable statute of limitations period for any employment claims arising from the event described.

3.1(f) Written Employment Policies

An employer either has written employment policies or it does not. Most employers have at least some written policies, but there are undoubtedly many policies that are not in writing. Some employers claim not to have any employment policies. These employers are only fooling themselves, as every employer has employment policies. The policies are either formalized by being written, or they are informal and consist of how things are actually done. If there are written policies, but actual practices vary from what is written, it is the actual practices that a court will determine to be the employer's policies.

Like written job descriptions, the employer should have sole discretion in preparing and modifying any employment policy. Information and recommendations can certainly be received and considered from employees and others, but the employer is the one held accountable for its policies. Therefore, the employer should always have the final say in what its written employment policies will or will not include.

Checklist 3.15
Identifying Written Employment Policies

❏ Collect ALL written policies that directly concern or affect the employer-employee relationship. This is not difficult to do if all such policies are printed in an employment manual. This may be more difficult if such policies are printed in different manuals, notebooks, files or if they are loose documents.

❏ Prepare a comprehensive table of contents for all written employment policies that have been collected.

❏ Determine how long it has been since each policy has been reviewed.

❏ Determine which policies have not been reviewed for at least 12 months.

❏ Determine which policies may need to be updated, modified or eliminated.

❏ Determine whether there are any issues not covered by written policies that should be covered by written policies.

❏ Describe how written policies are prepared.

❏ Describe how written policies are reviewed and how the decision is made to modify or eliminate a policy.

Form 3.5
Identifying Written Employment Policies

(To be used with Checklist 3.15.)

Name of Employer_____ Date_____

(1) Attach a copy of all written employment policies.

(2) Attach a copy of the table of contents prepared for all written employment policies.

(3) Determine the average length of time since each policy has been reviewed (in months & days):

_____ Months   and   _____ Days

(4) Identify which written employment policies have not been reviewed for at least 12 months:

_____   _____

_____   _____

_____   _____

_____   _____

(5) Identify which written employment policies need to be modified or eliminated, but action has not yet been taken:

_____   _____

_____   _____

_____   _____

_____   _____

(continued on next page)

(Page 2 - Form 3.5)

(6) Identify the issues not covered by written employment policies that should be addressed:

_____   _____

_____   _____

_____   _____

_____   _____

(7) Describe how written employment policies are created:

_____

_____

_____

_____

(8) Describe how written employment policies are reviewed and modified:

_____

_____

_____

_____

3.1(g) Unwritten or Informal Employment Policies

Even if an employer has no written employment policies, it definitely has unwritten or informal, employment policies. Tradition, custom, and the general perception that "this is just the way we do things around here" are the sources of informal policies. Informal policies exist when there are no written policies covering the same issue and when actual practices differ from the written policies that are supposed to cover the same issue.

Relying on informal employment policies is not inherently "bad," but unwise. Informal policies are often misunderstood, difficult to prove, viewed and experienced from different perspectives, and not reliable sources of information for reference or evidence. While it may be impossible and impractical to create and use written employment policies for every single issue, it is practical to create and use written policies for those issues that are most important to the employer. Relying on informal policies for incidental or less than crucial issues may be appropriate. The important point for the employer is that the issues which matter to the employer, which are necessary for a successful employer-employee relationship, and which lead to productivity should be made into formal and written policies that are actually implemented. Other issues may also become the subject of written policies, but it may be possible to let them continue as informal policies. As long as the employer knows all policies that are in force and has decided which ones to formalize in writing, and which to leave as unwritten, informal policies, the employer will maintain control over these issues.

Checklist 3.16
Key Issues Generally Covered
By Employment Policies

❑   Hiring procedure.

❑   Performance evaluations and consequences.

❑   Promotions, raises, increases in benefits, increases in authority, and other similar things that affect the status of an employee.

❑   Discipline and termination.

❑   Compensation and benefits.

❑   Use of company property, including vehicles, office equipment, office supplies, parking lots and facilities, electronic systems and communication methods, use of phone lines, and use or purchase of goods from company inventories.

❑   What is or is not a legitimate reason for being absent from work.

❑   Vacations, sick leave, and personal leave.

❑   Office or work space decoration.

❑   Use by the employee of their office or work space.

❑   Injuries and illnesses that occur on the job or that are related to the job.

❑   Maintenance of employee files and records.

❑   Access to and use of the firm's proprietary information, both during and after employment.

❑   Grievance policies and procedures (including anti-harassment policies).

❑   How specific emergencies or other particular situations are to be handled.

❑   The employee's appearance on the job and projecting a company image.

Checklist 3.17
Identifying Informal Employment Policies

❑   Begin with a review of the information from Form 3.5, Identifying Written Employment Policies.

❑   Determine what actual practices seem to be different than what is described in any of the written policies.

❑   Determine what actual practices seem to be in place for issues not specifically covered by written policies.

❑   Make the above determinations through: careful observation; interviews with employees and supervisors; by requesting anonymous, written opinions about what the informal policies are; and by watching, asking questions, and listening.

❑   Write out all informal policies that have been identified. There is likely to be more than one version of several or all of the informal policies. Be sure to write out all versions of informal policies.

3.1(h) Compensation and Benefits

What are the criteria for deciding which employees or positions will be paid what amount? The issue is not how much anyone is paid or what benefits are provided. Instead, the issue is the decisionmaking process that is used for determining compensation and benefits.

Once an employer has determined how it decides to compensate employees, it is necessary to determine what employees think are the criteria. Whether or not they are correct, what employees believe about how their compensation and benefits are set matters. It can help explain good or bad morale, why some employees may be angry about what they are paid, or why some employees do not believe what their employer says is the determined basis for increasing their pay. These and other issues need to be known by the employer so resulting problems can be addressed.

Checklist 3.18
Employer's Explanation of Decision Factors Behind Employee Compensation

❑ Are minimum wage employees paid that amount because the law will not allow a lesser amount to be paid?

❑ Determine which positions have a set pay scale, including a schedule for raises.

❑ Determine which positions do not have a set pay scale, including a schedule for raises.

❑ List in order from most to least important these characteristics of an employee as factors for determining the compensation of an employee in any given position: a) Formal education; b) Job related experience; c) Job performance in general; d) Ability to bring business to the firm; e) Degree of success in a project or assignment; f) Length of time on the job; g) Health of the employee; h) Insurability of the employee; i) Willingness of the employee to work long hours, extra hours, or overtime; j) Frequency of employee's absences not covered by paid leave; k) Financial stability of employee; l) Criminal record of employee; m) Employee's use of alcohol; n) Employee's use of illegal drugs; o) Employee's use of prescription medication pursuant to instructions in the prescription; p) The language ability of the employee; q) Other factors about the employee (specify):

_____

❑ List in order from most to least important the financial considerations by the employer as factors for determining the compensation of an employee in any given position in the firm: a) A range determined by what the employer can afford; b) Compensation rates paid by competition; c) Standard compensation rates in the industry; d) The availability of qualified persons for the position (paying higher or lower wages because there are not enough qualified people or no shortage of qualified people); e) Other financial considerations (specify):

_____

❑ Determine and describe other factors, along with their degree of importance, that are used to determine the compensation and benefits paid to employees.

Checklist 3.19
Employee's Explanation Of Decision Factors
Behind Employee Compensation

❑   Determine what factors are considered by employees as part of the decision process for setting wages and compensation.

❑   Make the above determination through: careful observation; interviews with employees and supervisors; by requesting anonymous, written opinions about what the factors are; and, by watching, asking questions, and listening.

❑   Write out all factors that have been identified. There is likely to be more than one version of several or all the factors. Be sure to write out all versions the identified factors.

Form 3.6
Factors for Determining
Compensation and Benefits

Name of Employer_____ Date_____

FACTORS IDENTIFIED BY EMPLOYER:

(1) Characteristics about the Employee Identified as Important Factors:

_____   _____

_____   _____

_____   _____

_____   _____

(2) Characteristics about the Employee Identified as Somewhat Important Factors:

_____   _____

_____   _____

_____   _____

(3) Financial Considerations Identified as Important:

_____   _____

_____   _____

_____   _____

_____   _____

(continued on next page)

(Page 2 - Form 3.6)

(4) Financial Characteristics Identified as Somewhat Important:

_____   _____

_____   _____

_____   _____

_____   _____

FACTORS IDENTIFIED BY EMPLOYEES:

(5) Factors Identified as Important:

_____   _____

_____   _____

_____   _____

_____   _____

(6) Factors Identified as Somewhat Important:

_____   _____

_____   _____

_____   _____

_____   _____

3.1(i) Maintaining Employment Records, Information, and Statistics

Every employer is required to maintain certain information for each employee. This includes Form W-4, Employee's Withholding Allowance Certificate; Form W-2, Wage and Tax Statement; Form I-9, Employment Eligibility Verification; the employee's name, address, and social security number; a description of the employee's job; information about their work schedule, pay period, rate of pay, and any benefits they receive; if an employee is claimed as exempt from minimum wage and hour laws, the employer must record the factors on which this claim is based. Records must be kept for all work-related injuries and illnesses of employees. These records must generally be kept by the employer for three years following the date of the employee's termination/resignation from the job.

Many employers also keep other information about some or all of their employees. Some employees compile and analyze various statistics and other data about their work force to assist in planning, productivity and other issues.

Whatever information about employees is compiled and maintained, the employer needs to know what information is being compiled, and how it is being maintained. All information an employer has about each of its employees must be considered absolutely confidential. An employer has good reason to know a lot about their employees and any employer acquires a significant amount of knowledge about each employee. For example, an employer knows each employee's full name, date of birth, social security number, home address, family status, amount of income, what deductions come out of their paycheck, employment history, educational background, the employee's health, the employee's medical history, the employee's insurability, whether the employee has a criminal record, whether the employee has a substance abuse history or current problem, family concerns of the employee, and so on. Most of this information is revealed through legitimate questions at the time the employee is hired. The rest is revealed by the employee when he or she uses health insurance, requests time off from work, or when the employee simply talks to their co-workers, supervisors, or employer. Some people are quick to give their entire life story, while others are more guarded, but an employer always acquires personal information about their employees.

The important issue is for the employer to keep track of what it knows about each employee. Access to this information must be limited to those who have a legitimate need to know, which includes the employee. The following checklist is designed to address these issues.

Checklist 3.20
Maintaining Employee Information

❑ Any information that identifies or can lead to the identification of a particular employee must be kept confidential.

❑ Compilations of statistics and other anonymous information about employees, personnel, the work force, or sections of the work force that are created and used for planning and analysis are probably not employee information for employment law purposes. While this may be considered as confidential, proprietary information, it is not confidential information for employment law purposes.

❑ Determine how employee information is acquired (i.e., from application forms, employee resumes, job interviews, insurance forms, accident or illness forms, employee requests for time off, etc.).

❑ Determine what employee information is maintained in hard copy format (such as in paper files or notebooks), even if some or all of the same information is also maintained electronically or in other forms.

❑ Determine what employee information is maintained electronically (such as in software programs), even if some or all of the same information is also maintained in hard copy format or otherwise.

❑ Determine what other methods of maintaining employee information are used (such as maintenance by a third party hired for this purpose), even if some or all of the same information is also maintained in hard copy format or electronically.

❑ Determine the number of physical locations that exist where access to stored employee information can be obtained (i.e., file drawers, computer disks, computer terminals, portable and hand held electronic devices, third party's office or facility, storage facility, etc.).

❑ Determine how access to each of the physical locations is obtained. This is not a determination of "who" has access, but what is the method of access to each location. For example, do you simply walk into the room and open the file drawer? Is a security system in place, such as a lock or a password?

❑ Determine who can access each of these physical locations. The answer is not necessarily limited to those who are authorized to have access. The real question is who can get access if they really want to?

❑ Determine what written policies are in place concerning compiling, maintaining, and accessing employee information.

Form 3.7
How Employee Information is Acquired and Maintained

Name of Employer_____ Date_____

I. HOW INFORMATION IS ACQUIRED

Identify which of the following are sources of information about employees:

____ Application Forms   ____ Employee Resumes   ____ Job Interviews

____ Applicant Testing   ____ Performance Evaluations   ____ Insurance Forms

____ Background Investigations   ____ Previous Employers and References

____ Requests for Time Off   ____ Requests for Employerprovided assistance

____ Alcohol/Drug Testing   ____ Monitoring of e-mail used by employees

____ News items from public sources   ____ Reports from other employees or third parties

____ Information that must be obtained pursuant to government regulation or order

____ Other (Specify)_____

II. HOW INFORMATION IS MAINTAINED

(1) Identify the types of information that are maintained in a hard copy format:

_____

(2) Identify the types of information that are maintained in electronic format:

_____

(continued on next page)

(Page 2 - Form 3.7)

(3) Identify the types of information that are maintained by other in-house methods:

_____

(4) Identify the types of information that are maintained by other methods off-premises:

_____

III. ACCESS TO INFORMATION

(1) Identify (by name or position) who has access to employee information:

_____

(2) Describe how access to information is controlled or limted:

_____

(3) How effective is access to employee information controlled or limited, as just described:

_____

(4) Attach copies of any formal policies, as well as descriptions of any informal policies, that are concerned with acquiring and maintaining employee information.

3.1(j) Claims, Complaints, and Grievances

These terms – claims, complaints, and grievances – include the following:

■   Lawsuits by a current or former employee (or job applicant) against the employer (whether in federal or state court);

■   An administrative action by a current or former employee (or job applicant against the employer (this is most likely to be an EEOC complaint or a complaint with the state human resources or human rights commission);

■   Worker's compensation case;

■   Unemployment compensation case (whether state or federal);

■   Any internal complaint or grievance made by an employee through a formal company procedure, including those made anonymously; and,

■   Any internal complaint or grievance made by an employee on an informal basis, including those made anonymously;

■   Any other issue of concern that has been brought to the employer's attention by a current or former employee about an employment matter, including those made anonymously.

While any claim, complaint, or grievance provides the opportunity for an employer to gain experience and to learn how to do things better, there are other effective, less expensive and less disruptive methods for gaining this experience. One of the primary goals of compliance planning is to significantly reduce claims, complaints and grievances. In order to evaluate its compliance planning, the employer must establish a base line of employee claims against which to measure progress. In addition, evaluating the types and nature of employee claims will tell an employer where particular weaknesses exist in its employer-employee relationships. It will also help determine whether such weaknesses are within the employer's control or outside of the employer's control.

An employer who has no employee complaints pending should make note of this fact.

Use the following form 3.8 to determine what employee claims currently exist.

Form 3.8
Employee Claims, Complaints, and Grievances

Name of Employer_____ Date_____

(1) If no employee claims of any type are currently pending, check here: _____

(2) Attach a list stating the court, caption, case number, and brief description of the nature of any pending lawsuits brought by current or former employees (or applicants) in any court.

(3) Attach a list stating the forum, caption, case number, and brief description of the nature of any administrative claims pending by current or former employees (or applicants) in any state or federal agency (this includes discrimination claims, wage and hour claims, worker's compensation claims, unemployment compensation claims, and other claims).

(4) Attach a list with brief descriptions of any formal, internal complaints or grievances that are pending and have been made by current or former employees. Indicate whether any such complaint or grievance is anonymous.

(5) Attach a list with brief descriptions of any informal, internal complaints or grievances that are pending and that were made by current or former employees. Indicate whether any such complaint or grievance is anonymous.

Note: Copies of any filed petitions or complaints, written grievances, or other documents may also be attached for purposes of describing the precise nature of the claim made.

3.2 Determining Trends

Once the current status of those issues identified in Section 3.1 has been determined, the employer can figure out if any trends are developing. Trends are determined by measuring what happens over time. It is necessary in the evaluation of trends to establish a benchmark, or baseline, against which to measure. The employer's current status, at least for compliance planning purposes, is the best place to start. Once current status is known, it is relatively easy to look backward in order to identify any trends, as well as to look forward to make plans.

An employer may pick several points in time and conduct the same evaluation described in Section 3.1 for each of those time periods. This will provide a great deal of information for identifying any trends. However, such a process is probably beyond most employers' budgets of time, money and other resources. Instead, an employer's time and resources will be better spent looking backward to identify any developing trends regarding specific issues. These issues are:

1) Complaints from current and former employees, as well as from job applicants.

2) Ability to attract and keep qualified employees.

3) Productivity.

When looking for trends in these or other issues, keep in mind that looking for and identifying trends is not an exact science. Also, a trend is simply a pattern of common factors in an issue. The trend may be good, bad or neutral. The point is to know whether trends are developing as the employer needs and wants. "Good" trends need to be kept; "bad" trends need to be stopped. Use the following checklist 3.21 to help identify any trends.

Checklist 3.21
Identifying Trends

❑   Look for trends in one issue at a time, making a list of the issues being investigated and analyzed.

❑   Determine how far into the past will be investigated. This time period should be long enough to be meaningful, but not so long that any results will be statistically skewed. A minimum of two years and a maximum of five years is suggested as the relevant time period, although different time periods may be more appropriate, depending on the needs of a particular employer.

❑   Review the current status of the issue being analyzed.

❑   Determine what events have occurred involving this issue during the relevant time period. For each occurrence identified, write a brief description of the relevant details (address the who, what, where, when, why and how).

❑   Review your descriptions of the occurrences. Are there common issues, causes, complaints, people or other factors? Or are the factors different in most or all of the occurrences?

❑   The discovery of common factors between occurrences tends to reveal the development of a trend or trends concerning that issue. Analyze what appears to be a trend and determine if common factors are merely coincidental or a likely trend. If an error is to be made in this analysis, err on the side of identifying a trend instead of a mere coincidence.

❑   Describe any trends that are identified in as much detail as possible.

By identifying trends, an employer acquires useful information for showing what is happening in the workplace. Reasons can be identified for the current status of issues investigated. It can become possible to determine the source(s) of a problem, and determine if it is long-standing or of recent development. Trend analysis helps an employer learn why it is in the situation it is in, as well as helping to determine if any policy could be changed to prevent the problem from recurring.

3.3 Current Methods of Planning for the Future

This section is not concerned with making a plan for the future, but with determining how an employer currently plans for the future.

Issues involved in future planning include:

1) Determining how many employees will be needed at various points in the future.

2) Determining what new jobs need to be created.

3) Knowing where qualified applicants can be found when needed.

4) Determining how to keep good employees.

5) Determining how to get employees to be as productive as possible.

6) How to control employment related costs.

7) How to control employment related risk and liability.

Knowing how future plans are made, for compliance planning purposes, enables an employer to determine if their planning methods are effective. In order to be effective, plans must be based on:

a) An accurate knowledge of the employer's current situation (which is determined through the methods described in Section 3.1);

b) By abandoning methods that do not work (which can be determined by identifying trends that are unproductive, see Section 3.2);

c) By keeping methods that do work (which can be determined by identifying trends that are productive, see Section 3.2);

d) By knowing the parameters within which the goals and objectives of future plans must be kept (which is one of the key purposes of compliance planning); and,

e) By staying in control of the above issues (which is another key purpose of compliance planning).

Use the following checklist 3.22 to determine how future employment related matters are currently being made.

Checklist 3.22
Determining How Future Employment
Related Matters are Planned

❑ Determine which "employment related matters" are currently the subject of planning in the firm. Be specific.

❑ Determine who (by name or position) is involved in the planning of employment related matters. Also, identify who has responsibility for what plans.

❑ Have each person describe in writing how they conduct their planning. They should include how they begin, how goals and objectives are set, how the plans are approved, whether they think their plans are implemented as prepared or are modified by others, how their plans are reviewed for progress, and anything else they want to include.

❑ Determine when planning is done for the various issues. Is it on a regular basis, is it ongoing, is it done on an "as needed" basis, or is it done by using a combination of these methods?

❑ Determine how plans are implemented.

❑ Determine how plans are monitored and modified.

❑ Determine how the effectiveness of planning is measured.

❑ Determine the effectiveness of planning, both in general and per issue.

The information obtained from the above checklist will establish a benchmark, or a baseline, of the employer's current methods of planning for employment issues.

CHAPTER 4
Analysis of Competitors' and Industry Standards

CONTENTS

4.1 Where to Begin

Business research, like legal research, begins with a question. The big question is: How does our competition, as well as the standards of our industry, deal with employment law issues? While this is the big question, it immediately leads to another question that must be answered before this analysis can begin. What are the employment law issues to be analyzed? Answering this question, as well as describing a method for analyzing the issues identified, is the focus of this chapter.

4.2 The Employment Law Issues to Analyze

Generally, the issues to analyze are the same as those that were the subject of the firm's self-analysis (see Chapter 3, especially Section 3.1). Ten employment law issues are identified in Section 3.1 as necessary for an employer's self-analysis. Here, those same ten issues are presented from the perspective of using them as the issues by which to analyze both the competition and industry standards.

Checklist 4.1
Adapting the Self-Analysis Issues to the
Analysis of the Firm's Competitors

[The "Firm's Competitors" are the firm's actual, closest competitors in the firm's market. Itdoes not necessarily include all "competition" throughout the firm's industry.]

❑ **Where Responsibility for Employment Issues Rests:** Do competitors have the same system or method of authority over employment issues? If there are any differences, determine what they are and what advantage or disadvantage the differences possess. In addition, how many competitors claim to have one method of authority, but a different system of authority actually exists? Of those whose actual authority is different than official authority, how many realize this? There are two goals when analyzing this issue: a) Is there an advantage to a different method for maintaining authority over employment issues that will work for the firm; and, b) Does a competitor have a built-in weakness in handling this issue that could give your firm a competitive advantage?

❑ **Size and Nature of the Work Force:** Is the firm larger, smaller or about the same size as its competition? Those competitors who have a significantly different work force size than the firm may have entirely different issues with which to deal. Even when the issues are the same, the decisions made on handling each issue may be different. As the discussion in Section 3.1(b) explains, employment law issues can be very different between firms with different size work forces. Use this issue to rate individual competitors. The most useful analysis will be of competitors who have similarly sized and composed work forces. For employment law issues, consider a competitor to have a similarly sized work force if its numbers are within 30%, higher or lower, of your firm's numbers. Use this standard whether comparing total numbers, numbers of part time employees, or full time employees, or administrative personnel, or independent contractors, or any other category or portion of the total numbers.

❑ **Location of the Work Force:** Determining where a competitor physically locates its work force is most useful for employment law purposes in determining how similar the competitor is to your firm. This is largely a jurisdictional issue (determining which state's laws apply to an employer and its work force) and those competitors who are subject to the laws of the same states as your firm are most similar for this analysis.

❑ **State and Federal Employment Laws that Apply to Competitors:** This issue is most useful to determine which competitors are most similar to your organization. Those competitors who are subject to the same state and federal laws as your firm are most similar for this analysis. Also, the analysis of this issue may reveal a better way to handle the issues of a specific law, or a weakness in how a competitor handles the law.

(continued on next page)

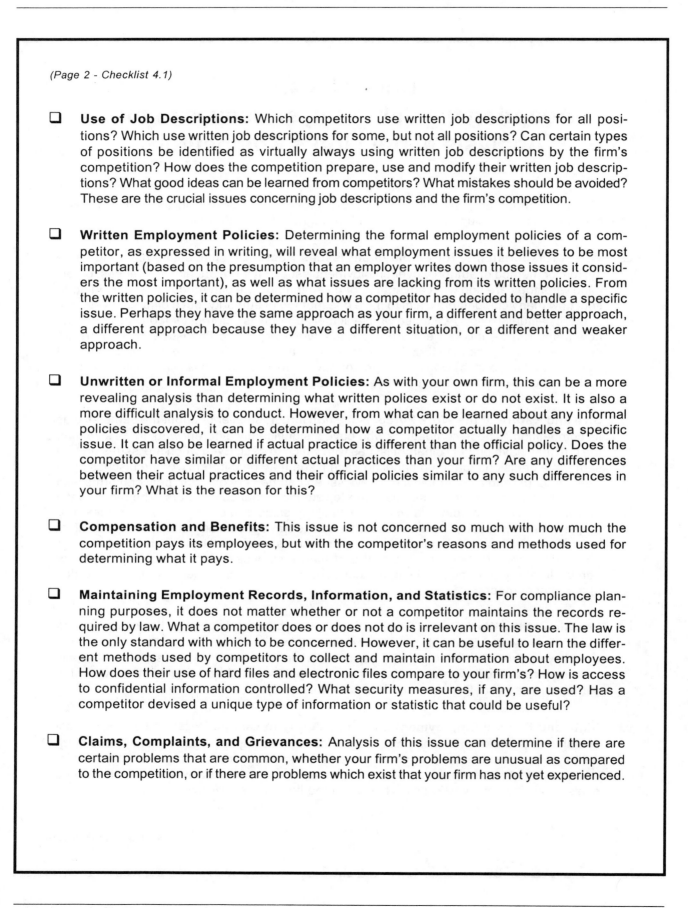

(Page 2 - Checklist 4.1)

❑ **Use of Job Descriptions:** Which competitors use written job descriptions for all positions? Which use written job descriptions for some, but not all positions? Can certain types of positions be identified as virtually always using written job descriptions by the firm's competition? How does the competition prepare, use and modify their written job descriptions? What good ideas can be learned from competitors? What mistakes should be avoided? These are the crucial issues concerning job descriptions and the firm's competition.

❑ **Written Employment Policies:** Determining the formal employment policies of a competitor, as expressed in writing, will reveal what employment issues it believes to be most important (based on the presumption that an employer writes down those issues it considers the most important), as well as what issues are lacking from its written policies. From the written policies, it can be determined how a competitor has decided to handle a specific issue. Perhaps they have the same approach as your firm, a different and better approach, a different approach because they have a different situation, or a different and weaker approach.

❑ **Unwritten or Informal Employment Policies:** As with your own firm, this can be a more revealing analysis than determining what written polices exist or do not exist. It is also a more difficult analysis to conduct. However, from what can be learned about any informal policies discovered, it can be determined how a competitor actually handles a specific issue. It can also be learned if actual practice is different than the official policy. Does the competitor have similar or different actual practices than your firm? Are any differences between their actual practices and their official policies similar to any such differences in your firm? What is the reason for this?

❑ **Compensation and Benefits:** This issue is not concerned so much with how much the competition pays its employees, but with the competitor's reasons and methods used for determining what it pays.

❑ **Maintaining Employment Records, Information, and Statistics:** For compliance planning purposes, it does not matter whether or not a competitor maintains the records required by law. What a competitor does or does not do is irrelevant on this issue. The law is the only standard with which to be concerned. However, it can be useful to learn the different methods used by competitors to collect and maintain information about employees. How does their use of hard files and electronic files compare to your firm's? How is access to confidential information controlled? What security measures, if any, are used? Has a competitor devised a unique type of information or statistic that could be useful?

❑ **Claims, Complaints, and Grievances:** Analysis of this issue can determine if there are certain problems that are common, whether your firm's problems are unusual as compared to the competition, or if there are problems which exist that your firm has not yet experienced.

Checklist 4.2
Adapting the Self-Analysis Issues to the Analysis of Industry Standards

["Industry Standards" includes formal policy statements in industry or professional organization or association writings, and/or, published standards as determined from statistical or other analysis of an industry. "Industry Standards" are industry-wide, not limited to a firm's closest competitors.]

❑ **Where Responsibility for Employment Issues Rests:** Compare the reasons for any industry standards on this issue to the reasons for the firm's method. Does the firm have the same or different reasons for what it does? Does the firm have a method that differs from industry standards because the factors on which the industry bases its standards do not apply to the firm?

❑ **Size and Nature of the Work Force:** How does the firm compare to industry averages? If the firm's characteristics on this issue are substantially different than industry standards, it could mean that industry standards are not all that relevant to the firm. The firm's characteristics are "substantially different" if they are 30% higher or lower than industry averages.

❑ **Location of the Work Force:** Are there industry policies or recommendations on how to physically locate the work force? Are there policies and recommendations that identify and address issues that arise when part of the work force does its work in places not owned, leased, or maintained by the employer, including in the employee's home? Determine why the firm does or does not substantially comply with any applicable industry standards.

❑ **State and Federal Employment Laws that Apply to the Industry:** This will be most useful in making the firm aware of additional employment laws that may not currently apply to the firm, but may in the future. Becoming ready for any likely need to comply with laws that are not currently applicable can be a relevant part of a compliance program.

❑ **Use of Job Descriptions:** Compare the reasons for any industry standards on the issue to the reasons for the firm's practices. Does the firm have the same or different reasons for how it handles the issue? Does the firm have methods and practices that differ from industry standards because the factors on which the industry bases its standards do not apply to the firm?

❑ **Written Employment Policies:** Compare the reasons for any industry standards on this issue to the firm's written policies. Does the firm have similar or different policies than established by industry standards? Does the firm have differences in policies because the factors on which the industry bases its standards do not apply to the firm?

(continued on next page)

(Page 2 - Checklist 4.2)

❑ **Unwritten or Informal Employment Policies:** Does the industry take a certain position on certain employment policies, but "everyone knows" it is different in actual practice "and for good reason?" If so, why is an "official" position taken that is different than industry practices? Is it an attempt to deceive? Is it a misunderstanding by the industry of actual conditions within the industry? Is the industry experiencing change that is hard to keep up with?

❑ **Compensation and Benefits:** Compare the reasons for any industry standards on this issue to the reasons for the firm's methods. Does the firm have the same or different reasons for what it does? Does the firm have differing methods from industry standards because the factors on which the industry bases its standards do not apply to the firm?

❑ **Maintaining Employment Records, Information, and Statistics:** It can be useful to learn the different methods used or recommended within the industry to collect and maintain information about employees. Does the firm use the same or different types of record keeping? Does the firm do some things differently from industry standards because the factors on which the industry bases its standards do not apply to the firm?

❑ **Claims, Complaints, and Grievances:** Analysis of this issue can determine if there are certain problems that are common in the industry, whether your firm's problems are unusual, or if there are existing problems that your firm has not yet experienced. In addition, what standards have been set or are recommended for preventing these problems, or for dealing with these problems when they arise? This could be a good source of information for preparing the policies to include in your firm's compliance program.

4.3 Trade Secrets

A trade secret is any information owned by a business that it desires to keep secret, whether or not any other business would want to keep the same information secret. Information can be the subject of a trade secret: a) if the business which owns it desires to keep it secret; b) if the information is not already public knowledge; and, c) if the firm treats the information as a secret through such methods as limiting access to the secret information within the firm, requiring those who know or have access to the information to guard it as secret, forbidding the sharing of the information to any person or for any reason except as authorized by the firm, and if the firm generally does what it can to keep the information secret and outside the sphere of general knowledge. Court opinions define a trade secret as:

> "A trade secret is defined as any formula, pattern, device or compilation of information which is used in one's business, and which gives the owner an opportunity to obtain an advantage over competitors who do not know or use it." *North Atlantic Instruments, Inc. v. Haber*, 188 F.3d 38 (2d Cir. 1999).

> "Trade secret law is unusual to the extent that it provides protection to the owner of a trade secret, but only while the information and knowledge remain secret . . . Although the subject matter of a trade secret need not rise to the level of novelty to the degree that it does in patent law, the information must be sufficiently novel that it is not readily ascertainable to the competitors in an industry . . . Although matters of general knowledge cannot be appropriated as secret, a trade secret may consist of a combination of elements even though each individual component may be a matter of common knowledge." *Rivendell Forest Products, Ltd. v. Georgia Pacific Corp.*, 28 F.3d 1042 (10th Cir. 1994).

One firm cannot legally get information that is the subject of the trade secret of another firm except in the following ways:

(1) The firm owning the trade secret voluntarily shares the information. Any conditions attached to this sharing of information must be observed.

(2) The secret information is made public.

(3) The firm wanting the secret information discovers it through their own analysis of legally obtained information. This is sometimes known as "reverse engineering."

Improperly obtaining trade secret information is known as misappropriation. This has been defined by the courts as:

> "Unauthorized use of trade secret information and unauthorized disclosure of trade secret information constitutes misappropriation . . . Trade secret protection extends not only to the misappropriated trade secret itself, but also to materials substantially derived from that trade secret." *General Electric Co. v. Sung,* 843 F.Supp. 776 (D.Mass. 1994).

> "Misappropriation occurs even where the trade secret is used only as a starting point or guide in developing a process." *Black, Sivalls & Bryson, Inc. v. Keystone Steel Fabrication, Inc.,* 584 F.2d 946 (10th Cir. 1978).

> "Misappropriation also occurs where a defendant uses a plaintiff's trade secret to understand what pitfalls to avoid." *Affiliated Hospital Products, Inc. v. Baldwin,* 373 N.E.2d 1000 (Ill.App. 1978).

The liability that can result from violating trade secret laws most often includes the granting of an injunction against the party that misappropriated the trade secret. An injunction is a court order to take some action or to stop some action. If a party ignores an injunction issued against it, the court can find that party in contempt of court and either put someone in jail until they come into compliance with the injunction, or issue a series of fines and/or penalties until they come into compliance. The exact nature of the injunction, or what it requires of a particular wrongdoer, will vary based on what the judge concludes is necessary to take any advantage away from the wrongdoer as a result of its misappropriation. This may include destroying or turning over all information it has derived, developed, or that it has in the process of research, which was based on or derived from the misappropriated trade secret. This could effectively destroy a compliance program.

There may also be criminal liability for misappropriation if state or federal criminal statutes are violated (this can include criminal penalties specifically included in trade secret statutes, as well as penalties for criminal activity used to obtain the secret information, such as burglary, theft, extortion, etc.)

4.4 Collecting the Information

Research methods already in use by a firm should be considered as the methods for gathering information for employment law compliance purposes. Any methods that show promise of success should be used, as the firm already knows how to work with such methods. The information presented below on collecting this information contains suggestions (although certainly not definitive statements on one specific method of collecting the information), as well as an evaluation on the likelihood of getting good information.

4.4(a) Collecting Information from Competitors

Businesses study their competition for a variety of reasons. Some information is willingly shared by a competitor; other information is the subject of trade secrets. Any information willingly shared by a competitor will not present legal problems concerning its acquisition or analysis. This statement assumes, however, that the person who shares the information is both authorized to have the information and to share the information with your firm. If either assumption is incorrect, there could be a trade secrets issue. Legal liability can result if a firm violates trade secret laws in acquiring information.

The following checklist describes methods of collecting information that can be effective for any issue or any type of information desired. Always consider these methods as viable options for collecting information (although not every listed method will work in all situations).

Checklist 4.3
Collecting Information from Competitors

❑ Ask the competitor for the information, either orally or in writing. Such requests for information are often granted on the basis of personal friendships, professional camaraderie or courtesy, because a favor is owed, because the reason for your request (preparation of a compliance plan) is considered a good reason or sometimes you may just not know the reason the information is being shared. Requests for information are often granted even when you are sure they will be denied. It never hurts to ask.

❑ Acquire and study all advertisements, literature and other written information released by the competitor. Businesses voluntarily release a great deal of information about themselves through: a) their advertisements; b) promotional materials; c) information describing themselves as an employer in order to attract job applicants; d) editorial comments or position statements on community and industry issues; e) their web site; f) press releases; and, g) through speeches and presentations by company personnel.

❑ Pay attention to all news items about competitors.

❑ Go to the courthouse and look through any court files in which the competitor is named as a party to a lawsuit. This is public information (unless a local court rule or court order has been issued to seal a particular case).

❑ Call your competitor, take them to lunch (or to a social event, or out hunting or fishing, or anywhere they like) and start talking and listening. It is amazing what people will share in social settings.

❑ Talk to their customers, their suppliers, or to anyone else who deals with the competitor. They may or may not have direct information about a given issue with which you are concerned, but they may be able to describe conditions or circumstances that will be helpful in making conclusions about the particular issue.

❑ Talk to any of *your* employees who recently worked for the competitor. Determine whether or not the individual is bound by a trade secret, and if not, ask them whatever you like. Ask such an employee if they will allow you to examine any written materials (such as employment policies) they may have. However, do not intimidate an employee into talking or sharing information. Respect the employee's willingness regarding cooperation.

(continued on next page)

(Page 2 - Checklist 4.3)

❑   Observe and study your competitors to establish how they appear to operate. What conclusions can be made, particularly about employment related issues that are likely to be as true now as in the past or in the future?

❑   Observe and study your competitors for any apparent changes. Pay attention to any changes in their operations, no matter how large, small or trivial the change may seem (such as changes in products or services offered, in pricing, whether they move from one location to another or add or close locations, etc.) Change in business is rarely done merely for the sake of change itself.

❑   Observe and study your competitors to determine if they do not make changes that seem to be occurring within your industry. Are they out of touch with their own industry or competition? Have they made different conclusions than others? Do they know something no one else knows?

4.4(b) Determining Industry Standards

Industry standards can be a reflection of what is actually occurring throughout the industry. The standards may be recommendations from industry organizations or associations on how to handle specific issues relevant to the industry, or they may be ethical ideals. Whatever they are, industry standards are generally much easier to determine than the activities of competitors.

Information collected by industry organizations and associations is, with rare exception, collected specifically for use by the members of the group that collected the information. This information may be data without much analysis, or it may be data with analysis. While any analysis offered by the organization can be useful, it should not be considered as a "sacred" analysis. Your firm should analyze all information itself. Draw your own conclusions and decide for yourself what the information gathered means to your firm.

Industry groups often publish notices or alerts concerning legal issues that are particularly relevant to members of the industry. Pay close attention to this information. While it may be too general for immediate use by your firm, these notices will identify and give some useful information about issues that your firm should be considering. However, information about legal issues often consists of opinions. As with all opinions, there is room for legitimate disagreement with some or all of the conclusions in a legal opinion. This does not mean a given legal opinion should be discredited or ignored. Even if disagreed with, it is an opinion that may be relevant for fully considering an issue that is part of your compliance program.

Another valuable source of information concerning industry standards are seminars and trade shows. Both speakers and printed information are almost always a part of these events. While the content of speeches and printed (or recorded) literature may not be specifically endorsed by the industry group sponsoring the event, the information will be quite useful. Information given at such events is, by nature, general and prepared in order to be relevant to as many members of the industry as possible. The result is current information that may be considered as approaching an industry standard. The response to such information is also valuable. What questions are asked? What answers are given? What exceptions are noted? What objections are made? In addition, what comments are made informally between members of the industry during social events or in other informal settings? These events are a prime opportunity to gather a great deal of information.

If an industry group polices itself to enforce ethical standards among its members, read everything released that describes how the group handles an issue. Determine the types of issues that are investigated and the consequences for violation of various issues. This information can be very revealing by showing the importance an industry group places on particular issues. There is always a hierarchy of ethical standards that determines what conduct will lead to serious consequences and what conduct will lead to less serious (or no) consequences. Although virtually every industry group will state that each ethical standard is equally important and that all are enforced equally, this is almost never true. While the hierarchy of ethical standards is undoubtedly informal, it can be determined by studying how ethical violations are actually handled. The result will be the industry's "true" code of ethics.

These and other methods for determining industry standards on employment law issues are described in the following checklist.

Checklist 4.4
Determining Industry Standards
On Employment Law Issues

❑   Read industry journals and other publications.

❑   Obtain copies of surveys, studies and other research sponsored by industry groups that concern employment and employment law issues within the industry.

❑   Attend seminars, trade shows and other presentations sponsored by industry groups. Listen to what speakers have to say and get copies of all available literature.

❑   Obtain copies of books, articles, videos and other publications that may not be sponsored or prepared by an industry group, but that are concerned with employment and employment law issues within the industry.

❑   Read letters to the editor and editorials in industry publications. These can illustrate the degree of support, the criticism of, and questions or differing opinions about employment issues relevant in the industry.

❑   If an industry group polices itself to enforce ethical standards among its members, read everything released that describes how the group handles an issue.

❑   If there does not appear to be a readily available source of information you need on a particular issue, write to the current president (or executive authority or other appropriate official) of the industry group(s) and ask for the information. There may or may not be an industry standard on the issue, but you will find out by asking.

4.5 Analyzing the Information Collected

The goal is to determine how competitors are handling the employment law issues that are a part of the firm's compliance program, as well as to determine the status of applicable industry standards for these same issues. Yet, neither industry standards nor what competitors are doing should become the standard with which to comply. That standard must always be what the law requires. Instead, the information from this analysis can be useful for learning effective methods of coming into and remaining in compliance with employment law. It can also show mistakes that are being made by others, the consequences of various conduct, as well as how well industry standards and the activities of the competition measure up to the requirements of employment law.

4.5(a) Organizing the Information

Organize the information by issue. The issues should already have been determined before collecting information, so in one form or another, create a file for each issue and put everything learned about that issue in that file. Separate the information for each issue into that which concerns competitors and that which concerns industry standards. Subdivisions within each file may then be made on the basis of any subissues identified as being part of the main issue, chronology, geography, or on any other basis that has significance to the firm. The data within each issue or any subdivision in each issue may be further organized by type, such as statistics, interviews, published reports, etc. The goal in organizing information is to create a system where all information on the relevant issues can be readily accessed when needed.

4.5(b) Quantifying the Information

Quantifying information means to give it value, to make it usable, and to determine its relevance to the preparation and implementation of the compliance program. If the firm already has a successful method for quantifying information from research, use this method. If not, any or all of the following methods can be useful:

(a) Make lists in which factors are rated by their place on the list;

(b) Create graphs to show the frequency of factors;

(c) Create tables or charts for comparing different types of data;

(d) Prepare flow charts to illustrate lines of authority and communication, as well as procedures for handling different things;

(e) Compile statistics prepared by others into a master statistical analysis;

(f) Compile your own statistics from the information gathered;

(g) Summarize or paraphrase narrative statements; or,

(h) Maintain narrative statements in their original form, but organize them by issue, sub-issue, or on some other useful basis.

Whatever methods are used to quantify the information gathered, the overriding goal should be to evaluate the information in order to draw conclusions about it.

4.5(c) Making Useful Conclusions

A conclusion is useful if it is accurately drawn from the information gathered, if it is specific, and if it addresses the issues that are relevant to the compliance program. It should be possible to know what information is the basis for each conclusion. This is commonly done by referring directly to the source of information relied upon within the body of each conclusion (either by some method of citation or by use of footnotes).

CHAPTER 5
Analysis of the Market Place

CONTENTS

5.1 Market Place Issues Relevant to Employment Law

The demands of the market place are among the most influential factors behind business decision making. While it is certainly wise to pay close attention to these demands, there are employment law issues that cannot be decided by the market place. For compliance planning purposes, it is not necessary to do additional research into the likes and dislikes of the firm's customers than is already done (assuming, of course, that the business is engaged in at least some efforts to determine the preferences of its customers). Instead, use what is already known about the firm's customers and all other demands of the market place on the firm. Before making plans to meet those demands, analyze them against the relevant employment law issues. These issues are identified in the following checklist and are discussed in the sections after the checklist.

Checklist 5.1
Key Market Place Issues Relevant
To Employment Law

❏   Race, color, national origin or sex of employees.

❏   Age or disability of employees.

❏   Religion of employees.

❏   Dress of employees.

❏   Grooming and cleanliness of employees.

❏   Demeanor and attitude of employees.

❏   Language ability of employees.

❏   Hours of work.

❏   Duties and responsibilities of an employee.

5.1(a) Race, Color, and National Origin of Employees

Federal law and the laws of every state prohibit the making of any employment decision on the basis of race, color or national origin [Title VII of the Civil Rights Act of 1964, 42 U.S.C. 2000e *et seq.*]. There are no exceptions to this prohibition regarding the issues of race or skin color. There *may* be an exception on the basis of national origin, but any such exception will be extremely rare and should only be made after obtaining a legal opinion from an attorney stating a situation exists which would justify basing the employment decision in question on national origin. Generally, any demands from the market place, regardless of their nature, subtlety, aggressiveness, earnestness, naivete, or any other characteristic of the demand or of the source of the demand, which concern the race, skin color, or national origin (which includes ancestry) of past, current or future employees must be ignored. It is not necessary to chastise a customer who brings up this issue, nor is it necessary to throw out or to stop doing business with such a customer. However, how to deal with such a customer is an issue to consider for the compliance plan.

5.1(b) Sex, Age or Disability of Employees

Federal and state law prohibit making employment decisions on the basis of sex, age or disability [Title VII of the Civil Rights Act of 1964, 42 U.S.C. 2000e *et seq.*; Age Discrimination in Employment Act of 1967, 29 U.S.C. 621-634; and Americans with Disabilities Act of 1990, 42 U.S.C. 12101 *et seq.*]. Customers are not always slow to let you know that they would rather have someone take care of them or of their needs who is a man instead of a woman or who is a woman instead of a man, who is younger or older, or who is not handicapped or disabled, etc. In addition, market research does clearly indicate that customer preferences do exist on these issues, depending on the situation. Some airlines, for example, argued in court during the early 1970's that being young and female was a necessary qualification to hold the job of stewardess (now generally referred to as flight attendant). Evidence of customer surveys from male and female customers of all ages, as well as psychological evidence about the comforting effect of young women as stewardesses was introduced at the trial court level. In one of the landmark cases on this issue, the court ruled,

> "[W]e apply a business *necessity* test, not a business *convenience* test. That is to say, discrimination based on sex is valid only when the essence of the business operation would be undermined by not hiring members of one sex exclusively . . . The primary function of an airline is to transport passengers safely from one point to another. While a pleasant environment, enhanced by the obvious cosmetic effect that female stewardesses provides as well as, according to the findings of the trial court, their apparent ability to perform the nonmechanical functions of the job in a more effective manner than most men, may all be important, they are tangential to the essence of the business involved. No one has suggested that having male stewards will so seriously affect the operation of an airline as to jeopardize or even minimize its ability to provide safe transportation from one place to another." *Diaz v. Pan Am World Airways, Inc.*, 442 F.2d 385 (5th Cir. 1971).

A market place preference alone will not be legally sufficient as the basis for an employment decision on sex, age or disability. There must be legitimate reasons for such a decision that are based directly on the actual requirements of the job. This issue is discussed in detail in Part Three.

5.1(c) Religion of Employees

Federal and state law prohibit employment decisions from being based on religion [Title VII of the Civil Rights Act of 1964, 42 U.S.C. 2000e *et seq.*]. However, as with the issues of sex, age or disability, this is not an absolute prohibition if there are legitimate reasons for such a decision that are based directly on the actual requirements of the job. Such reasons are referred to as *bona fide occupational qualifications* (BFOQ), which simply mean a good faith occupational qualification. For example, no law anywhere in the United States will prohibit the members of a synagogue from insisting that their rabbi be Jewish. However, customer preferences that the employees of a kosher deli all be Jewish cannot be followed. A deli is kosher because of the way it handles and prepares its food, not because of who it employs. As stated in the *Diaz v. Pan Am* case above, the court applies "a business *necessity* test, not a business *convenience* test. That is to say, discrimination based on [any protected class] is valid only when the essence of the business operation would be undermined by not hiring members of [any protected class] exclusively."

5.1(d) Dress of Employees

Market place preferences on the dress of employees may be a legitimate basis for employment decisions on this issue. Not only do some jobs require the wearing of protective clothing and equipment, many jobs require a certain dress because customers expect or like a certain type of dress. For example: a coat and tie for men and comparable attire for women can be required in office settings as well as in retail settings; a particular style of dress or an actual uniform can be required in delivery services, restaurants, retail stores, warehouses and in many other businesses; requiring a style of dress to fit the theme of a business can be required, such as western wear in a western clothing store.

In addition, certain types of dress, jewelry or accessories can be prohibited by an employer. For example, all jewelry but a single ring (usually a wedding ring) and a watch may be prohibited; or forbidding the wearing of pierced jewelry anywhere that can be seen except for a single earring in each ear; prohibiting the wearing of sandals or of any type of shoe that does not cover the entire foot (this is often a health code requirement); or prohibiting the wearing of anything except the uniform required by the employer.

While the employer cannot control how the employee dresses when not actually at work, the employer can generally require or prohibit while a work a certain dress. The only potential exceptions to this control of the employer occur in some instances when a particular item is worn by the employee because of religious belief or because of national or cultural identity. To control the wearing of such items *may* be a type of religious or national origin discrimination pursuant to Title VII of the Civil Rights Act of 1964. For example, an employer cannot stop an employee from wearing a cross on a necklace because it may offend its non-Christian customers, but an employer can control the wearing of religious items if the law requires certain safety clothes or equipment to be worn on the job. If possible, the employer must try to accommodate employees' desire to wear religious items. Such an accommodation may include the wearing of the item under mandated clothing or equipment, or, perhaps, wearing it along with the required clothing.

5.1(e) Grooming and Cleanliness of Employees

Generally, the demands of the market place that an employee be clean and adequately groomed can be followed. Many types of work, in fact, require high levels of cleanliness, such as food handling, health care, and many manufacturing processes. Even if a particular type of work does not require a minimal level of cleanliness, there is no real legal prohibition stopping an employer from simply wanting clean and groomed employees. There are jobs, however, which by their very nature cause employees to become dirty. While it is absolutely unreasonable to insist that an employee remain clean in a dirty work environment, it may be proper to set different standards for cleanliness, grooming, and dress in portions of the work site that do not involve the "dirty" work, such as offices.

5.1(f) Demeanor and Attitude of Employees

The market place almost always insists on common courtesies, normal levels of patience, and common respect. An employee does not have to like their job, their employer or their employer's customers, but an employee can be required to act with common courtesy and respect for others while on the job. An employee whose demeanor and attitude are not up to the required standard set by the employer based on market place demands can be terminated.

5.1(g) Language Ability of Employees

Most business transactions in the United States are done in English. However, market place demands may include language abilities in many other languages. Employers are not prohibited from meeting the language demands of their market, as long as that demand is based on a legitimate need, such as doing business with a particular country where that language is used, or doing business with a particular customer group who only speak that language. A particular language ability, therefore, can easily be a legitimate requirement of holding a job. If so, the precise language ability necessary should be included in that position's written job description. However, do not require a particular language ability if that ability is not a business *necessity*. In addition, being a native speaker of a particular language will probably *not* be a legitimate job qualification. Language ability as a job qualification should be judged on the basis of fluency, not whether or not the applicant is a native speaker. The quality of fluency required must also be based on actual requirements of the job. For example, in a restaurant it may only be necessary to understand the menu, how to count money, and how to respond to customer requests.

Another issue regarding language ability or use is an employer's control over what language is spoken on the job. For example, can employees who use English when actually doing their work, communicate with each other in another language? The answer generally is yes. Employees can be required to use English or another language (either spoken, written or both) when there is a legitimate, job related purpose. Otherwise, employees can use any language they like.

5.1(h) Hours of Work

If the market place rewards a particular business for being open for business at certain hours, that business should be open during those times. In addition, the business should be open for as much additional time as it takes to prepare for being open to its customers' demands during certain times. Employment law does not prohibit a business from setting any hours of operation that it wants. Any schedule from 24 hours a day, 7 days a week, 365 days a year, or less, is appropriate as determined by the business. The only employment law issue on this factor is the actual hours worked by a particular employee. Child labor laws set the standards for work schedules of minors of various ages and in various types of work. The Fair Labor Standards Act of 1938 [29 U.S.C. 201 *et seq.*], commonly known as the "wage and hour law," sets a minimum hourly wage for all employees defined as "non-exempt" under this act (see Part Two for a full discussion of this issue) and requires the payment of overtime pay (which is one and a half times the non-exempt employee's regular hourly wage) for every hour worked over an average of 40 hours per week per pay period. The regulations of the Occupational Safety and Health Act (OSHA) [29 U.S.C. 651 *et seq.*] may also set requirements for some jobs that affect how long an employee can work. The real issue, therefore, is not what hours of operation a firm sets, but ensuring that they comply with applicable laws when scheduling certain employees to work those hours.

5.1(i) Duties and Responsibilities of an Employee

The market place does expect certain duties and responsibilities to be fulfilled by each type of job. The market place expectation also changes over time for many positions. An employer can and should respond to these demands. The use of written job descriptions, as well as the regular review and modification of written job descriptions is the best method an employer can use to handle this issue.

5.2 Relevant Compliance Planning Factors

Meeting the demands of the market place is one of the keys to business success. Any business should do whatever it can to achieve success, except for those things which violate applicable employment law. When creating the policies of its compliance plan, the firm must use certain guiding principles for dealing with market place issues. These principles are described in the following checklist:

Checklist 5.2
Compliance Planning Factors for Planning
To Meet Market Place Demands

❑ Courts tend to consider market place demands, by themselves, as business conveniences. A convenience is subordinate to a necessity. Business necessities include complying with applicable law, and setting business policies that are actually necessary to fulfill legitimate (lawful) needs.

❑ There is no legal basis for making employment decisions on the basis of race or skin color.

❑ There is little, if any, legal basis for making employment decisions on the basis of national origin or ancestry.

❑ Employment decisions cannot be made on the basis of religion, sex, age or disability unless there is a good faith occupational qualification based on such a factor for the job in question. Such qualifications will be considered suspect by the courts and will be examined closely.

❑ Employers can, set and enforce standards concerning the general appearance, attitude and behavior of employees. Such standards are often based on market place demands.

❑ Market place demands regarding actual language ability can generally be met.

❑ Setting the hours of operation of a business is within the sole discretion of the business. The only real employment law issue is not working employees in positions or for a schedule prohibited by law for that type of employee (child labor laws and the wage and hour law).

❑ By properly using and maintaining written job descriptions, an employer is generally free to match the responsibilities of a particular position with the expectations of the market place.

❑ Customers who make demands that an employer cannot legally meet can remain customers at the discretion of the employer. However, the compliance plan should describe how to respond to customers making such demands. This also applies to suppliers, competitors, and others with whom the firm and its personnel must deal.

❑ An employer does not need to become an outspoken advocate for the employment laws it must follow. However, it must be clear by its policies and actual practices that the employer complies with applicable employment law.

❑ Demands and preferences of the market place are always subordinate to legal requirements on the firm, including state and federal employment law.

CHAPTER 6
Employment Law

CONTENTS

6.1 The Purpose of Employment Law

Employment law is a specialized area of the law that serves two primary purposes: First, it defines the employer-employee relationship; Second, it describes the obligations, rights and liabilities in the employer-employee relationship.

The body of employment law has not been created to put employers out of business, nor does it exist to frustrate business planning. It may seem that these are the real purposes of employment law, but many other issues in business cause difficulties (i.e., taxes, products liability, customer preferences and competition). Employment law issues are simply another set of factors that must be understood and dealt with by business people. Unlike some business issues, employment law has principles, concepts, and rules that can be read and studied. The employer can plan for and comply with the law, which is the premise of this book.

6.1(a) Defining the Employer-Employee Relationship

This area of employment law addresses these questions: What is meant by the terms, "employer" and "employee"; who is the employer; who is the employee; who is the employer of a particular employee at a given point in time; when does the relationship begin and when does it end; what is the nature of the relationship; and, in which jurisdiction(s) does the relationship exist?

6.1(b) Obligations, Rights and Liabilities in the Relationship

The employer has more obligations toward the employee, and the employee has more rights. This is because the employer has more power and control in the relationship than does the employee. The strongest party in any relationship has, by nature, the most responsibility in that relationship. It is the employer who creates the job, who decides on the qualifications for the job, who lets it be known that the job is available, who selects the person to be hired into the job, who sets standards for the job and evaluates the employee's performance, and who decides whether the employee will continue in the job or be terminated. However, the employee also has obligations toward the employer. The employee must do the job they are hired to do, they must comply with the employer's policies and procedures, and they must follow the employer's instructions.

When either the employer or the employee violates their obligations toward the other, they will become liable for the consequences. This usually means loss of a job for the employee, although there are situations when the employee may be required to pay damages to the employer in addition to losing their job. For the employer, violation of their duties in employment law can mean paying damages to employees or job applicants, having to reinstate a terminated employee, along with payment of back wages and benefits, being required to change certain practices or procedures or, in extreme cases, bankruptcy or jail.

The issues in this area of employment law address all aspects of the employment relationship. Hiring, evaluations, promotions, discipline, termination, injury and illness, discrimination, employee absence, insubordination, commission of crimes, safety, conditions of the workplace, wage and hour issues, benefits, confidentiality, trade secrets, definition of the worksite, and a host of other issues are all addressed by state and federal employment law.

6.2 Sources of Employment Law

Employment law is not new. Some principles, such as *employment-at-will*, have been recognized by the law for centuries. Others, such as enforceable prohibitions against discrimination based on race, sex, religion, or disability, date from the last decades of the twentieth century. The twenty-first century will undoubtedly see new and different issues defined and regulated by the law. Employment law may be old, but it is constantly evolving as society and the market place evolve.

The employer-employee relationship was originally known as the master-servant relationship. In fact, use of the term *master* for *employer*, and *servant* for *employee*, is still in common usage in legal opinions, texts and in the courtroom. These terms are used interchangeably in many sources of employment law, although the terms *employer* and *employee* will be used throughout this book unless *master* and *servant* are the terms used in a quoted source. In addition, it is recommended that employers (as well as lawyers and consultants) use the terms *employer* and *employee* in everyday practice. The reason is that *master-servant* terminology carries implications and meanings to many people that, while not legally accurate, are degrading and confusing.

The following chapters describe the key issues in employment law. All sources are cited in the text and in a table of cases and statutes in the appendices of this book. In general, the sources of employment law are: statutes and rules; common law; and public policy.

6.2(a) Statutes and Rules

The United States Congress and the President must work together to create a federal statute. Likewise, the statutes of each state are created by the combined efforts of a state's legislature and governor. Each statute that is created is a written statement of law. Typically, statutes provide definitions, describe procedures for specific things, and encourage or prohibit certain behavior. A primary source of employment law is federal and state employment statutes.

Rules are similar to statutes, but are subordinate. For example, Title VII of the Civil Rights Act of 1964 is a federal statute that, among other things, prohibits discrimination in employment and creates the Equal Employment Opportunity Commission (EEOC). The EEOC is an agency of the federal government that is empowered to do certain things. These things are described in the statute that creates the agency (Title VII, in this case), and an agency is always given authority to create rules. The rules created by an agency are primarily for explaining how the agency operates and to give detailed instructions on how to comply with the statutes that created the agency. For example, the statutes in Title VII simply prohibit discrimination in employment based on race, color, religion, sex, or national origin. The rules of the EEOC, however, provide a great amount of detail in how to engage in behavior that will avoid the types of discrimination prohibited by the statutes. Therefore, read a statute to learn what the law is on a particular issue. Read the rules that correspond to the statute for detailed information on the meaning of the statute and on how to comply with the statute.

Federal statutes are created by the federal government and are applicable throughout the United States. Federal statutes are published in the *United States Code* (referred to as the U.S. Code, or as U.S.C.), which is an official publication of the United States government. The U.S. Code is available in law libraries and in many of the larger public libraries. It is also available on the Internet.

State statutes are created by state governments and are only applicable in the state in which they are created. For example, New York statutes only apply to actions that occur within the geographic limits of the State of New York. An employer in Pennsylvania would have no reason to study a New York statute unless it intended to transact business in New York. This means there are 50 sets of state statutes in the United States, plus separate statutes for U.S. territories and the District of Columbia. In addition, each state creates its own state agencies, which in turn create their own rules.

An employer must be aware of the statutes and rules in its own state, as well as in any other state where it operates, and it must be aware of federal statutes and rules. If there is a conflict between a federal statute and a state statute, the federal statute prevails. (Article 6 of the United States Constitution makes this clear in its "supremacy clause," which states: "This Constitution, and the laws of the United States which shall be made in pursuance thereof . . .shall be the supreme law of the land . . . anything in the constitution or laws of any state to the contrary notwithstanding.") This clause has been interpreted to mean that while a state can impose additional requirements through its statutes to any federal statute, it cannot authorize less strict or contrary requirements. States are also generally free to create any statute desired on any issue not covered by a federal statute. As a result, state employment statutes are usually more strict than federal employment statutes, especially in stating which employers the statute covers. These issues will be described in the following chapters.

6.2(b) Common Law

The common law of the United States and of each state is descended directly from English common law (along with our entire legal system). The common law is a large body of law not found in statutes. Instead, it is found in the opinions and decisions of appellate and supreme court cases, or in case law. Federal and state statutes and rules do not cover every issue in employment law. For example, there are very few statutes covering employment contracts. When no statute applicable to a legal issue exists, the common law applies.

To find the relevant common law it is necessary to research case law, a task that can be more time-consuming than simply looking up a statute. In addition, research into case law is also very helpful in finding judicial opinions that interpret the meaning or application of both statutes and rules.

Common law principles are much older than statutory principles, although many statutes are derived from common law principles.

6.2(c) Public Policy

Public policy is any concept or principle that is generally good for the public as a whole, even if individuals or a small group might have to give something up for the benefit of the majority. Public policy is reflected by statutes and rules, but it is not specifically contained in statutes and rules. Likewise, the common law reflects public policy, but it does not necessarily spell out public policy on specific issues. By researching case law, it can be possible to find out whether or not a public policy is described for a given issue, but public policy is better characterized as a concept that encourages conduct that benefits the public.

In employment, if an issue arises that is not clearly covered by a statute, a rule, or by relevant common law, the course of conduct to take should be whatever appears to comply with public policy. For example, does an employer have any control over whether an employee uses tobacco products? There are no specific statutes that either give or deny this type of control to an employer. However, there is a Constitutional right of privacy and an expectation that an adult may use tobacco if they wish. Tobacco products can be legally used by adults, although there are safety rules that prohibit smoking in certain situations. Some statutes and rules do state where tobacco products may or may not be used, but they do not prohibit their use. Case law is also scarce on this issue. An employer, therefore, must try to determine what the public policy is regarding its ability to control the use of tobacco products by its employees.

Public policy is almost always a general type of policy. It sets guidelines for conduct, while statutes and the common law are much more specific in their requirements. However, an employer who is found by a court to have violated public policy, even when statutes and common law have little to say on the subject, can be held liable to those who are legally damaged.

6.2(d) A Hierarchy of Sources of Employment Law

To find the status of the law on a particular issue, first determine if a statute applies to the issue. Check for both federal and state statutes and comply with the one which more specifically applies to the issue (making this decision is not that difficult in practice and is discussed whenever relevant in the following chapters). Along with the relevant statute, read any applicable rules for further discussion of the legal requirements. Case law should also be researched to determine how to properly interpret and apply the statute and/or rule. If there is not a statute that applies, research case law to find the common law. In the event the most relevant statutes or common law do not seem to provide all the guidance necessary to handle the issue, determine from research what public policy would seem to require. Reliance on public policy alone is not a very common necessity. Instead, public policy is most often used to add weight to conclusions made by statutory and common law sources.

CHAPTER 7
Creating the Employment Relationship

CONTENTS

7.1 Hiring Employees

The process of hiring an employee includes creation of the position, advertising to fill the position, reviewing applications and interviewing, testing, and deciding which applicant to hire. Each of these issues will be discussed in this section.

7.1(a) Creation of the Position

Unless the owners of a business do everything necessary to operate their business themselves, they will need one or more employees. Creating any position, or job, therefore, occurs when a business recognizes that certain skills, talents, abilities or other qualifications that it does not already have (or does not have enough of) are needed to meet its goals. This is true whether the job is truly unique to the business or whether it is an already well-defined position in an industry. It is also true whether the position is new to the business or is one that has a long history and, perhaps, thousands of people already holding the job in the business. Positions are created, or continued, to meet some need of a business.

The Need for a Job Description

Once the need for a particular job is recognized, it is necessary to define or describe that job. Therefore, preparation of a job description must be the first thing done by the employer. The process can be compared to deciding where to eat. Once hunger is acknowledged, it is helpful to describe what taste will best satisfy the hunger. If it is pasta that is wanted, the search for the best restaurant serving pasta can be made. If a search for a restaurant is undertaken without really identifying the type of food that is being craved, it will be more luck than design if the restaurant finally selected fully satisfies the taste buds. It is similarly difficult to hire just the right employee if it has not already been determined exactly what need must be met.

Failing to prepare a written job description is a mistake made by many employers. It is a failure that unnecessarily increases risk for trouble (i.e., hiring an unqualified or even incompetent applicant, passing over the ideal person for the job even if the person hired is adequate, or not having an objective standard for performance evaluation). Preparing and using written job descriptions accomplishes the following:

(1) It forces the employer to think about the job. Whether it is a brand new position or an old position that has (or is about to become) vacant, some thought should go into deciding what the job will be. If it is an old position within the company, is it best to continue with an old job description (provided there is one), or are the demands of business suggesting that a change in the old description is necessary?

(2) It provides the best opportunity for identifying the actual qualifications necessary to do the job. If an employer can describe what a particular job is supposed to accomplish, it becomes relatively easy to determine the qualifications needed for the job. Like selecting a tool, it is necessary to know what must be done before it is possible to know which tool is best for the job.

(3) It focuses the employer's attention on the demands of the job and on the qualifications necessary to do the job, which is very helpful in avoiding discrimination issues during the hiring process. For example, it may be determined that a particular sales representative position requires: frequent travel over a specific geographic area; the need to use various forms of electronic devices; the analysis of financial statements and information; working with an expense account; a great deal of personal contact with customers and potential customers; and working independently. Knowing this position's description is a great help in determining the qualifications necessary to do the job well. These qualifications could include: being able to travel; a minimum level of education and/or experience in sales and/or accounting; communication skills; an ability to work closely with people; and a certain degree of self-discipline. Determining these qualifications, and focusing on the qualifications to do the job, translates into a higher degree of likelihood that applicants will be evaluated on whether or not they possess these qualifications. The likelihood that personal biases of the employer will be most responsible for making the selection are correspondingly reduced. The less that personal bias is a part of the hiring process, the lower the risk that illegal discrimination will also be part of the hiring process.

(4) If ever examined in court, in an administrative hearing, during an internal company investigation of a claim by an employee, or in any other situation, having used such a process of describing a job and determining the qualifications of the person to do the job prior to hiring an employee adds credibility to the employer. The failure to do this makes it appear as though the employer is, at best, naive and careless (and somewhat lazy), or, at worst, trying to hide discriminatory conduct. Either conclusion can lead to decisions against the employer and in favor of a job applicant or employee.

(5) Having and using written job descriptions provides a definite standard for evaluation of job performance, for determining whether a job should be changed or even eliminated, and for knowing who is responsible for what.

(6) The Americans with Disabilities Act, at 42 U.S.C. 12111(8), has this to say about job descriptions: ". . . consideration shall be given to the employer's judgment as to what functions of a job are essential, and *if an employer has prepared a written description before advertising or interviewing applicants for the job, this description shall be considered evidence of the essential functions of the job*." [emphasis added] Federal law specifically acknowledges the significant value of written job descriptions.

Preparing a Job Description

A good job description is clearly written, describes the key elements of the job, and is no longer than necessary. It is neither necessary nor possible to prepare a job description that describes everything required of the person in the job.

Job descriptions can be written for new positions and they can be written for positions that have existed for years in the company, but have never had a written description. In addition, any position in any business, regardless of the position, needs a job description.

The purpose of a job description is to be a usable reference for knowing what is expected from the position described. Therefore, it must be written in a style and format that make sense to the employer, to the employee in the position, and to applicants for the position. For this reason, the employer should prepare the job description in the style that will be most effective for the position. However, while the "look" of a job description, as well as the amount and type of information included in the job description may vary from employer to employer (or even from job to job with the same employer), there are certain things that should be common to all job descriptions. These things are set out in the following checklist:

Checklist 7.1
Preparing a Job Description

❑ The employer prepares the job description, not the employee or anyone else. It is the employer who knows best what the company needs from a given position. In addition, it is the employer who is held accountable for what is in a job description. While input from others may be solicited and actively considered, the employer must be the one who makes the decisions about what will and will not go into the job description.

❑ While preparing the description, remember exactly what the job is supposed to accomplish.

❑ Do not use cliches, idioms or slang. Such things are too easily misunderstood.

❑ Use a standard American English vocabulary, grammar, spelling and punctuation.

❑ Write for your intended audience, which includes applicants for the job and persons who will hold the job. Therefore, a description for an unskilled labor position would be written in a different style than a description for a position of high authority requiring post-graduate education.

❑ While it can be acceptable to use general language in some job descriptions, never be so vague that the description has no real meaning. It is better to be specific, but general language is probably unavoidable for at least part of the description.

❑ Focus on the key responsibilities of the job, not on describing everything required of the person in this job.

❑ The job description can be written in a narrative format, in a series of short statements, in outline form, in combinations of styles or in any other format that is clear and effective.

❑ Key qualifications expected of applicants for the job may be described. Be sure, however, that any qualification described is actually necessary. Be able to answer this question, "What is the specific reason for requiring each qualification?"

(continued on next page)

(Page 2 - Checklist 7.1)

❏   If qualifications are described, do not include any that are based on race, color, sex, religion, national origin, age, or disability, unless you already have a legal opinion stating such a qualification is a "bona fide occupational qualification" for this position. (See Chapter 9, Discrimination, for more information on this issue.)

❏   Pay and benefits can be included in the description, but are certainly not a necessary part of any job description. Instead, reference can be made to some other source where this information is provided, such as an employment manual.

❏   Give the job a title — the briefer the better.

❏   When finished, review the description and be sure you can explain the exact meaning of the entire job description with a straight face to anyone, including a hostile attorney and a judge and jury. You may have to do so one day.

Preparing a job description for a new position may seem easier than preparing one for a position that already exists, particularly when the position has been occupied by the same person(s) for a number of years and no changes in personnel are anticipated. In fact, many employers become very reluctant to write a job description for such a position. The theory behind this reluctance seems to be, "if the plumbing already works, don't fix it." This is flawed logic. Remember, the purpose of a job description is to inform everyone of what the job must accomplish and what the person in that job must be able to do. If the analogy of plumbing is continued, it could be said that everyone knows that water flows through the pipe in question. However, over time, the pipe comes to be seen as a convenient place to hang laundry as it dries. The kids will eventually discover they can have fun swinging from the pipe. It may also serve as the center-pole for a blanket that is really a tent being used in some make-believe adventure. A number of uses will be found for the pipe in addition to its primary function of being a water pipe. Even if the pipe never seems to object to the additional uses placed on it, it will wear out faster from such extra work. While any pipe, or employee, may occasionally be required to do more than originally intended, there is always a limit. A point is always reached when too much is expected. By having and using a job description, or a clear understanding of the purpose of the job and the person in the job, the long-term effectiveness of the position and of the employee is less likely to be degraded. It is never too late to write a job description.

Checklist 7.2
Preparing a Job Description for a
Position that Already Exists

❑ Review Checklist 7.1, *Preparing a Job Description*. The information in that checklist applies here as well.

❑ It is not necessary to tell the employee that a job description is being prepared for the position, although there is no real reason not to tell the employee.

❑ Determine what the employee in the job actually does. Do this by observation, by reviewing any records or paperwork generated by the employee or as a result of the employee's work, by talking with the employee, by talking with the employee's supervisor, by reviewing the employee's performance evaluations (if any), or by other methods that would be helpful.

❑ Compare the information learned about what the employee really does to what is expected from the employee's position.

❑ If the employee is essentially doing what is expected of their position, write a job description accordingly.

❑ If the employee is doing a job similar to what is expected, but not necessarily exactly what is expected, there is an option. Determine whether the position is most useful to the company as expected, or as it is actually being done by the employee. Write the job description accordingly.

❑ If the employee is doing a job substantially different than what is expected, the same option described in the previous step exists.

❑ When the newly written job description is finished give it to the employee. It may be necessary to retrain the employee to some extent. It may also be necessary to tell the employee that the job they had been doing is no longer needed and the job description describes the position that is needed. As appropriate, either offer the employee the "new" position or lay them off.

❑ At all times during this process, the employer must remember that it is the employer who has the authority and the responsibility for making all decisions.

Job Description Forms

The following forms are different formats for the same job. Following the last format is a critique of the information contained in these forms.

Form 7.1
Office Manager (Narrative Format)

This is a full time, administrative position with some supervisory authority. The primary purpose of the position is to oversee and coordinate the daily functioning of the company's business office. This includes responsibility for: maintenance of filing systems; maintenance of computers and communications systems; stocking office supplies; preparing and implementing a budget for operation of the office; coordinating vacation and other leave time of office personnel; hiring temporary help as needed; being a source of information for inquiries about wages, benefits and of employment policies in general; being a source for receiving employee grievances; and, such other responsibilities and activities that are necessary to the smooth operation of the business office.

The qualifications for this position include a bachelor's or higher degree in administration, management, or similar field of study. Specific abilities necessary to do this job include budget preparation and implementation, working with people in a supervisory capacity, written and oral communication skills, handling stress and stressful situations, preserving the confidentiality of privileged communications, and being on the job as required. Although there are set office hours, this position does not have a specific beginning or ending time each day, nor a specific schedule each week. The person in this position must be present in the office during office hours (unless on scheduled leave or out of the office to fulfill some function of the position), and is expected to meet the obligations of this position in a timely manner. Unless inappropriate for business purposes, work may be done at home or elsewhere out of the office before or after office hours.

The compensation and benefits for this position are described in the company's employment manual.

Form 7.2
Office Manager (Bullet Format)

This is a full time, administrative position. The primary purpose is to manage and coordinate the daily functioning of the firm's business office. Responsibilities include, but may not be limited to:

■ Maintenance of filing systems, computers and communications systems.

■ Preparing and implementing a budget for operation of the office.

■ Coordinating vacation and other leave time of office personnel.

■ Handling inquiries about wages, benefits, and employment policies in general.

■ Taking employee grievances and forwarding them as appropriate.

■ Such other responsibilities and activities as necessary.

Qualifications and abilities necessary for this position include, but are not necessarily limited to:

■ Bachelor's degree in administration, management, or similar field of study.

■ Budget preparation and implementation.

■ Effective written and oral communication skills.

■ Preserving the confidentiality of privileged communications.

■ Being present in the office during office hours (unless on scheduled leave or out of the office to fulfill some function of the position).

■ An ability to meet the obligations of this position in a timely manner.

■ As appropriate, work may be done at home or elsewhere out of the office.

■ The compensation and benefits for this position are described in the company's employment manual.

Form 7.3
Office Manager (Outline Format)

I.   Type of Position

    A. Full time, administrative position with some supervisory authority

II. Primary Purpose of Position

    A. To oversee and coordinate the daily functioning of the company's business office

III. Key Responsibilities of Position

    A. Maintenance of filing systems

    B. Maintenance of computers and communications systems

    C. Ensuring that office supplies are ordered and stocked

    D. Preparing and implementing a budget for operation of the office

    E. Coordinating vacation and other leave time of office personnel

        1. Hiring temporary help as needed

    F. Handling inquiries from company employees, managers, and supervisors about the following:

        1. Wages, benefits, and employment policies in general

        2. Status of the business office

        3. Grievances and claims

    G. Such other responsibilities and activities as necessary

(continued on next page)

(Page 2 - Form 7.3)

IV.   Qualifications Necessary to this Position

    A.   A bachelor's or higher degree in administration, management, or similar field of study

    B.   An ability to prepare and implement a budget

    C.   Working with people in both a supervisory capacity and in a subordinate position

    D.   Strong written and oral communication skills

    E.   An ability to handle stress and stressful situations

    F.   Preserving the confidentiality of privileged communications

    G.   Ability to be present in the office during office hours (unless on scheduled leave or out of the office to fulfill some function of the position)

    H.   An ability to meet the obligations of this position in a timely manner

V.   Compensation for Position

    A.   The compensation and benefits for this position are described in the company's employment manual, but include:

        1.   Initial salary range of $_____ to $_____

        2.   Paid annual vacation

        3.   Paid sick and personal leave

        4.   Health and life insurance

        5.   Retirement plan

A Critique of the Information in Forms 7.1, 7.2, and 7.3:

It is not the format or style of the job description that is crucial. It is the information in the forms that matters. Notice what type of information is *not* contained in these forms: Nothing about the employer; nothing to indicate that this position is to be filled by a person of a particular race, color, religion, sex, national origin, age, or disability; nothing about anyone who has previously held (or who is currently holding) this position; no statements, opinions, or theories about what makes a good employee; no promises of continued employment, of advancement, or of anything; no warnings or threats; no attempt to set a standard of how good the person in the position must be; and no attempt to do anything except to describe the position.

The job description is not the place for theory, for a history of the employer, for a history of the position and of those who have held it, or for how performance of the position is to be evaluated. The place for these things is the employment manual.

Notice what type of information *is* contained in the preceding forms: the position's title; a statement of its primary purpose to the employer; general statements of responsibilities to be fulfilled by this position; general statements of relevant qualifications for this position; and a reference to where information about the pay and benefits for the position can be found. While this information is all general, it is nevertheless specific to this position. Enough of a description has been given that a reasonable person could read any of the above formats and have a good idea of what the position is all about. This is all that is necessary.

Maintenance of a Job Description

Once written, a job description is not a finished work. Very few positions with any employer stay the same from year to year. While certain aspects of the position may not change, others will be constantly evolving. Every level of business is dynamic and is effected by changes in the market place, by competition, by change (or lack of change) in the law, by local and national economies and events, and by many other factors. With such potential for change, it is ill-advised to believe that a job description can be written and then left alone.

At least once a year, such as following an employee's performance evaluation, each job description must be reviewed and modified as necessary. Perhaps additional responsibilities should be added, or taken away, or the employee may have completed additional education or acquired additional abilities that would justify a change in their position. If it is in the best interests of the business to do so, modify the job description.

Checklist 7.3
Modifying a Job Description

❑ The guiding principle is to do what is in the best interests of the employer's business.

❑ Review each job description at least once each year. An ideal time for such a review is during the performance evaluation of the employee who holds the position.

❑ When a position becomes vacant (or is about to become vacant) and a new employee will be sought to fill the position, review the job description and change it to fit the needs of the business. This is perhaps the easiest time to change any job description as a new person will be taking the position and will not necessarily be used to the job as it was previously described.

❑ The information in the previous checklists, *Preparing a Job Description* and *Preparing a Job Description for a Position that Already Exists*, continues to apply when modifying a job description.

❑ When the modified job description is finished, give it to the employee and retrain or review their responsibilities as necessary.

❑ Be sure those who need to know are aware that a particular position has had its description modified (such as supervisors and subordinates).

7.1(b) Advertising to Fill the Position

Once the job description is complete, the employer is ready to fill the position. It is necessary to begin with a completed job description, as it provides the best guide for finding a qualified person.

Deciding *What* to Look For

The caption for this section is "Deciding *What* to Look For," instead of "Deciding *Who* to Look For," to emphasize the point that the guiding principle in advertising to fill a position is to look for qualifications, not for a particular person or kind of person. (This does not mean that there is necessarily anything inappropriate with hiring a specific individual and then creating a position for them. As long as a particular individual is wanted because of the qualifications they possess and not because of their race, color, religion, sex, national origin, age, or disability status, it is generally proper to design any position for any individual.)

Look to the job description to determine what qualifications are needed for the position and set out to look for those qualifications. Look in places where people with the necessary qualifications are most likely to be found. Use methods that qualified people are most likely to respond to. Design the advertisement in such a way that qualified people will understand that it is their skills, talents, education, experience, and abilities that are being sought. It is necessary to know *what* you are looking for in order to know where and how to find what you need.

How to Look

There are many effective and proper methods to advertise a job opening. An employer is generally free to use any method or combination of methods that they decide is best for them. Whether the search for qualified applicants is done with want ads in a general circulation newspaper, a trade journal, a magazine, at job fairs, at schools and universities, on the Internet, through radio and television advertisement, billboards, posting notices at the place of business, by spreading the word through associates that an opening exists (so called, "word of mouth" advertising), or by any other method or combination of methods that might be imagined, the crucial legal issue is not the method(s) used. Instead, the real issue is the actual goal of the employer in their choice of methods for finding employees.

The preceding paragraph could have been written about a company's product. A business advertises its products or services in whatever ways it believes will result in the most sales. The specific methods for advertising or marketing any product depend a great deal on the product. Is it a luxury item, a necessity, something expensive, or not so expensive? These and other factors will be considered in deciding how best to sell the product. When attempting to attract qualified applicants for a position, it is the nature of the position and of the qualifications necessary that should dictate how to advertise the job opening. The law does not forbid any particular method of advertising for new employees. The law only requires that the search focus on actual qualifications instead of on race, color, national origin, sex, religion, age or disability.

Consider the information in the following checklists when planning how to advertise for a job opening.

Checklist 7.4
Methods of Advertising for Applicants

❏ **Want ads in a general circulation newspaper.** This can be an effective way for making the position known throughout a given geographic area.

❏ **Want ads in a trade journal.** Whether a newspaper, magazine, newsletter or other style of publication, if it is read by people within a certain industry, activity or trade, this is an effective way of advertising a position among people already in the field.

❏ **Radio and television ads.** This is effective for reaching the general public in the listening or viewing area of the particular station. With many radio stations and cable television stations being designed to attract certain demographics (information that is available through ratings services and which is readily provided by the station), it is also possible to focus advertisements for certain segments of the public. But be aware, this also makes it possible to discriminate in deciding which demographics will or will not learn of the advertisement.

❏ **Job fairs.** These include events sponsored by a single company, by an industry or professional organization, by community groups, or by any group who wants to allow employers to set up a table or booth to advertise openings they may have. Depending on the sponsor and the location of a job fair, it can be designed to attract attention from the general public or from a targeted group or segment of society. It is not necessarily inappropriate to participate in a job fair sponsored by any particular group (i.e., an ethnic organization or a religious group), as long as such a specifically targeted job fair is not the only method used to advertise the job opening (would a business overlook an opportunity to sell its product to a targeted group, but would the business also limit their advertising to a targeted group?).

❏ **Schools.** Conducting interviews of soon-to-be-graduates at their college, university, trade or other school can be an extremely effective method for finding new employees for positions that require specialized education or training.

❏ **Billboards and other publicly posted signs.** One such sign, or a number of these signs in similar demographically organized neighborhoods is not public advertising. It is targeted advertising, which is not necessarily inappropriate, but recognize it for what it is. A series of signs throughout a particular city or geographic area might qualify as general advertising.

(continued on next page)

(Page 2 - Checklist 7.4)

❑   **The Internet.** Anyone with access to a computer terminal and a phone line can, in theory, find a want ad posted on the Internet. Businesses typically post notices of openings on their own Web page, or on other Web sites maintained or sponsored by other organizations. This can be effective, particularly for positions actually requiring use of the Internet. However, it is possible to "hide" any information on the Internet by limiting direct access to it through the use of specifically selected search words or phrases.

❑   **Notices at the job site.** Whether posted in areas frequented by employees, by customers, or both, advertising a job opening at the business itself can be quite effective. Special interest retail stores and businesses may prefer this method of advertising, as only people who already have an interest in their special interest business will see the ad. However, this can also be a method of avoiding advertising of the job in places where people "who don't look like us" would never see it. That could be a discriminatory practice.

❑   **Word of mouth advertising.** It is frequently stated that the best jobs and career opportunities are never advertised. In fact, some businesses may never formally "look" for anyone to ever fill certain types of positions. Instead, they let it be known that they are always interested in reviewing resumes, or in talking to well-qualified people, or that there is always room for the "right" person. This is all legitimate. It is also a system that is easy to abuse. Federal employment law does not prohibit such "advertising." However, the law will define such advertising as unlawful discrimination when it can be shown that it results in certain characteristics (i.e., race, color, national origin, sex, religion, age, disability) being a part of the process for considering or hiring anyone.

❑   **Other.** Any other method of giving notice that there are openings, or that interest exists in people with certain qualifications, will be legitimate if the method is not merely an overt or subtle method for unlawful discrimination. The bottom line is being able to give an affirmative answer to this question, "Is the method used an honest, good faith effort to find people who might be qualified for the position in question, and nothing more or less?"

Checklist 7.5
Advertising for the Right Person

❑ Begin with the written job description. This will identify the qualifications needed.

❑ Structure the advertisement t o attract the qualifications needed.

❑ Always use clear language, whether oral or written, to describe what qualifications the right person will possess. Again, this will be based on the job description.

❑ When deciding what methods to use, where to look, how and when to look, as well as the language used while looking, never let any part of the process include considerations based on race, color, national origin, religion, sex, age or disability. The only exception to this is when you have a legal opinion in hand that clearly states such a consideration is a bona fide occupational qualification.

❑ Clearly describe what qualifications you are looking for, or clearly describe the available position. This does not need to be a lengthy description. In fact, it may be most effective if it is quite brief. The point is to communicate clearly, to avoid confusion and misunderstanding as much as possible.

❑ Prepare the advertisement for the intended audience, which is the pool of people who have the qualifications being sought.

❑ Select one or more methods of advertising that should be most effective in reaching the largest number of qualified people. Do not target demographics that result in unlawful discrimination. At the same time, however, when looking for a rabbi there is no point in advertising in a Catholic magazine.

❑ If specific educational or experience requirements are given in the advertisement, be sure these requirements are supported by the job description. This can be an issue resulting in discrimination if the goal is simply to ensure that a particular group of people will not be qualified. This can occur whenever there is no more than a slight possibility that anyone in the targeted group would have the education or experience "required."

(continued on next page)

(Page 2 - Checklist 7.5)

❑ When competition for qualified persons is high between employers, the advertisement may focus on selling the idea of having a career with the employer's company. Mention of specific positions may be limited or even omitted. The ad may simply state that anyone interested in joining the company should contact the company with their ideas.

❑ Be sure to include information on how an interested person can apply for the position. As appropriate, having more than one way to apply can be preferable. This is not necessarily a legal requirement. It might become a legal necessity, though, if a particular method of applying would likely eliminate or reduce applications from people based on race, color, national origin, religion, sex, age, or disability. For example, requiring applications to be made in person in the men's room at the top of three flights of stairs and above the military training barracks for the American Nazi party. Such a location will probably mean no applications can be made by women, or by disabled persons who do not have use of their legs, or by anyone targeted by Nazis. This is a method of applying for a job that is nothing more than unlawful discrimination.

Want Ad Formats

The following are examples of various formats for advertising the office manager position described in the previous section of this chapter.

<u>In a newspaper or magazine:</u>

Wanted: Office Manager. Call 555-1234 to schedule an interview.

-or-

Office Manager. Bachelor's degree in business or related field, experience preferred. Duties include supervision of business office, budgeting and close work with others. Send resume and letter to: (give address).

<u>At a job fair or at a school:</u>

The person representing the company can describe the opening based on the job description. In addition, this person can have copies of the actual job description to distribute to those interested, along with instructions on applying for the position.

<u>Notice posted on signs:</u>

Opening for Office Manager. For information call: 555-1234, or write to: (give address).

<u>On the Internet:</u>

Employment Opportunities (click here).

—This could then go to a link containing the titles of all open positions, and by clicking on a title, there would be a link to the complete job description for the title selected, along with instructions for applying via the company's web site or through some other method.

As can readily be seen, legally appropriate advertising about a job opening can be very brief, but it can also be as detailed as the actual job description. It is also proper for the employer to add information to an announcement that attempts to "sell" potential applicants on the employer's company in general. Particularly in competitive businesses where there are more openings than truly qualified people, a want ad must also convince the reader that the employer is a better place to work than other employers. In fact, most or all of the advertisement may be about the employer's company, with only a short notice at the end on how to find out more about employment or career opportunities.

7.1(c) Reviewing Applications and Interviewing

Applications

An application for a job should be considered any communication from anyone expressing an interest in the job or position, or in coming to work for the employer in some unspecified capacity. This includes unsolicited letters, communications in response to advertisements for openings, a completed application form used by the employer, a resume (whether solicited or not), or an appearance in person at the employer's door.

Applications are generally made in response to an advertisement about an opening, or because the employer maintains a personnel office that accepts applications at any time, or because someone wants to work for a particular employer and makes an unsolicited application for a position that may or may not exist.

However they are made, or for whatever reason they are made, all applications should be taken seriously and handled appropriately. Even if an application is ridiculous (such as by a hopelessly unqualified person), treat the person with respect and common courtesy and put the application through the normal procedure. This is not to say that a person would have a reason to successfully sue an employer for being rude to them and for throwing their application away in front of them, because such action alone probably will not support a lawsuit. However, a person can still make a claim against an employer that will have to be defended. Even winning a case, including winning the case fairly early in the process, has a cost that should be avoided. Any lawyer who handles employment cases can give examples of claims made only because the person was treated rudely, whether or not their claim had much merit. By handling all applications pursuant to a prescribed procedure, almost all such nuisance claims can be avoided.

While there are different methods for handling applications, this checklist contains factors that should be a part of any method of handling job applications.

Checklist 7.6
Handling Applications

❑   Always have a procedure for accepting and reviewing applications for any job or position.

❑   Different procedures for different types of positions are appropriate and even logical.

❑   Once a procedure is in place, always use it. If a particular application is to be handled differently than the normal procedure for that type of application, be able to explain exactly why the application calls for different treatment.

❑   Legally, it makes no difference whether an employer prefers to use pre-printed application forms, custom application forms, or no forms at all. Likewise, it does not matter whether the employer prefers resumes instead of application forms, application forms with resumes, or applications instead of resumes. The nature of the forms or paperwork wanted by the employer is not the issue. It is the information wanted from the applicant that is the issue.

❑   Appropriate information to be solicited from an applicant generally includes (but is not necessarily limited to): Applicant's name; an appropriate way to contact the applicant about their application (such as a mailing address, telephone number, e-mail address); information about any experience the applicant may have that is relevant to the position in question; information about education or training the applicant may have that is relevant to the position in question; information about other relevant qualifications the applicant may have; an acknowledgment from the applicant that they can legally work in the United States; an acknowledgment from the applicant that there is no legal reason that they are aware of that would prohibit them from holding the job in question; an acknowledgment from the applicant that, if hired, they would be able to be present for work as required; and an acknowledgment from the applicant that, if hired, they would agree to submit to any required medical examination, drug testing, or background check.

❑   Inappropriate information to request or demand from an applicant generally includes   (but is not necessarily limited to): information about their race or skin color (even though seeing the person reveals something about this issue); information about their religious faith, beliefs, or practices; anything about their age, whether direct or indirect (such as asking, "when did you graduate from high school" or, "who was your favorite music group while you were in school"); anything about the applicant's ancestry or national origin (whether or not simply seeing the person *seems* to give information about this issue); whether or not they consider themselves to be disabled (instead, all applicants should be advised at some point that reasonable accommodations for any disability will be made as requested); the marital or family status of the applicant; whether the applicant has children, the ages

(continued on next page)

(Page 2 - Checklist 7.6)

of their children, or their plans for children (and the same issues concerning grandchildren); whether the person has ever made a worker's compensation claim; the applicant's political beliefs; whether the applicant is serving or has served in the armed forces of the United States; and, other information that does not concern a good faith inquiry into the person's qualifications for the position for which they have applied.

❑ Applicants can be eliminated from consideration for the position if they are not actually qualified; if they have not followed the instructions for applying for the position, even if otherwise qualified; if their dress and/or demeanor is entirely inappropriate for the position; or if they refuse or fail to provide relevant information necessary for consideration of their application, even if otherwise qualified.

❑ Be consistent in how applications are handled. Do not make exceptions unless there is a clear reason for doing so.

Resumes

Resumes are often preferred to a job application form by employers (and even by many applicants) because they usually contain more information about the applicant than would be asked by an employer. The applicant usually prepares their own resume, deciding which format to use and what information to include, which usually results in more detailed information than would be requested on an application form.

The fact that people may volunteer information about themselves in their resume that would not otherwise be asked does not necessarily authorize an employer to rely on all the information given. For example, one person may list the organizations they belong to and include religious or ethnic groups. It is not a problem for the employer that the person chose to add this information to their resume, but it could be a problem for the employer to use such information in evaluating the person's application. This is because it may appear to have been a decision based on the applicant's religion or national origin. However, there is also the position that a membership in such organizations indicates merely that the person is involved in the community, which may be a relevant factor in evaluating their application. The point is that, unfortunately, this is not always a clear issue.

The best way to resolve this dilemma is to refer again to the written job description. Since the job description shows the relevant qualifications for holding the position, using it as the standard for evaluating the information in the resume can reduce much of the risk. Some employers handle this issue by having personnel who are not a part of the decision making process review each resume. The purpose of this review is to "edit" the resume to remove any photographs or other information that could not legally be part of the evaluation of the applicant. This practice is a legitimate method for handling this dilemma, but it is not necessary in all situations. Most people who review a resume and compare the qualifications in the resume to those required in the job description can make a proper evaluation.

There is the question, though, of which is better to use, an application form or a resume? Legally, the answer depends on what is the best and most practical way to gather valid, relevant information about an applicant's qualifications. A resume is probably more effective, but there are many jobs where applicants do not traditionally prepare and use resumes. The answer to this question is up to the employer.

Interviewing

An interview is the part of the application process where the applicant and the employer ask each other questions relevant to the position, and where each gives the other information relevant to the position. Interviews can be formal or informal. They may occur in a face to face meeting, over the telephone, over the Internet, or through just about any method of communication (real time or not) that is satisfactory to the employer. Interviews are sometimes a lengthy process, consisting of several meetings with various people. There is no real standard, at least not a legal standard, for how a particular interview process should be organized. The point to remember, however, is that an interview, in whatever form it takes, is a method for exchanging information. The employer's legal obligation is to make sure the exchange of information is limited to those issues and topics that are relevant to evaluating the applicant's actual qualifications for the job.

Regardless of the form an interview takes, the following factors should be a part of the interview process:

Checklist 7.7
Conducting an Interview

❑   The actual interview should be private. While there may be one or more people present on behalf of the employer, each applicant should be interviewed one at a time.

❑   Whenever possible, interviews should take place at the employer's place of business during regular business hours. It can also be appropriate to conduct an interview at a job fair, a school, or some site other than the employer's office, depending on the circumstances of the employer or applicant.

❑   Use the job description during the interview to focus the exchange of information on the position and on the necessary qualifications. Do not be afraid to discuss other issues that invariably arise (such as "small talk" types of things like weather, sports, current news events, etc.), but always return the conversation to the position in question.

❑   Have a copy of the applicant's application form, resume and any other paperwork provided by the applicant.

❑   The interviewer has the obligation to control the interview. Decide ahead of time how the interview will progress, what general issues will be discussed, what issues concerning the particular applicant, if any, will be discussed, and how to conclude the interview. Never let the applicant take control of the interview.

❑   Use common courtesy and respect for the applicant throughout the interview, even if these are lacking from the applicant.

❑   Do not bring up issues that are not appropriate. If the applicant brings up such an issue, steer the conversation back to the position and the relevant qualifications. If the applicant resists this or insists on engaging in inappropriate conversation or behavior, end the interview. Inappropriate issues are anything that concern race, color, national origin, sex, religion, age or disability, unless you already know one or more of these is the subject of a bona fide occupational qualification.

❑   If the applicant appears to be under the influence of alcohol or drugs, cancel or reschedule the interview. In this situation, the interview could be canceled and the applicant would no longer be under consideration for the position.

(continued on next page)

(Page 2 - Checklist 7.7)

❑   If the applicant appears at the interview in inappropriate dress, is dirty or foul-smelling, is rude or behaving inappropriately, cancel or reschedule the interview. In this situation, the interview could be canceled and the applicant would no longer be under consideration for the position.

❑   The interview is not an opportunity for sexual flirtation, religious or political debate, or for anything but an exchange of information about the position. If it becomes anything else, the interview can be stopped and rescheduled. If it is the applicant who continues to pursue improper conduct or issues during the interview, this can be a legitimate basis to cancel the interview and to remove the applicant from consideration for the position.

7.1(d) Testing

Various types of tests are given to applicants as part of the application process. These are typically limited to tests designed to measure skills and abilities necessary to perform the duties of the position. Such tests are legitimate and useful. The legal issue involved in this type of testing is that the test must be designed to actually measure a relevant skill or ability. It cannot be a pretext for eliminating certain groups or classes of people. If a person states they are disabled and requests an accommodation or assistance in performing the test, a reasonable accommodation may have to be provided (see Chapter 15 for discussion of the Americans with Disabilities Act. Required testing must be required of all applicants for the same position (unless it is a test with results that remain valid for a specific period of time and the applicant had previously taken the test and has results that are still valid). Generally, the employer must provide any materials needed for taking or completing the test, pay for the testing and for analysis of the test results; and, keep the results of all such testing confidential. Only the person taking the test and the employer would be entitled to know test results.

Other types of testing are conducted only after a person has been offered the position, conditional on achieving specified results in the testing. Such testing includes medical examinations, psychological testing, drug tests and background criminal checks. All such testing must be professionally administered and evaluated. This type of testing must also have a legitimate, job related purpose, such as ensuring the person is healthy enough to do the work, or that they qualify for required insurance coverage. If a person's test results do not meet or exceed the results specified as necessary, the job offer can be withdrawn. The employer must keep all information about such testing, including the results, confidential.

One type of testing is specifically limited, and even prohibited to most employers by federal law. Polygraph (lie detector) testing is controlled by the Employee Polygraph Protection Act of 1988 [29 U.S.C. 2001 *et seq.*]. This act prohibits an employer from using polygraph examinations, or from threatening the use of polygraph examinations, on employees or applicants for any purpose, unless specifically authorized to do so by the terms of this act. Only certain types of employers are allowed under this law to use polygraph examinations. These are: the United States Government, any State or local government, or any political subdivision of a State or local government; any employer engaged in the business of providing armored car personnel, personnel engaged in the design, installation, and maintenance of security alarm systems, or other uniformed or plainclothes security personnel; any employer authorized to manufacture, distribute, or dispense a controlled substance as defined by federal law (Schedule I, II, III, or IV of Section 812 of Title 21, United States Code).

Another type of testing is to actually have an applicant go to work in the position for which they have applied. This is an effective method in determining how well a person can do the job. The length of time for such a test can be determined by the employer to be appropriate, from one day to several days or longer. During such a test, the applicant must be paid for the work they do. It is not necessary that they be given the full compensation and benefit package that would go with the position, but they must be paid at least the minimum wage (when applicable), or more likely, some compensation that would entice an applicant to devote the required time to such an employment test. At the conclusion of the test period, the applicant would be evaluated based on performance (which can include their compatibility with others who are already employed). Those applicants not hired would not become eligible for unemployment compensation or any other unemployment benefits. This is strictly a type of pre-employment testing and must be handled as such.

Checklist 7.8
Types of Testing

❏ **Ability Testing.** Used to determine the abilities, experience, talent and overall skill of an applicant to perform the job. Such testing may be specific to the use of a machine or equipment. It could be designed to see how the applicant handles particular duties that are required of the position or how well the applicant performs the actual job.

❏ **Temporary Employment.** This is a variation of ability testing. One or more applicants are actually hired to work in the position. After a period of time, ranging from part of one day to several days or even longer, the employer will have a very good idea of how well the applicant can actually do the job. It is necessary to pay applicants during such a test, although it is not necessary to offer the full compensation package until an actual job offer is made. Not all applicants will be willing to agree to this type of test. It may seem to some applicants to be too much of a commitment (even though no more than a few days or so) just to determine if they get a job or not.

❏ **Medical Testing.** Regardless of the reason, an applicant must first be offered the position before requiring that they undergo any medical testing. The offer can be conditional on achieving results within a specified range. The offer could even be withdrawn if the applicant refuses to take the test after receiving an offer. The employer should pay for any required medical testing and all results must be kept confidential.

❏ **Psychological Testing.** This can include aptitude testing, assessments, psychological evaluations, or other testing methods given and analyzed by a psychologist or a psychiatrist. It is important that only professionally prepared testing be used, that it be administered as designed by the professional(s) who prepared the test, and that it be professionally analyzed. The employer should pay for any psychological testing and all results must be kept confidential.

❏ **Drug and Alcohol Testing.** An offer of employment may be conditioned on the successful completion of drug and alcohol testing. This could include urinalysis examinations, blood tests and/or assessments or evaluations given by an appropriate professional. A person who tests positive for the use of illegal drugs or alcohol can be excluded from further consideration. However, a person with a past drug or alcohol problem cannot necessarily be excluded on that basis alone, as long as they are clean and sober at the present time. A past history, with no current usage, can be a disability under the Americans with Disabilities Act.

(continued on next page)

(Page 2 - Checklist 7.8)

❑   **AIDS Testing.** Acquired Immune Deficiency Syndrome (AIDS) is a medical condition, but it is also a civil rights issue. Unless a real risk of transferring AIDS during the normal performance of the job is present, any legal basis for requiring AIDS testing as part of the hiring process is unlikely to exist. This is because there is such a strong social stigma attached to persons who have AIDS or HIV. In addition, having a diagnosis of AIDS or HIV is considered a disability under the Americans with Disabilities Act, and employment decisions cannot be made on the basis of whether or not a person has or is believed to have AIDS or HIV unless there is a clear bona fide occupational qualification that applies.

Checklist 7.9
Factors to Include in Any Testing

❑ There should be a specific reason for giving any type of testing. Testing should not be done because it has always been done, because another employer does it, because someone read an article about it, or for any vague or general reason. A test is given to test something specific. Unless there is something specific that needs to be tested, do not give any tests.

❑ Whatever is being tested must actually be relevant to the position. If changing technology or other changing standards means a once necessary test has become obsolete, stop using that test.

❑ Do not give tests, even if relevant, when the results will not actually be considered. Not every employer wants to use tests to hire for certain positions, even though others use testing for the same position in their company. If the results of a test are not going to be used, there is no reason to give the test.

❑ Tests should be designed to actually measure or evaluate the object of the test.

❑ Use professionally designed testing methods and observe all required procedures for each type of test. Test results should also be professionally analyzed.

❑ Keep all test results confidential, especially any medical, psychological, drug and alcohol, AIDS, or other clinical testing.

7.1(e) Deciding Who to Hire

Eventually it will be time to decide who to hire and who not to hire. Many ways exist to make a good decision about which applicant to hire. Some people even have a special talent for identifying exactly the right person to hire. The legal issue here is not concerned with how good decisions are made. The law's only concern is that decisions are not based either wholly or partially on prohibited factors.

When evaluating the information that has been obtained about an applicant for any position, whether they are the only applicant or one of many, do not base any part of the decision on the applicant's race, color, national origin, religion, sex, age or disability status. It is true that a bona fide occupational qualification may exist for basing a hiring decision on an applicant's religion, sex, age or disability status, but this must be a clearly defined and legally supportable basis for a job qualification. There is no legal justification to base any part of an employment decision on a person's race or skin color; and there is probably no justification to base a decision on national origin (although it has been allowed for national security issues).

Other factors that are prohibited from being the basis for the decision to hire include whether the person has made prior worker's compensation claims; whether they have a history of job related illness or injuries, regardless of whether or not they have made worker's compensation claims; whether they have made a claim against a current or former employer for any reason (such as a Title VII discrimination or harassment claim); whether they have testified as a witness in a court or other legal proceeding against a current or former employer; whether they have a history of union participation or involvement; whether they are in the National Guard or the armed forces of the United States on active or inactive duty, or on reserve status; whether they are planning to have children, already have children, are of child-bearing age, or do not like children; whether they are married, single, divorced, widowed, dating or not dating; and, generally, any other factor not relevant to the qualifications necessary to do the job as described (or as implied) in the written job description.

Among the legally justifiable reasons for a hiring decision are decisions based on which applicant appears to have or has demonstrated the best qualifications; how well the applicant followed instructions for applying for the position and completing any testing or other aspects of the application process; the applicant's demeanor; the appropriateness of their dress; and whether or not they actually want the position.

Many employers have no trouble properly identifying those applicants who are not qualified for the position or who can be properly eliminated from consideration for one reason or another. The concern expressed by employers tends to be how to decide between two or more apparently equally qualified persons who want the position. Sometimes there simply is not an easy answer. However, this can be a situation where the equally qualified candidates are asked to work the job for a week or a pay period to determine which one actually handles the position best. If one of the applicants refuses to participate in such a test, they can be eliminated. Also, further interviews or other testing could be scheduled. It may be a matter of devising a method for getting more information about the contenders and then deciding. A common consequence of gathering additional information in this situation is that one or more of the applicants may withdraw themselves from consideration. As long as such a process is not a disguised attempt to frustrate a particular applicant into giving up, there usually is nothing wrong with wanting more relevant information on which to base the decision.

Once the decision is made, it is simply a matter of notifying the person(s) selected. Usually, the applicants who are not initially selected are not told the bad news until the person being offered the position accepts the job. This is for the obvious reason that the position needs to be filled before all the good applicants are told they did not get the job. Remember, no applicant ever has a legal duty to accept any position just because they go through the entire application process and are offered the job. In fact, someone may lead you to believe they will accept the position, only to refuse the offer when actually made. Even if this causes difficulty for the employer, there is nothing the employer can do. Applicants are generally free to accept or refuse any position, at any time, for a good reason, a bad reason, or no reason at all. An applicant can even refuse to accept a job offered to them on the basis of race, color, national origin, religion, sex, age or disability status of potential supervisors and co-workers. These prohibitions apply only to employers.

Checklist 7.10
Making the Decision on Whom to Hire

❑ Review the job description to make sure you understand the qualifications for the position. The employer should be intimate with these qualifications by this point, but it is still prudent to re-read the job description.

❑ Eliminate applicants who do not have the necessary qualifications, as compared to the job description.

❑ Eliminate applicants who did not follow the instructions for applying for the position, including responding to any advertising, information requested in the application or resume, appearing on time for interviews, completion of testing, and so on.

❑ Eliminate applicants with testing results that do not fit into the pre-determined range for a successful test.

❑ Eliminate applicants who cannot legally work in the United States in the position under consideration.

❑ As necessary, ask for additional information, testing, or interviewing to help in determining which of closely qualified applicants should be offered the position.

❑ At some point, make the decision. Be able to explain why the decision was made to offer the job to a particular person. Also, be able to explain why the decision was made not to offer it to the others.

Checklist 7.11
Factors Which Cannot Form Any Part
Of the Hiring Decision

❑ In general, any factor which does not demonstrate the actual or apparent qualifications of the applicant for the position. Use the job description as the standard for determining what qualifications are necessary. Use information acquired about the applicant during the hiring procedure to compare what is learned about their qualifications to what is required by the job description.

❑ The person's race or skin color under any circumstances for any position.

❑ The person's national origin or religion, unless the employer has a current legal opinion stating this factor is a bona fide occupational qualification for the position in question.

❑ The person's sex or age, unless there is a bona fide occupational qualification for either factor.

❑ The person's disability status, unless they have a disability that cannot be reasonably accommodated by the employer.

❑ Marital status.

❑ Children and family status.

❑ Any history of worker's compensation claims.

❑ Any history of having made claims of discrimination against any employer, or of having participated in such a case as a witness.

❑ Status of service in the National Guard or in the United States armed forces.

❑ History of union activities.

7.1(f) Federal Hiring Guidelines [29 C.F.R. 1601 *et seq.*]

Federal regulations do address how several issues should be handled during the hiring process. These issues are set out below:

Sex: None of the paperwork to be completed during the hiring process, whether it is completed by the applicant or company personnel, may require language which identifies the applicant's sex. The exception would be if being of a particular sex is a legitimate qualification for the job (a bona fide occupational qualification). Therefore, do not use, these terms on the application form or on any other paperwork: Mr., Mrs., Miss, Ms., Male, Female, or any other language that identifies gender.

Marital Status: Knowledge of a person's marital status is legally irrelevant during the application process, unless marital status is a bona fide occupational qualification.

Pregnancy and Childbirth: It is unlawful discrimination to make any employment decision based on whether or not an applicant is pregnant, plans to become pregnant sometime in the future, is of child-bearing age, or has a medical condition related to pregnancy or childbirth, unless it is a bona fide occupational qualification.

Religion: It is unlawful discrimination to make any employment decision based on religion. Employers must make *reasonable* accommodations for an employee's religious practices (such as excusing them from work related duties in order to partake in religious observance or other practice). In limited situations, religion may be a legitimate qualification for a job (i.e., a rabbi must be Jewish).

National Origin: An applicant's national origin, ancestry, the nationality of their name, whether or not they are a member of or support particular national or cultural organizations or activities, or any other aspect of their life connected to national origin (whether or not their own national origin) is legally irrelevant. The exception would be those limited circumstances when national origin is a bona fide occupational qualification.

English Language Requirements: It is proper for an employer to require that an applicant and an employee use written and/or spoken English (or any other language, for that matter) on the job when this is a legitimate requirement to do the job. However, an employer may not necessarily require an employee to use English (or any other language) at all times during the hours of employment. If two or more employees speak the same language, they can usually use their common language with each other as long as it does not interfere with their job responsibilities and is not disruptive to the workplace. They must, however, use English when necessary for their job.

U.S. Citizenship: Whether or not an applicant is a U.S. citizen at the time of application or by the beginning of employment is irrelevant. The real issue is whether or not the applicant can legally have the job, regardless of their national citizenship. All that can be asked of an applicant is whether or not they can legally work under United States law. They may also be asked to verify their statement.

Unfair Testing: 29 C.F.R. 1607.14(8) states, "When members of one race, sex or ethnic group characteristically obtain lower scores on a selection procedure than members of another group, and the differences in scores are not reflected in differences in a measure of job performance, use of the selection procedure may unfairly deny opportunities to members of the group that obtains the lower scores." Therefore, job testing in the hiring process must be designed to measure actual or potential skills and abilities. If a trend develops in the test scores that members of one race, sex, or ethnic group are scoring lower than other applicants of other races or ethnic groups, the test may be unfair. Basing employment decisions on such unfair testing is an unlawful discriminatory practice.

Prior Training or Experience: Prior training and experience is a legitimate qualification for a job. There must be a direct correlation between the prior training and experience demanded by the employer and the essential functions of the job.

Education and Official Licenses or Certifications: Education and having (or being eligible for) official licenses or certifications is a legitimate qualification for a job. However, there must be a direct correlation between the education, official license or certification demanded by the employer and the essential functions of the job.

7.2 Employment at Will and Employment Contracts

7.2(a) Employment at Will

The *Employment at Will* Doctrine has existed in American law since its beginning. This doctrine states that an employer can hire or fire any person at any time, for any or no reason, and that an employee can accept any employment or resign from any employment at any time, for any or no reason. While this doctrine is still the law in all states, it does have two significant exceptions. The employment at will doctrine does not justify the violation of any applicable state or federal employment statute, and the doctrine does not apply if part or all of the employment relationship is covered by an employment contract. Because of these two exceptions, it is often stated that employment at will is largely a thing of the past. However, when no statute or contract applies to a given situation, employment at will is still enforced by the courts as the applicable law.

"(I)n the absence of a contract covering the duration of employment, the employment is terminable at the will of either party, and the employee has no cause of action by alleging he was discharged." *Anco Const. Co., Ltd. v. Freeman*, 693 P.2d 1183 (Kan. 1985).

Under the "general rule of at-will employment...either party may terminate the relationship with or without cause or justification." *Cunningham v. Dabbs,* 703 So.2d 979 (Ala.Ct.App.1997).

State law generally "presumes employment to be at will, (although) the at-will doctrine is subject to agreements to the contrary." *Goodyear Tire & Rubber Company v. Portilla*, 879 S.W.2d 47 (Tex.1994).

When employment at will applies (or at-will employment as it is also called), the courts will rule that the action of the employer in the case at hand is proper. This doctrine is the legal justification supporting the actions of an employer in dealing with any or all of its employees, as long as a statute or contract does not apply to the situation. For compliance planning purposes, employers must understand when a contract covers a given employee, and when a statute covers a given situation. This is not as difficult an issue as it may at first appear. The next checklist describes the issues covered by statutes. The section immediately following the checklist describes how contracts affect employment at will.

Checklist 7.12
Employment Issues Covered by State
Or Federal Statute

❑ **Discrimination.** The employment at will doctrine will never justify any employment decision made either partially or completely on the basis of race, color, national origin, religion, sex, age or disability.

❑ **Minimum wage and hour issues.** State and federal statutes both require a minimum hourly wage be paid to employees with certain types of jobs (see Chapter 10 for a full discussion of this issue). In addition, these statutes require covered employees to be paid an overtime wage (time and a half) for every hour worked that is over an average of 40 hours per week per pay period. These statutes only set minimum standards and except for complying with these minimum standards, the employer is in control of wage and hour issues.

❑ **Benefits.** Whether an employer offers benefits to its employees, or what benefits an employer decides to offer, are issues entirely in the control of the employer. Statutes only apply to require that offered benefits are actually paid, that they are offered on a consistent (i.e., non-discriminatory) basis, and that proper record keeping is done.

❑ **Employee absence.** Statutes require an employer to allow employees time off only for specific things. These include: jury duty, reporting for service in the National Guard or armed forces, an order from a court to appear in that court, when the Family and Medical Leave Act applies, observance of a religious practice based on a genuine religious belief, or when the employer has a policy that allows an absence for the reason given by the employee.

❑ **Workplace safety.** Statutes set minimum standards for the maintenance of the workplace and safe operation of equipment at the workplace.

❑ **Use of polygraph testing.** This is prohibited by statute unless the employer or the nature of the employer's business is specifically exempted by the Employee Polygraph Protection Act.

❑ **Compliance with worker's compensation laws.**

❑ **Compliance with unemployment compensation laws.**

❑ **The employment at will doctrine does give legal justification for an employer to make any decision it desires about an issue not covered by a statute or that is not in violation of any minimum standards set by the statute.**

7.2(b) Employment Contracts

A contract is basically an agreement between two or more parties that is enforceable by law. An employer must always know when it is a party in an employment contract. To become a contract, the agreement must include an exchange of value. Each party to the contract must receive some value from the agreement, as well as give some value to the other party. This exchange of value is referred to in contract law as *consideration*. The existence of consideration is the difference between a mere promise and a contract. A promise is generally not enforceable at law because only one party to the transaction has agreed to give something of value to the other party. The nature of a promise is that when it is given, nothing is expected in return. A contract includes not only promises to exchange value, but an expectation of receiving value in exchange for the value given. This mutual exchange of consideration is necessary to create any contract.

In an employment contract, the parties are the employer and the employee. The employer exchanges money for the performance of specific services from the employee. The employee exchanges his or her performance of services for the employer's money. In addition, there are often other terms to an employment contract in addition to the exchange of services for wages. A common issue described in an employment contract by such additional terms is how and when the employment can end.

Employment contracts are either express or implied. An express contract is an oral or written contract that is understood to exist by the parties. They negotiated it, discussed it, and agreed to it. They know they have a contract. An implied contract is one that the parties may or may not know they have. Whether or not an implied contract exists is determined largely by the conduct of the parties. If they act as if they have a contractual agreement on one or more specific issues, courts will find that an enforceable contract exists which covers those particular issues. Implied contracts are a major issue in employment, particularly on the issue of how and when employment ends.

Express Contracts

Unless an express contract of employment exists between the employer and the employee, a presumption exists that there is no contract covering the relationship and that the employment at will doctrine applies. This presumption means that the employer has sole discretion (except for applicable statutes) in determining how much to pay, the hours of work, what the work will consist of, when the employee can be absent from work, how to evaluate the employee's performance, when to end employment, and how to end employment. Therefore, an employer who does not want to use or be covered by employment contracts with its employees should not make express contracts, whether orally or in writing. The next checklist describes how to avoid creating express employment contracts.

Checklist 7.13
Avoiding the Creation of Express Employment Contracts

❑ Do not prepare a written contract with the employee.

❑ Do not prepare a written memo, letter, e-mail, or other document in hard copy or electronic format that contains express agreements between the employer and the employee about the terms and conditions of employment.

❑ A written job description, by itself, is not an express employment contract. It is, instead, the employer's unilateral statement describing expectations for the specified position. As long as it is not negotiated with the employee, the written job description will not be a contract.

❑ An employment policy, by itself, is not necessarily an employment contract. It is, instead, the employer's unilateral statement(s) about how it will handle various issues with its employees. As long as they are not negotiated with employees, and as long as they do not have "contractual characteristics" (discussed below), employment policies will not be a contract.

❑ Verbal and other non-written communication between an employer and an employee will not be an express contract to the extent that there is no negotiation between the employer and the employee.

Implied Contracts

An implied contract is one that exists because the conduct of the parties makes it clear (at least to a judge) that they have intended to create a contract with each other. It does not matter whether the parties understand this, it only matters that they have implied an agreement on one or more specific issues because of how they treat those issues between themselves. In employment, an implied contract may exist on only one or two issues between a particular employer and employee. In virtually every employment relationship, for example, there is an implied contract as to the basics of the employee's initial duties to the employer and how much the employee will be paid at the beginning of the relationship. This is because, at the time of hiring, the employer said words to the effect of, "I'm offering you this job for this much money;" and the employee said, "Okay, I'll take it." The fact that an employment relationship exists where a particular employee will have a certain job for a certain rate of pay with a particular employer will be based on an implied contract. However, every other term and condition of that employment relationship may not be covered by an implied contract. This means the employment at will doctrine applies and the employer can change the nature of the job, the rate of pay, the hours of work, and whether or not the employee can continue holding the job.

Whether or not an implied contract of employment exists is something that must be proven in court. Whichever party claims that an implied contract exists, usually the employee, is the party with the burden of proof, or the party who must prove the implied contract exists. Unless the implied contract is proven, no such contract exists and the employment at will doctrine will control the situation, unless a statute applies.

> "Where no definite term of employment is expressed, the duration of employment depends on the intention of the parties as determined by circumstances in each particular case. The understanding and intent of the parties is to be ascertained from the written or oral negotiations, the usages of business, the situation and object of the parties, the nature of the employment, and all the circumstances surrounding the termination." *Kistler v. Life Care Centers of America, Inc.*, 620 F.Supp. 1268 (D. Kan. 1985)

> "A promise, or offer, that supports an implied contract might be found in written representations such as an employee handbook, in oral representations, in the conduct of the parties, or in a combination of representations and conduct . . . When such a contract is implied, it is implied in fact. An implied-in-fact contract term is one that is inferred from the statements or conduct of the parties . . . An implied contract is created only where an employer creates a reasonable expectation. The reasonableness of expectations is measured by just how definite, specific, or explicit has been the representation or conduct relied upon." *Hartbarger v. Frank Paxton Company*, 857 P.2d 776 (N.M. 1993).

The most likely sources of proof that an implied contract exists are described in the next checklist.

Checklist 7.14
Likely Sources of Implied Contracts

❑ A letter or other communication, verbal or written, offering a job to an applicant. This communication can become an implied contract if the employee actually begins working for the employer in the position offered, but only to the extent of any terms contained in such an offer, such as what job the employee will have, when employment begins, and the rate of pay and any offered benefits.

❑ Written employment policies of the employer. However, policies are considered on a policy-by-policy basis to determine which policies, if any, can become an implied contract. Factors most likely to create an implied contract from an employment policy include: If the policy was negotiated with employees; if the policy clearly states certain consequences will result from specific conduct, whether or not they are for the good of those being addressed in the policy; if termination of employment is specifically conditioned on listed factors or by the terms, "good cause" or "for cause"; if the policy is described in detailed, specific, and thorough language; or if the policy describes things the employer will do "if" or "on the condition that" or "when" (or other similar language) the employee does certain things. Each of these factors are characteristics of a contract, not of a unilateral policy statement by an employer about how it handles its employment issues.

❑ Unwritten or informal policies of an employer that have contract characteristics similar to those just described for written policies. These can include traditions and customs.

❑ Communications between an employer and an employee that clearly show an agreement on how a particular issue is to be handled.

The real issue about implied contracts for the employer is that the employer recognize when an implied contract exists. It really does not matter whether a communication or a policy becomes an implied contract. What matters is that those communications and policies that the employer does not want to become implied contracts do not become implied contracts. Likewise, those communications and policies intended to be followed and enforced by the employer as contracts should actually be contracts.

For compliance planning purposes, the entire employment contract issue comes down to this statement: Any express or implied employment contract, whether it is a comprehensive contract or a contract limited to a single issue, must exist only because it is the intent of the employer for it to exist.

7.3 Employment Policies and Policy Handbooks/Manuals

7.3(a) Description

An employment policy is the employer's statement of how it handles a particular employment issue. A policy handbook or manual is a compilation of policies. Policies can be written or unwritten, general or specific. Every employer has unwritten employment policies and many employers have written policies. To determine the unwritten policy on any issue, ask and determine how a given issue is or would be handled. The answer is the policy, or at least the basis for determining the policy. A better method for determining the unwritten policy on any issue is to examine how that issue is actually handled, even those issues that are described by written policies. Actual practices are always the best evidence of what a policy is or is not. Courts will readily conclude that an employer's policy on an issue is not what the employer writes or says about the issue, but what the employer does and has done about the issue. In other words, substance always controls over form.

7.3(b) How to Create an Employment Policy

Courts will always determine what an employer's policy is on a particular issue when necessary to resolve a claim against the employer. Therefore, employers should not waste time in denying the existence of policies. They exist. However, it is not necessary for each policy to be put in writing and compiled into a handbook. As a matter of fact, it would be impossible to identify every policy and successfully and accurately describe it. Instead, a better plan is for an employer to identify those issues that it determines are important enough to put in writing and then do so. This is never a completed project and written policies should be reviewed on a regular basis. Additional policies may be required or existing policies may need to be changed or deleted. The creation and maintenance of employment policies should be a part of the compliance plan. In fact, the policies that make up much of the compliance program are employment policies. The following checklist describes how to create employment policies.

Checklist 7.15
Creating Employment Policies

❑ The employer prepares all policies, not the employee or anyone else. It is the employer who knows best what the company needs from a given policy. In addition, it is the employer who is held accountable for its policies. While input from others may be solicited and actively considered, the employer must be the one who makes the decision about what will and will not go into any policy.

❑ While preparing the policy, remember exactly what it is supposed to accomplish.

❑ When writing a policy, do not use cliches, idioms, or slang. Such things are too easily misunderstood. Use standard American English vocabulary, grammar, spelling and punctuation.

❑ While it is acceptable to use general, or vague language for many policies, never be so vague that the policy language has no real meaning.

❑ Decide whether the policy is to be contractual in nature, which means it is one that must be followed by everyone, including the firm, as written. If it is to be contractual, be clear and as specific or detailed as necessary. Do not include elements that the firm would not want to follow. If it is not to be contractual, be sure to use more general language and do not attempt to fully describe the issue.

❑ The policy can be written in a narrative format, in a series of short statements, in outline form, in combinations of styles, or in any other format that successfully communicates the policy.

❑ Give the policy a title, a number, or a code so it can be specifically referred to.

❑ When finished, review the policy and be sure you can explain it with a straight face to anyone, including a hostile attorney and a judge and jury. You may have to one day.

7.3(c) When Policies Might be Interpreted as Implied Contracts

Although it requires a lawsuit and a judge to formally declare that a particular employment policy is to be enforced as an implied contract, an employer should understand from the moment a policy is created whether or not it is enforceable as a contract. For compliance planning purposes, this is essential. There are three issues on this point.

(1) Do Not Create a Policy You Do Not Intend to Follow: Employers create a policy, whether written or unwritten, because it explains how the subject of the policy is to be handled. Employees, at least those affected by the policy, are expected to comply with the employer's policy. This is a natural, logical, and enforceable expectation. Employees who do not comply may suffer consequences, including termination from their employment. The employer should also comply with its own policies. There is absolutely no reason why an employer should consider itself exempt from its own policies and immune from any consequences of not following its own policies. After all, the employer is the one who created the policy. If the employer does not want to be bound by a policy, don't create the policy! If a policy is created and circumstances later change so that the employer no longer intends to follow the policy (whether the policy has become irrelevant or the employer simply chooses to ignore the policy for any reason), the employer should change the policy! As long as the employer remains in control of its policies, it retains full discretion to create, change, modify or eliminate any policy it considers appropriate for the firm's interests. Failure of a firm to comply with its own policies sends a clear signal to employees and any others who become aware that the firm does not follow its policies that the firm's policies simply do not mean much. It then looks like hypocrisy to react to employees who do not comply with a policy when the employer does not comply. Firm hypocrisy on any issue never sits well, and is bad for business.

(2) Types of Policies that are Contractual by Nature: Certain types of employment policies are most likely to become the subject of an implied contract. These policies are contractual in nature, which means they necessarily involve a "this for that" element. The basic structure of any contract can be stated as, "if you do this for me, I will do that for you." Employment policies with this inherent structure may still be created, modified, or eliminated at the employer's sole discretion, but while they exist they will be susceptible to being interpreted by a court (should a court ever become involved) as an implied contract. Therefore, with these types of policies, the employer should take the most care to comply. The following checklist describes policies that are contractual by nature.

(3) Factors used by the Courts to Determine Whether a Policy is an Implied Contract: This issue has been litigated often. As the case summaries following this checklist will show, there are specific factors that can elevate any mere policy into an implied contract.

Checklist 7.16
Inherently Contractual Employment Policies

❑   Any policy describing pay scales for particular types of positions. These indicate that if an employee holds one of the positions described or referred to, their wages will be within a specific range.

❑   A policy explaining that paid leave is available for vacations, illness or any other reason. This indicates that an employee who meets the condition stated in the policy will be allowed to be absent from work for the length of time described, and will be paid on the basis described.

❑   Statements of eligibility to receive certain benefits, including bonuses, raises, promotions, health insurance, life insurance, disability benefits, retirement benefits, profit sharing, educational opportunities and any other benefit offered by the employer. These policies indicate that once an employee meets the conditions described, they will receive the benefit described.

❑   Descriptions of performance evaluations. This type of policy indicates the frequency, method, and often the consequences of employee performance evaluations. Such policies can provide the basis for determining whether or not an employee is adequately performing their job.

❑   Methods of employee discipline. These indicate the procedure that will be followed in the giving of warnings, face-to-face meetings, counseling, how much time may be given to improve performance, and types of discipline that will be used. This type of policy is often the subject of an employee claim against the employer on the basis of breach of implied contract.

❑   Policies describing the reasons for termination of employment. These indicate that employment will continue unless and until the employee does one of the things that are described as a reason for being fired. This type of policy is the most frequent subject of an employee claim that the employer has breached an implied contract.

Checklist 7.17
Legal Factors for Determining if a
Policy is an Implied Contract

❑ The policy has an inherent, contractual nature.

❑ The policy was created through negotiation with employees, either directly or through a representative of the affected employees.

❑ The policy is detailed in its descriptions and clearly indicates that the existence of certain conditions will result in certain benefits or consequences.

❑ The policy contains lists of factors which will become the basis of decisions by the employer, especially if the list of factors is detailed and appears to be comprehensive.

❑ The existence of language in a policy handbook, or in an individual policy, that none of the policies are to be considered as creating a contract between the employer and any employee, and that employees are employed "at will," can be effective in preventing the conclusion that policies are implied contracts. However, this type of disclaimer by itself is not always effective. It is necessary to write policies in such a manner that they are not likely to be interpreted as implied contracts.

❑ Finally, the finding of a court that an employer's policies are implied contracts can be made concerning a single policy or any number of the employer's policies. Usually, an implied contract case concerns only one, or at most a small number of the employer's employment policies.

The following are relevant case summaries on this issue:

"Where it is alleged that an employment contract is one to be based upon the theory of implied in fact, the understanding and intent of the parties is to be ascertained from several factors which include written or oral negotiations, the conduct of the parties from the commencement of the employment relationship, the usages of the business, the situation and objective of the parties giving rise to the relationship, the nature of the employment, and any other circumstances surrounding the employment relationship which would tend to explain or make clear the intention of the parties at the time the employment commenced. . . . A disclaimer in a supervisor's manual that 'nothing in this policy manual should be construed as an employment contract or guaranty of employment' did not, as a matter of law, create an unqualified employment-at-will relationship in absence of evidence that the disclaimer was brought to the personal attention of employees, or was intended to create an unqualified employment-at-will relationship in view of other provisions in the manual and statements made by the employer to supervisors and employees." *Morriss v. Coleman Co., Inc.*, 738 P.2d 841 (Kan. 1987).

While state law "presumes that employment is at-will, a handbook may alter this presumption if its terms reasonably create an expectation that the employee will not be fired except for just cause." *McIlravy v. Kerr-McGee Corp.,* 119 F.3d 876 (10th Cir.1997).

"(A)n employee handbook may modify the presumption of employment at will if it promises specific treatment in specific situations." *Wlasiuk v. Whirlpool Corp.*, 914 P.2d 102 (Wash.App.Div.1 1996).

"While an employer may restrict its ability to fire at-will employees by instituting a company-wide personnel policy, a general statement of policy does not create an enforceable contract. In this case, the company's manual listed examples of misconduct and contained no promise disallowing employment termination for other reasons. The employer retained its discretion to fire employees without using (its) disciplinary procedure." *Ross v. Times Mirror, Inc.,* 665 A.2d 580 (Vt.1995).

"An employment manual which fails to include a clear and prominent disclaimer may create an enforceable contract even when the employment is otherwise terminable at will. If the manual is sufficiently definite to raise the reasonable expectations of employees concerning job security provisions, the provisions may be construed as contractual promises." *Witkowski v. Thomas J. Lipton, Inc.,* 643 A.2d 546 (N.J.1994).

"Employment at will is presumed . . . This presumption may be overcome when systematic disciplinary procedures or other language of an employee handbook unambiguously create an employment contract. However, a disclaimer may prevent the modification of at will status if it is conspicuous and unambiguous." *Lincoln v. Wackenhut Corp.,* 867 P.2d 701 (Wyo.1994)

"Throughout the handbook, the employer had placed clauses that retained its right to terminate the employment relationship at any time. Further, the night crew leader had signed a receipt for a copy of the handbook which stated: 'I recognize that either [the store] or I may terminate the employment relationship at any time for any reason.' . . . (This) employment handbook did not create a contract of employment." *French v. Foods, Inc.,* 495 N.W. 2d 768 (Iowa 1993). See also, *Hart v. Seven Resorts Inc.,* 947 P.2d 846 (Ariz.App.Div.1 1997), holding that an employment manual which conspicuously notifies employees that their employment is at-will is not an implied contract; *Talanda v. KFC Natl. Mgmt. Co.,* 863 F.Supp. 664 (N.D.Ill, 1994) holding that an employment handbook with a disclaimer advising employees that employment could be terminated at will by either the employer or the employee, and which expressly disclaimed that the handbook created an employment contract, was not an implied contract; and *Robins v. Flagship Airlines, Inc.,* 956 S.W.2d 4 (Tenn.App.1997) holding that an employee handbook containing a specific reservation of the employer's right to discharge employees and which also declared that the employment relationship remained at will, is not an implied contract.

7.4 Employee Files

This issue concerns the information about employees that is acquired and maintained by employers. Some information is required by law to be kept, other information is obtained because it is useful to the employer, or because the employee voluntarily gives the information. For compliance planning, the issues that must be addressed are: a) what information must be kept by law; b) how the information is kept; c) access to the information; and, d) consequences of not acquiring and maintaining information properly.

7.4(a) Information Required by Law

For All Employees:

- Form I-9, Employment Eligibility Verification, which verifies that the employee can legally work in the United States.

- Form W-4, Employee's Withholding Allowance Certificate, which is the employee's statement of how many deductions he or she is entitled to claim for income tax withholding purposes.

- Form W-2, Wage and Tax Statement, which is the employer's annual statement to the employee of the total wages and deductions from wages of the employee.

For Employees Not Exempt from the Federal Wage and Hour Law, whether they are paid hourly or not (29 U.S.C. 201 et seq.):

■ The employee's full name, address, social security number, date of birth (if the employee is less than 19 years old), and the sex of the employee.

■ A description of the employee's job.

■ The employee's regular work schedule, as well as a schedule of hours actually worked by the employee.

■ Total of overtime hours worked and overtime wages paid, as well as a total of non-overtime hours worked and non-overtime wages paid.

■ A description of the pay period (weekly, monthly, etc.), and the total wages paid to the employee each pay period.

For Employees Exempt from Federal Wage and Hour Law (29 U.S.C. 201 et seq.):

■ The factors on which the employer bases its conclusion that the employee is exempt from the federal wage and hour law.

For All Employees in Specific Circumstances:

■ Whenever a court order has been issued requiring certain information to be kept in employee files.

■ Whenever the employee and/or the employer are covered by a specific state or federal statute that has specific record keeping requirements. These can include records of on-the-job injury or illness to the employee, the results of drug and alcohol testing, the results of medical examinations related to employment, the results of polygraph testing, etc.

When employers do not keep proper records about their employees, as required by the Fair Labor Standards Act (the wage and hour law), there are consequences. In *Herman v. Palo Group Foster Home, Inc.*, 976 F.Supp. 696 (W.D.Mich.1997), the court ruled that the employer who did not keep statutorily-required records was not entitled to make the defense that its violation of the statute should be mitigated since it was attempting to comply with the law in good faith. *Basic to a good faith attempt at compliance with the law is proper record keeping* (emphasis added). In *Arias v. United States Serv. Industries, Inc.*, 80 F.3d 509 (D.C.Cir.1996), the employees successfully sued their employer to recover unpaid wages. Since the employer had failed to maintain accurate records, as required by the FSLA, the court ruled that the evidence presented by the employees at trial was sufficient to establish the amount of unpaid wages. "Where employer records are inadequate or inaccurate, courts may not penalize employees by denying them any recovery based on inability to precisely prove their damages."

7.4(b) How to Keep the Information

All information should be kept absolutely confidential and released only on a "need to know" basis, or as required by law (see the next section on access to information). In addition, the information should be organized so it can be easily located and controlled. The following checklist describes good methods for keeping employee information.

Checklist 7.18
Maintaining Employee Information and Files

❑ Be sure each employee file has the information required by law. In addition, each file should include the employee's application and resume, their job description, correspondence between the employee and the employer, performance evaluations, and any other information determined by the employer to be relevant to that employee.

❑ Information may be kept in hard copy, electronically, or in a combination of paper and electronic files.

❑ Unless necessary for a specific reason, do not keep duplicate copies of employee files in different locations. Controlling access to the file is more difficult with multiple copies.

❑ Organize each file by some method useful to the firm.

❑ To the extent possible, keep all files in one location because controlling access to the files is easier this way.

❑ If back-up files or systems are used as a precaution against lost information (such as for electronically stored information), treat such files the same as the primary or original files.

❑ Each file must be kept for three years following the date the employee's employment ends, regardless of the reason the employment ended.

❑ When destroying files, be sure to use a method that obliterates the information, such as shredding or burning. Do not just toss them into the trash.

7.4(c) Access to the Information

The information contained in employee files, in whatever format it is kept, is confidential. Access to the information must be controlled and it is the employer's legal responsibility to control access. Information in employee files should only be released to personnel in the firm who have a legitimate need to know. Depending on the firm, this may or may not be a fairly large number of people. Whether it is one or many people who have such a legitimate need to have access to employee information, each person must understand that the information is absolutely confidential. The firm's policy should be that anyone who breaches that confidentiality, whether accidentally or intentionally, may be terminated from employment.

In order to ensure employee information is confidential, the information should be treated accordingly. This includes keeping the files in a locked file cabinet or drawer; keeping the files in a central location; having a check-out system to get to the information; using secure passwords to get electronically stored information; and not leaving notes, documents, or other sources of information laying around.

Access to employee files should only be granted: to authorized personnel in the firm; to the employee; or when required by court order.

An employee does have the right to see what information is in their file, but the employer has the right and the obligation to set the conditions under which an employee can view the information in their file. For example, an employer can determine: a) a schedule or the time for viewing the file; b) the location where the file can be viewed; c) restrictions on copying the information in the file; d) whether the employee can have anyone view the file with them; and, e) whether the employer wants to have someone present while the employee views their file.

7.4(d) Consequences

An employer who does not treat employee information as confidential can become liable to the employee on the basis of invasion of privacy. Invasion of privacy is the release of confidential information without legal authority or without the consent of the person who the information concerns. If an employee consents to the release of information, the employer should have the employee sign a written consent form allowing the release, which describes the information to be released, to whom the information is to be released, and the purpose of releasing the information.

An employer will have legal authority to release information in an employee file, whether the employee consents or not, when a court order has been issued to release the information as described, when the information is relevant to a claim against the employer by the employee, or when a state or federal statute requires certain information about employees to be reported to a state or federal agency.

7.5 Determining Who is an Employee

This issue concerns knowing whether someone working for the firm is actually an employee or an independent contractor. Employers are liable for the actions of their employees, but are generally not liable for the actions of independent contractors. Determining who is your employee is easy, as whoever an employer considers to be its employee is its employee. Determining who is not an employee and is instead an independent contractor is not as easy. A person is or is not an independent contractor based on certain factors determined by law, not just because the employer decides to treat someone as an independent contractor.

The factors described in the following checklist are used to determine this issue.

Checklist 7.19
Factors for Determining Whether Or Not a Person Is an Employee or an Independent Contractor

❑ Instructions. An employee must follow the employer's instructions. The employer has the legal right to control what work is to be done, how the work is to be done, and the results to be achieved. An independent contractor is only responsible to achieve the result wanted by the employer. How they achieve this result is up to the independent contractor.

❑ Training. Employees are trained by the employer to do their work as the employer wants. Independent contractors use their own methods and do not receive any training or instruction from the employer on how to do their work.

❑ Hiring of Assistants. Employees do not hire assistants to help them do their work for their employer. Independent contractors can and often do hire their own assistants or employees to help them in their work.

❑ Continuing Relationship. Employees have a continuing relationship with their employer. While the length of their employment may never be guaranteed, they are hired to do a job on an ongoing basis until the relationship ends. Independent contractors are generally hired on an as needed basis. Once the independent contractor has achieved the specified result, the relationship ends unless and until hired again.

❑ Hours of Work. Employees work pursuant to a schedule set by the employer. Independent contractors generally set their own work hours.

❑ Payment. Employees are paid a wage on some regular basis, such as by the day, week, or month. Independent contractors are generally only paid after they submit a bill for their services.

❑ Tools and Materials. Generally, an employer provides the tools and materials needed by the employee to do their job. Independent contractors provide their own tools and materials.

❑ Number of Employers. An employee generally works for one employer at a time and can even be prohibited by the terms of their employment from having another employer. An independent contractor routinely works for more than one employer at the same time.

(continued on next page)

(Page 2 - Checklist 7.19)

❏ Self-Employment. Unlike an employee, an independent contractor is self-employed and has characteristics consistent with being self-employed, such as offering their services to the public or to a specific market, investing capital in their own business, showing a profit or a loss on their investment, and paying for their own taxes, social security, Medicare/ Medicaid, insurance, retirement, and other benefits.

❏ Contract. An employee may or may not work pursuant to a contract. An independent contractor always works pursuant to a contract covering every issue of their work, although this contract may be oral or written.

❏ Right to Terminate the Relationship. An employee's employment can be terminated virtually anytime, by either the employer or the employee. With an independent contractor, however, the relationship can only be terminated pursuant to the terms of the contract controlling the relationship.

Courts have dealt often with the issue of when the employment relationship has been created and whether a person is an employee or an independent contractor:

> "In determining whether an employer-employee relationship exists, the court looks to the right of control, either actually exercised or reserved. In the last analysis, it is the right of control rather than its actual exercise that provides the answer. The factors tending to demonstrate a right of control are: (1) direct evidence that demonstrates a right of the exercise of control, (2) the method by which the (employee) received payment for his services, (3) whether the equipment is furnished by the alleged employer or not, and (4) whether the individual has the right to terminate." *Curry v. Interstate Express, Inc.,* 607 So.2d 230 (Ala. 1992).

> "One who is in the general employ of one party may be in the special employ of another despite the fact that the general employer is responsible for the payment of wages, has the power to hire and fire, has an interest in the work performed by the employee, maintains workers' compensation for the employee and provides some, if not all, of the employee's equipment. Relevant to resolving the issue is who controls the employee's manner of working and the details of the work. Employees who are employed and paid by one person may nevertheless be employees of another with respect to a particular transaction even where the general employer is interested in the work. A special employee is one who is transferred for a limited time of whatever duration to the service of another. The presumption is that the general employment continues in the absence of clear proof of surrender of control. The question is frequently one of law. However, where the elements of the employment or of the particular work being done bespeak both general and special employment, the question is one of fact for the jury." *Brooks v. Chemical Leaman Tank Lines, Inc.,* 422 N.Y.S.2d 695 (N.Y.App.Div. 1979).

> "An independent contractor is defined as one who, in exercising an independent employment, contracts to do certain work according to his own methods, without being subject to the control of his employer, except as to the results or product of his work. The primary test used by the courts in determining whether the employer-employee relationship exists is whether the employer has the right of control and supervision over the work of the alleged employee, and the right to direct the manner in which the work is to be performed, as well as the result which is to be accomplished. It is not the actual interference or exercise of the control by the employer, but the existence of the right or authority to interfere or control, which renders one a servant rather than an independent contractor . . . The question of whether an individual is an employee or an independent contractor is considered a question of fact for the jury or trier of facts . . . Ordinarily an employer is not held to be vicariously liable for the negligence of an independent contractor it hires." *Mitzner, by and through Bishop v. State,* 891 P.2d 435 (Kan. 1995).

"A court, in determining whether a hired party is an employee or an independent contractor . . . must consider the hiring party's right to control the manner and means by which the product is accomplished; among the other factors relative to this inquiry are (1) the skill required; (2) the source of the instrumentalities and tools; (3) the location of the work; (4) the duration of the relationship between the parties; (5) whether the hiring party has the right to assign additional projects to the hired party; (6) the extent of the hired party's discretion over when and how long to work; (7) the method of payment; (8) the hired party's role in hiring and paying assistants; (9) whether the work is part of the regular business of the hiring party; (10) whether the hiring party is in business; (11) the provision of employee benefits; and (12) the tax treatment of the hired party; no one of these factors (being) determinative." *Community for Creative Non-Violence v. James Earl Reid*, 490 U.S. 730, 109 S.Ct. 2166, 104 L.Ed.2d 811 (1989).

CHAPTER 8
Discipline and Termination of Employment

CONTENTS

8.1 Discipline

This section concerns methods taken by an employer to deal with employees whose job performance is not adequate. The goal of discipline should be to inform an employee that his or her job performance is inadequate, how their performance can be improved, and the consequences of inadequate performance that is not improved (not including termination of employment). The risks to an employer of not handling this issue properly include: a) job performance remains inadequate, which can hurt productivity and cost money; b) discipline is handled inconsistently, which can result in claims of discrimination; c) discipline is inappropriate, which can result in claims of harassment; d) discipline is handled contrary to company policy, which can result in claims of breach of implied contract; and e) discipline is handled contrary to an applicable express contract, which can result in claims of breach of contract.

8.1(a) Types of Discipline

Warnings: This is the most common type of discipline used and it is generally effective. A warning is notice from the employer to the employee that improvement is needed in the employee's job performance. Sometimes a notice also includes a description of consequences that can result if the employee does not show improvement within a specified period of time. The key for employers is to develop a method of giving warnings that produces an improvement in the employee's performance. For most employees, this requires little more than telling them why their performance is not good enough and how to improve their performance. Most people will respond to such a warning. When this method is ineffective, however, the warning may need to include a deadline for improvement or a specific consequence will result. The consequence can include termination of employment, reassignment of duties with or without a cut in pay, or some other action designed to improve the employee's performance or to remove the employee from that particular job. The following checklist outlines the issue of warnings for employers.

Checklist 8.1
Giving Warnings to Employees

❑ The goal of any warning is to give notice to an employee that their job performance is not adequate, to inform them of how to improve their performance, and make clear that if their performance does not improve within the allowed period of time, certain consequences may result.

❑ Warnings should be given in private. Verbal warnings should be given out of the hearing of other employees. Written warnings should be given directly to the employee.

❑ Regardless of the form it takes, a warning should clearly communicate the problem to the employee. Deadlines for improvement, consequences that may result, and any other information the employee needs to know should also be communicated clearly and accurately.

❑ A warning based on an employee's inadequate performance, violation of some policy or contract, or a warning that is otherwise based on a written standard, should include a reference to the specific written standard (a written warning should include a copy of the standard). The written standard for evaluating the employee's performance is their job description and the conclusions of any recent evaluations.

❑ Give warnings on a consistent basis. An employee's personal situation as known by the employer can be taken into consideration when deciding how to handle the employee's performance problems. However, inconsistent use of warnings sends a signal to other employees that the employer has favorites or makes exceptions in some cases. These signals often result in rumors that can easily lead to problems of their own, sometimes resulting in claims of discrimination.

❑ Keep all warnings as simple as possible. Do not adopt complex procedures or set standards that are impractical. Remember the goal of giving warnings.

Consequences: Besides warnings, only one other type of discipline exists — the consequences of poor performance. The goal of any consequence used by an employer should not be to punish an employee. Instead, the goal should be to either improve the employee's performance, or to remove the employee from the job they were doing.

Improving performance can be accomplished by requiring the employee to be retrained, to be placed under the supervision of someone else, by checking on the employee's performance on a frequent and regular or irregular basis, or any combination of these methods. The use of any of these methods may, but probably would not include a pay cut.

Removing the employee from the job can be accomplished by giving them a different job which they can handle better, by taking away one or more of the responsibilities they have shown they cannot adequately perform, or by terminating their employment. Any of these methods often includes a cut in pay to match the reduction in responsibilities.

While punishment of an employee is not recommended as a method of discipline, some employers do engage in this practice. This is particularly true of the state or federal government as an employer, or when dealing with employees covered by a collective bargaining agreement. The methods of punishment used include: a) suspension from work for a specific period of time, with or without pay; b) a cut in pay; c) a loss of benefits; d) a demotion, with a corresponding loss of responsibility and pay; or, e) reassignment to another geographic location, another department, or to another position. There could be other forms of punishment as well. The problem with taking action that has a primary purpose of punishing an employee, no matter how much the employee may deserve it, is that it exposes the employer to unnecessary risk. While an employee may "accept" a loss of their job because of their poor performance, they are highly likely to resent being disciplined. Resentment leads to anger by both the employee being punished and any other employees who believe the punishment to be an inappropriate response to the problem. This often leads to hostility in the work place and even more problems. Punishment is not something that employers generally do well. Instead, the consequences of poor performance are better handled by showing the employee how to do their job properly or by removing them from the job.

Checklist 8.2
Consequences of Inadequate Job Performance

❑   The goal of any consequence used by an employer should not be to punish an employee. Punishment exposes an employer to unnecessary risk.

❑   The goal of consequences for inadequate job performance should be to either improve the employee's performance, or to remove the employee from the specific job.

❑   Use consequences on a consistent basis. An employee's personal situation as known by the employer can be taken into consideration when deciding how to handle performance problems. However, inconsistent use of any consequences sends a signal to other employees that the employer has favorites or makes exceptions in some cases. These signals often result in rumors that can easily lead to new problems, which sometimes result in claims of discrimination.

❑   Keep the consequences as direct and as simple as possible. Do not adopt complex procedures or set impractical standards. Remember the goals of the implemented consequences.

8.1(b) Deciding How to Use Discipline

The methods and procedures used by any employer are a source of risk to that employer. In addition to improving job performance, the goal of employee discipline should include keeping the employer's risk as low as possible. This is best accomplished by having a clear policy, but the policy should allow the employer flexibility in handling various situations. The following factors are important in developing such a policy:

Avoid too much detail: A policy that describes specific conduct that will result in discipline — even if the descriptions are general — tends to be interpreted as an implied contract. While this is acceptable for having authority to discipline for the conduct described, it may mean no other conduct can be disciplined. Likewise, details about the methods and procedures to be followed during the discipline process may be interpreted as an implied contract. Therefore, the employer must follow the methods and procedures described *all the time*. The methods and procedures may work at first, but situations will arise where additional procedures may be deemed appropriate, or when only some of the procedures described are needed. An employer must reserve the necessary flexibility to adapt its policies to the situation as much as possible. Too much detail usually results in contractually locking the employer into a system that proves to be frustrating.

Be careful with progressive discipline procedures: Progressive discipline is a series of steps taken in response to inadequate performance that usually begins with a warning, progresses to additional warnings, then to relatively minor consequences, and on to more serious consequences which can include termination from employment. Progressive discipline procedures are usually interpreted to be implied contracts. This means the employer must faithfully follow its process for discipline *all the time*. If the process has more than two or three steps, it will invariably prove to be unworkable. Progressive discipline takes flexibility away from the employer. It also allows an employee who learns how to work the system to remain employed even if the employee no longer should be. An employer needs to be able to deal with problems effectively and as quickly as possible. Progressive discipline does not generally allow this.

Avoid the use of promises or guarantees in the policy: Do not use statements that specifically state or imply certain conduct will or will not result in discipline. For example, avoid the use of statements like, "Employees who have satisfactory performance evaluations will not be disciplined;" or, "The failure to meet productivity quotas will result in discipline." An employee may have satisfactory performance evaluations while most others have exceptional evaluations. When "exceptional" performance results are the standard, a "satisfactory" performance is no longer satisfactory. The employer with this policy cannot do anything about the employee who is just meeting the minimum standards to keep from being disciplined. An employee who does not meet productivity quotas may be in a situation that explains the problem to the employer without the need for discipline (such as illness, family problems, a slump after a period of surpassing their quotas, or a decline in productivity overall). Using promises or guarantees in a policy tends to create implied contracts that lock the employer into consequences they may legitimately know are inappropriate.

Be clear when describing the policy: Whatever the policy, use clear language. Do not leave room for misinterpretation and do not be so vague that the policy says nothing.

Use warnings in the policy: In any situation that is not going to result in immediate termination from employment, give the employee a warning that there is a problem. Verbal warnings are appropriate. Written warnings should be reserved for more serious issues or if previous warnings have had little or no effect. Copies of written warnings should be placed in the employee's file.

Use reasonable consequences: The goal should be to improve the employee's performance or to remove the employee from the situation. Let the consequence fit the problem.

Be consistent: As with all policies, warnings and consequences should be used consistently. If a warning or a consequence is not given when it normally would, be able to explain the reason for the exception. Do not let the exception be based on race, color, national origin, religion, sex, age or disability.

Be firm: Once a decision has been made, follow through. It can be very difficult to follow through with discipline at times, but the employer is the person who must be firm. Failure to follow through with its own policies makes it appear as if the employer is being inconsistent and, perhaps, discriminatory.

Listen to the employee: When addressing a problem with an employee, ask for and listen to any response they may have. They may have information or be operating under circumstances not known by the employer that are relevant to the problem. What the employee has to say could be irrelevant, or it could result in the employer deciding on a different course of action.

Consider other policies: When preparing or carrying out discipline policies, do not forget about other employment or firm policies that may affect the situation. There may not be any other such policies, but if there are, coordinate the requirements of those policies with the discipline policies.

Consider express contracts: Employees who are working under an express employment contract, including collective bargaining agreements, must be disciplined pursuant to the applicable terms of their contract. Failure to comply may be a breach of contract that gives the employee a remedy against the employer.

8.1(c) Discipline Policies

Here are sample discipline policies:

Form 8.1
Discipline Policy

Any employee who fails or refuses to comply with any company policy, or who does not meet expected levels of performance in their job, may be subject to discipline. The employer will determine the appropriate discipline in each situation, which may include, but is not necessarily imited to, one or any combination of the following: warnings, retraining, reassignment, or termination of employment.

Form 8.2
Discipline Policy

Whenever it appears to the employer that an employee is not meeting the employer's expectations in their job, a warning will be given to the employee regarding the problem. The nature of the warning will be appropriate to the circumstances, as determined by the employer. If the employer determines that the employee has not resolved the problem described in the warning, action will be taken as deemed appropriate by the employer.

Form 8.3
Discipline Policy

Employees may be disciplined based on any one or more of the following factors:

❑ Job performance;

❑ Not following company policies applicable to the employee;

❑ Improper use of company property;

❑ Insubordination;

❑ Excessive absences;

❑ Violation of the law, regardless of the nature of the violation and whether or not the violation occurs on the job; or,

❑ Any other factor determined to be relevant by the employer.

The types of discipline that may be used include any one or more of the following, as determined most appropriate to the situation by the employer:

❑ Verbal or written warnings;

❑ Requiring specific improvement within a given period of time;

❑ Change in responsibilities or in job;

❑ Change in pay or benefits;

❑ Termination of employment; or,

❑ Anything else the employer determines to be appropriate.

8.2 Termination of Employment

8.2(a) Pursuant to Contract

Express Contracts: An employee who works pursuant to an express employment contract can only be terminated according to the terms of the contract. Whether the employee or the employer terminates the employment by a method that is contrary to the contract, it is a breach of contract. The other party then has a claim for breach of contract. The remedies for such a breach of contract could include a judgment for money damages caused by the improper termination of employment, or the issuing of an injunction or court order requiring the breaching party to do or to cease doing some act. For example, an employee who quits in breach of the contract may be required to return to work or to quit working for any new employer; an employer who "fired" the employee in breach of the contract may be required to rehire the employee or to pay the employee everything they would have received under the contract had there been no termination of employment. In *King v. PYA/Monarch, Inc.*, 453 S.E.2d 885 (S.C.1995), an employer and employee expressly agreed in writing that the employee would receive copies of written reprimands and that three or more reprimands could be considered cause for termination. However, the employer attempted to terminate the employee without giving all three contractually required reprimands. The court stated: "the employer could not deviate from its promise to follow its own employment procedures. The employer had breached its employment contract by failing to give the representative three written warnings and failing to place them in his personnel file."

Implied Contracts: When the court rules that an employer terminated an employee's employment in violation of a policy that is interpreted to be an implied contract, the employer will be liable to the employee for breach of contract. The employer may be ordered to pay the employee monetary damages proven to have resulted from the breach of implied contract, or the employer may be ordered to rehire the employee.

The bottom line in either situation is that employment pursuant to a contract can only be terminated as described in the contract.

8.2(b) By Employee

Unless an express or implied contract applies to the employee, an employee is free to resign or to quit their job at any time, for any reason or for no reason, and the employer can do nothing about it. The issue is simple from the employee's perspective. If the employee wants to quit their job, they can quit without liability to their employer.

The real issue when an employee quits is how the employer will handle the resignation. The following checklist describes how to handle this situation.

Checklist 8.3
Handling the Resignation of an Employee

❑ Confirm that the employee is actually resigning. If they are unclear or vague or having trouble saying the words, ask them to be specific. As appropriate, ask them to give you their notice of resignation in writing.

❑ If the employee's notice of resignation includes a date in the future when their resignation will become effective, it is not necessary to honor the effective date. The employer may tell the employee that their resignation is effective immediately, or that it is effective at any time up to the date given by the employee. The employer is in charge, not the employee. Therefore, the employer has the discretion to honor the employee's choice of effective date for their resignation. Just be sure to tell the employee when their resignation is actually effective.

❑ Handle the resignation professionally, whether or not the employee has. Deal with your frustration and anger or joy away from the employee. Responding in an unprofessional manner can result in something being said or done that is later regretted.

❑ Even though it is the employee who has decided to quit, it is the employer that is in control of how the resignation will occur. The employer must instruct the quitting employee on when and how to return company property, when and how they can take their property home, and what insurance or other documents the employee must sign. The details of severing the relationship must be under the control of the employer.

8.2(c) By Employer

(1) Firing

"Firing" is a term that means an employer is terminating the employment of an employee because the employer has decided to do so, regardless of whether or not the employee wants their employment to continue. As long as the employer does not violate an applicable statute, or any terms of an applicable express or implied contract, the employer can fire the employee at any time and for any reason. It is not legally necessary to fire an employee only for cause or because they have done something specific to cause the firing. The key issues to consider when firing an employee are: a) make sure the decision does not violate a statute, which is fairly easy; b) make sure the decision does not violate an express or implied contract, which is also fairly easy; and, c) handle the firing in an appropriate manner. Each of these issues is addressed by the following checklist.

Checklist 8.4
Firing an Employee

❑ Determine why the employee is to be fired. The reason(s) may be general, specific, detailed, or even vague. The employer must have one or more reasons for wanting to fire an employee. If the firing results in a claim against the employer by the employee, the employer's reasons will become relevant.

❑ Determine if the reasons for firing the employee involve or include the violation of any applicable state or federal statute. Research and talk to an attorney as necessary. If the answer is yes, firing the employee may not be an option.

❑ Determine if the reasons for firing the employee involve or include anything that is in violation of an express or implied contract that covers the employee. If the answer is yes, firing the employee may not be an option.

❑ If the reasons for firing the employee are based on job performance, review the employee's file. Does the file contain evaluations or other information that tend to indicate his or her job performance is acceptable? If yes, firing at this time may not be an option. Information in an employee's file should be consistent with any decision to fire that employee.

❑ Tell the employee in private that they are being fired, or in as private a setting as possible. Do not mince words; if they are being fired, tell them so.

❑ Be prepared for the employee's likely response. Have help standing by as necessary to deal with overly emotional responses, medical symptoms, anger or whatever response seems most likely.

❑ Handle the firing professionally. While it is certainly appropriate to be as gentle or sympathetic as possible, you are firing someone. They will not be happy. Do not become emotional with them or in response to their behavior, do not be condescending, do not feel compelled to comfort them, and do not offer any opinions or information that is unnecessary in handling the matter professionally.

❑ If the employee wants to say something in response to being fired, unless what they have to say could change the decision about firing them, tell them to send a letter with their comments and any questions.

(continued on next page)

(Page 2 - Checklist 8.4)

❏ Be prepared to follow through with the firing immediately after telling the employee they are fired. Any paperwork that needs the employee's signature, any information about their insurance or other details should be ready. The employee must also be able to leave the premises and get home. Help them arrange transportation, if necessary. Tell them when and how they can return company property and take their own property home. Be prepared to handle any situation.

❏ The employer must remain in charge of the firing at all times.

(2) Lay Off

A lay off is the decision by the employer to terminate an employee's employment for reasons that are usually based on business conditions, instead of reasons directly concerning the employee. For example, a decrease in business, a loss in profits, a change of products or services being offered, or other factors that are generally outside the control of the employees being laid off. Employees who are laid off generally have an expectation of being rehired when business conditions improve, and they often are.

The federal statute that directly deals with lay offs is the Worker Adjustment and Retraining Notification Act [29 U.S.C. 2101 *et seq.*]. If an employer has a work force of 100 employees or more, this act requires the employer to give all employees who are to be laid off a minimum of 60 days notice before the lay off begins.

Title VII of the Civil Rights Act of 1964 [42 U.S.C. 2000e *et seq.*] also applies to lay offs. The decision on which employees to lay off, which ones to rehire, and any other decision to be made concerning the lay off must be based on factors that do not include race, color, national origin, religion, sex, age or disability.

(3) Elimination of Job

The elimination of a job or position within a firm occurs for different reasons. It is a legitimate business practice to eliminate jobs on the basis of financial decisions, operational decisions, or any other business reason. Typically, employees whose jobs are eliminated are laid off and should be considered as laid off employees. Absent a contract covering an affected employee, there is no legal requirement for an employee whose job is being eliminated to be reassigned to another job in the firm. However, elimination of a job cannot be a legitimate basis to get rid of an employee for a discriminatory reason.

(4) Constructive Termination

Constructive termination is a legal term that describes the situation where an employer's actions compel an employee to quit. It does not matter what the employer does. If the objective is to create an environment which is hostile enough that the targeted employee or employees decide to quit, then the employer has forced its will on the employee. This is constructive termination and it is considered a firing, as well as a cowardly way to get rid of an employee.

In a constructive termination, the issue becomes the employer's reason for wanting the employee to quit. Courts tend to be suspicious of any case of constructive termination, as it always appears that the employer is hiding something. The presumption is that an employer with a legitimate reason to fire an employee will simply fire that employee. Constructive termination is only resorted to, the presumption continues, when the employer does not have a legitimate reason to get rid of an employee. Often, the real reason behind constructive termination is unlawful discrimination. Employers should never, under any circumstances, resort to any method of constructive termination.

This issue was considered by the court in *Ramsey v. Derwinski*, 787 F.Supp. 8 (D.D.C. 1992): "To establish a claim of constructive discharge, (the employee) must show that (the employer) deliberately made her working conditions . . . so intolerable that a reasonable person in her situation would have concluded that she was forced to resign . . . To demonstrate intolerable working conditions (the employee) must do more than prove an actionable instance of discrimination. There must be aggravating factors, such as continuous and pervasive discriminatory treatment, spanning a substantial period of time."

In *Borque v. Powell Electrical Manufacturing Company*, 617 F.2d 61 (5th Cir. 1980), the court discussed the issue this way: "The general rule is that if the employer deliberately makes an employee's working conditions so intolerable that the employee is forced into an involuntary resignation, then the employer has encompassed a constructive discharge and is as liable for any illegal conduct involved therein as if it had formally discharged the aggrieved employee . . . (In this case) Defendant urges, with some supporting authority, that in order to constitute a constructive discharge, the imposition of intolerable working conditions must be with the purpose of forcing the employee to resign . . . Nevertheless, such a rule is inconsistent with authority in this Circuit and, we believe, with the realities of modern employment . . . To find constructive discharge we believe that the trier of fact must be satisfied that the working conditions would have been so difficult or unpleasant that a reasonable person in the employee's shoes would have felt compelled to resign."

(5) Wrongful Termination

Wrongful termination, or discharge, refers to the termination of an employee by any method that violates the law or public policy. While a termination in violation of a statute, a contract, or that is a constructive termination is wrongful, the term wrongful discharge is generally reserved for terminations in violation of the common law or of public policy. The following case summaries illustrate this issue.

In *Reynolds v. Ozark Motor Lines, Inc.*, 887 S.W.2d 822 (Tenn.1994), when employees refused the demand of their employer to operate vehicles in a manner that violated the state Motor Carriers Act, the employees were terminated. The court ruled that, "Tolerating the retaliatory discharge of these employees for observing the safety provisions of the act would impair the legislature's declared policy of protecting the public."

"An employer may be held liable for wrongful dismissal of an employee where the termination is for the exercise of a legal right or interest (such as making a workers' compensation claim)." *Groce v. Foster*, 880 P.2d 902 (Okl.1994)

State law has made an "exception to the general rule of at-will employment – it allows a cause of action for wrongful termination when the employee has been discharged for refusing to perform an illegal act." *Amador v. Tan,* 855 S.W.2d 131 (Tex.App.1993)

CHAPTER 9
Discrimination

CONTENTS

9.1 A Legal Description of the Term

Discrimination simply means to choose one thing, or person, instead of another. Therefore, discrimination is not necessarily good or bad; it is simply an action being taken, a decision being made. *Unlawful* discrimination occurs when the choice being acted upon violates the law. In employment law, unlawful discrimination refers to making choices between or decisions about job applicants or employees on some basis prohibited by statute. Lawful discrimination is the making of choices between or decisions about job applicants or employees on any basis not prohibited by statute.

As a result of the various state and federal employment law statutes that prohibit certain types of discrimination, all employers have a legal duty not to discriminate unlawfully. It can be a difficult duty to fulfill at all times, for reasons that have nothing to do with the honest desire of an employer not to discriminate unlawfully. Unlawful discrimination is a condition. To illustrate, compare unlawful discrimination to the flu. A normal person does not want to get the flu. They take reasonable steps to avoid catching a flu virus; they may read articles on how to prevent the flu; they may consult with their physician for specific instructions on how they can best stay healthy; they may get a flu vaccine and take other actions to help make sure they do not catch the flu; and they may be very diligent in all their efforts to avoid the flu. However, if in spite of all their efforts, this person wakes up one morning with the flu, they have the flu. It will not do any good to argue about everything that was done to avoid the flu. When the flu strikes, the patient has to deal with the illness. It is likely that the specific flu viruses targeted for prevention did not make the person sick, but there are many flu viruses out there. The flu is an illness, or a condition, that can make an appearance no matter how hard a person works to stay healthy. It is often true that a person who has tried to stay healthy is in a much better position to combat the flu. They may still be sick, but the symptoms are not necessarily as severe as they might have been. Their recovery to full health is also likely to be faster than if they had not attempted to stay healthy.

An employer who actively tries to prevent unlawful discrimination in its workplace will avoid many types of discrimination. However, they are always susceptible to some type of discrimination. If this condition is found, the employer has no choice but to deal with it in order to resolve the particular problem, as well as to prevent that type of discrimination from recurring. In addition, if the employer has been trying to prevent the condition of unlawful discrimination, its efforts are very likely to reduce or mitigate any potential consequences. No employer is ever a helpless victim of the legal system who must simply wait its turn to fight a claim of discrimination and then hope it survives. An ancient legal maxim from Roman Law applies directly to this issue: *Vigilantibus et non formientibus jura subvenient.* The law aids the vigilant, not those asleep on their rights.

Employment law compliance planning is the best thing an employer can do for itself to prevent unlawful discrimination, as well as the other problems discussed throughout this book.

9.2 Unlawful Descrimination

This section includes in checklist form the statutes that describe the types of discrimination prohibited in employment. Chapter 15 describes these and other employment statutes in detail, including applicability of the statute, cases explaining the statute, and potential damages for violation of the statute. All quoted language is from the indicated statute.

9.2(a) Statutes Prohibiting Discrimination

9.2(a)(1) Equal Rights Under the Law [42 U.S.C. 1981-1988]

Checklist 9.1
Discrimination Prohibited By §1981 *et seq.*

❑ "All persons" have the same right in every state and territory of the United States "to the full and equal benefit of all laws and proceedings for the security of persons and property as is enjoyed by white persons."

❑ "All persons" means any human being who is within the jurisdiction, or authority, of the United States, wherever that may be. This statute applies equally to U.S. citizens, residents, visitors, and to those who may be anywhere within the U.S. illegally.

9.2(a)(2) Title VII of the Civil Rights Act of 1964 [42 U.S.C. 2000e *et seq.*]

Checklist 9.2
Discrimination Prohibited by Title VII

❑ It is an unlawful employment practice for an employer "to fail or refuse to hire or to discharge any individual, or otherwise to discriminate against any individual with respect to his compensation, terms, conditions, or privileges of employment, because of such individual's;"

❑ Race;

❑ Color;

❑ Religion;

❑ Sex; or,

❑ National Origin.

❑ It is also an unlawful employment practice for an employer "to limit, segregate, or classify his employees or applicants for employment in any way which would deprive or tend to deprive any individual of employment opportunities or otherwise adversely affect his status as an employee," because of the same five factors listed above.

❑ There are some exceptions to this statute (see Chapter 15).

9.2(a)(3) Age Discrimination in Employment Act [29 U.S.C. 621-634]

Checklist 9.3
Discrimination Based on Age Prohibited

❑   The prohibitions in this statute are limited to persons who are at least 40 years old.

❑   It is an unlawful employment practice for an employer to "fail or refuse to hire or to discharge any individual or otherwise discriminate against any individual with respect to his compensation, terms, conditions, or privileges of employment, because of such individual's age."

❑   It is also an unlawful employment practice to "limit, segregate, or classify his employees in any way which would deprive or tend to deprive any individual of employment opportunities or otherwise adversely affect his status as an employee, because of such individual's age."

❑   It is also an unlawful employment practice to "reduce the wage rate of any employee in order to comply with this statute."

❑   There are a number of exceptions to this statute (see Chapter 15).

9.2(a)(4) Americans with Disabilities Act of 1990 [42 U.S.C. 12101 *et seq*.]

Checklist 9.4
Prohibition of Discrimination
Against Disabled Persons

❑   An employer cannot discriminate against "a qualified individual with a disability because of the disability of such individual in regard to" —

❑   Job application procedures;

❑   Hiring;

❑   Advancement;

❑   Discharge from employment;

❑   Compensation;

❑   Job training; and,

❑   Other terms, conditions, and privileges of employment.

❑   The term "qualified individual with a disability" means "an individual with a disability who, with or without reasonable accommodation, can perform the essential functions of the employment position that such individual holds or desires."

❑   This statute, and the case law concerning this statute contain further definitions and rules of application for whether or not an individual is "disabled," whether they are "qualified," when an accommodation is "reasonable," and other issues relevant to this statute (see Chapter 15).

9.2(a)(5) Equal Pay Act of 1963 [29 U.S.C. 206(d)]

Checklist 9.5
Prohibited Discrimination Regarding
Employees' Wages

❑ An employer cannot discriminate between employees on the basis of sex by paying one employer lower wages than another employee of the opposite sex when —

❑ They work in the same establishment;

❑ They do equal work in jobs which require "equal skill, effort, and responsibility, and which are performed under similar working conditions."

❑ There are a number of exceptions to this statute (see Chapter 15).

9.2(a)(6) Veterans' Employment and Reemployment Rights Act [38 U.S.C 4301 *et seq.*]

Checklist 9.6
Discrimination Prohibited Against Members
Of the Armed Forces

❑   This statute protects any person "who is a member of, applies to be a member of, performs, has performed, applies to perform, or has an obligation to perform service in a uniformed service."

❑   Such persons "shall not be denied initial employment, reemployment, retention in employment, promotion, or any benefit of employment."

❑   This statute has a number of exceptions (see Chapter 15).

9.2(a)(7) State Statutes

Each state has its own versions of the federal, anti-discrimination statutes. The same types of discrimination are prohibited by state law as by federal law, but there is a significant difference between state and federal statutes. Federal law only applies to employers with a minimum number of employees and the lowest minimum is fifteen. This means federal law does not apply to employers with less than fifteen employees (or whatever number is the minimum stated in the language of the statute). State law also has a minimum number of employees requirement before it applies to an employer, but the minimum numbers under state law are much lower than under federal law. Depending on the state, state law usually applies to employers with a minimum of two to four employees.

Generally, an employer with fifteen or more employees is covered by federal anti-discrimination statutes. The same employer is also covered by their state's anti-discrimination statutes. This means that an employee with a claim of unlawful discrimination against such an employer can make their claim in either state or federal court. The decision of whether to pursue the claim in state or federal court is entirely up to the employee. The basis for deciding between state or federal court is to pick the one that offers the best chance of success for the employee. Important factors that an employee should consider in making this decision include: a) federal court usually takes longer, is more expensive, and can be more difficult than the state court process, which makes state courts look attractive; b) federal court can result in higher damages being awarded to an employee who wins their case, which makes federal court more appealing; c) and, by starting in federal court, a settlement more favorable to the employee can be made than by starting in state court, as the employer generally is more eager to avoid the cost and time involved in defending a federal case, which makes federal court look attractive. This decision, regardless of the factors considered and the reasons for the decision, is the employee's decision. Although an employer can attempt to have a case moved from federal or state court to the other, such attempts are usually unsuccessful unless the basis is jurisdictional – i.e., the number of employees the employer has.

An employer with under fifteen employees can only be sued in state court, as federal court does not have jurisdiction over such an employer.

An employer with less than the minimum number of employees required by state statute is not free to discriminate. Although the language of the state statute may clearly state an employer must have four employees to be covered by the statute, the case may still be heard by the court on the basis of "public policy."

9.2(a)(8) Public Policy

This is a term that refers to an implied legal requirement for promoting the general interest and welfare of the public. Likewise, public policy includes the implied legal requirement of not doing anything that would seem to harm the general interest and welfare of the public. Public policy is not necessarily written down anywhere, but it is based on written sources, such as statutes and case law. For example, an employer with only one employee may not be covered by either state or federal discrimination statutes. This fact does not give that employer a license to discriminate. A court could, and probably would, conclude that a public policy against discrimination in employment exists. Further, the basis for public policy includes state and federal statutes, as well as the abundant case law concerning these statutes. While a particular employer may not fall under the technical requirements for applicability of a statute, when public policy requires or prohibits conduct based on established law, it is in the general interest and welfare of the public that the requirements of the statute be applied to the employer. Public policy can, therefore, be the basis for enforcing statutes prohibiting employment discrimination against any employer.

While public policy can be used to close a loophole that would seem to allow an employer to discriminate, it cannot be the basis for filing a case in federal court when it should clearly be filed in state court due to the employer's number of employees. The goal of public policy is to close technical loopholes that might otherwise deprive an injured party of any legal remedy, not to allow an injured party to pick a different and legally unavailable remedy because they believe it might be better than the legal remedy available to them.

9.2(b) Proving Unlawful Discrimination (the *McDonnell Douglas* test)

Whether an employment discrimination case is filed in state or federal court, the method to be followed for proving whether or not unlawful discrimination actually occurred is now established and is referred to as the *McDonnell Douglas* test. This test was first described by the U.S. Supreme Court in *McDonnell Douglas Corporation v. Green*, 411 U.S. 792, 93 S.Ct. 1817, 36 L.Ed.2d 668 (1973). (The name comes from the name of the employer.) An employee, Percy Green, had been laid off as part of a general lay off. The employee believed he had been selected for lay off because of his race and his participation in anti-discrimination demonstrations against his employer. Sometime after the demonstrations, laid off employees were rehired, but Mr. Green was not. Believing the decision not to rehire him was based on his race, he filed a claim against his employer pursuant to Title VII of the Civil Rights Act of 1964. The case went all the way to the U.S. Supreme Court, which ruled against Mr. Green. Of most significance is the test the Court described for proving whether unlawful discrimination has occurred. The test is:

An employee must first establish a minimal level of proof of discrimination. This is done by the employee showing: (1) That he is a member of a protected class (i.e., race, color, national origin, religion, sex, age, or disability); (2) That he suffered an adverse employment action; (3) That he was qualified for the position in question; and, (4) That the basis of the adverse employment action taken against the employee was being a member of a protected class. Showing these four things raises an inference of unlawful discrimination only because of a presumption that the decision, if otherwise unexplained, is more likely than not based on unlawful discrimination. Once an employee has made this initial proof, a rebuttable presumption arises that the employer unlawfully discriminated against the employee and the burden of proof shifts to the employer to articulate some legitimate, nondiscriminatory reason for its actions. If the employer is able to articulate such a legitimate, nondiscriminatory reason for its actions, the employee must then prove that the employer's reason is nothing more than pretext, or a cover-up for discrimination. The employee can prove pretext either by directly persuading the court that a discriminatory reason more likely motivated the employer, or indirectly by showing that the employer's explanation for its actions against or affecting the employee is unworthy of credence.

In addition to *McDonnell Douglas,* see: *Texas Department of Community Affairs v. Burdine*, 450 U.S. 248, 101 S.Ct. 1089, 67 L.Ed.2d 207 (1981); and *United States Postal*

In addition to *McDonnell Douglas,* see: *Texas Department of Community Affairs v. Burdine*, 450 U.S. 248, 101 S.Ct. 1089, 67 L.Ed.2d 207 (1981); and *United States Postal Workers Board of Governors v. Aikens*, 460 U.S. 711, 103 S.Ct. 1478, 75 L.Ed.2d 403 (1983).

An employer can best prepare policies in its compliance plan for dealing with discrimination issues by both knowing what actions and conduct are described by statute as unlawful discrimination, and by understanding the test by which a court will evaluate whether or not unlawful discrimination has occurred in a particular case. These issues are discussed further in Chapter 15.

CHAPTER 10
Wages and Benefits

CONTENTS

10.1 Wages

"Wage" is a legal term that means the compensation paid by an employer to its employee. A wage can be paid on any basis, with hourly, daily, weekly, bi-weekly, or monthly wages being the most common. For employment law purposes, an employee's wage is usually determined on an hourly basis, even if it is not determined and paid on an hourly basis. This is done by using a simple formula: EMPLOYEE'S TOTAL WAGES FOR ONE PAY PERIOD ̥ TOTAL HOURS WORKED BY EMPLOYEE IN THAT PAY PERIOD = HOURLY WAGE FOR THAT PAY PERIOD. Therefore, an employee who receives a salary of $2000 per month and works, on average, 170 hours per month, is paid an hourly wage of $11.76. An employer who is not paying overtime wages to an employee who must be paid overtime (see Section 10.1(a), below), will find that the court uses this formula to determine that employee's hourly wage. Then, based on the hourly wage determined, the overtime wage will be set, which is always 1½ times the hourly wage.

"Salary" is a term that usually indicates an employee's compensation is determined by the employer on some basis other than hourly, such as annually. Whether an employee is considered by the employer (and/or by the employee) to be paid a wage or a salary is irrelevant for employment law purposes. The relevant issue is whether the employee is "exempt" from wage and hour statutes, or "non-exempt" from wage and hour statutes. Non-exempt employees must be paid at least the legally required minimum wage and must also be paid overtime wages for each hour worked over an average of 40 hours per week per pay period. Exempt employees can be paid anything and worked any number of hours, and they usually are. The rules for determining whether an employee is exempt or non-exempt are described below. However, paying an employee a "salary" as opposed to an "hourly wage" is not one of the factors described in the statutes for determining if an employee is exempt or non-exempt.

10.1(a) The Fair Labor Standards Act of 1938 [29 U.S.C. 201 *et seq.*]

This federal statute is commonly referred to as the "wage and hour law." The basic provisions of this act require that, effective September 1, 1997, employers are required to pay their employees a minimum wage of $5.15 per hour [29 U.S.C. 206(a)(1)]. Newly hired employees who are less than 20 years of age, may be paid a lower, "training wage" of no lower than $4.25 per hour for the first 90 days of their employment [29 U.S.C. 206(g)]. In addition, this act sets a maximum work week of 40 hours per week. An employee who works more than 40 hours per week is to be paid an overtime wage of 1½ times their hourly wage for the hours they work in excess of 40 hours per week [29 U.S.C. 207(a)(1)]. There are other minimum hourly wage provisions of this act that apply to specific situations. There are also other criteria for determining when the overtime wage must be paid that apply to specific situations. Both of these additional requirements for other minimum wages and for payment of overtime wages are discussed in Chapter 15. Most employers in the United States, however, are covered by the basic provisions of this act.

Another key part of this act is its definitions of which employees are exempt from the minimum wage and maximum hour requirements. This tends to be the most confusing part of this act. If an employee is *exempt*, as defined by this act, that employee can be paid any wage and worked any number of hours that the employer can get away with. In fact, during some busy weeks, an exempt employee may determine their actual hourly wage (by using the formula set out above) to be much less than the minimum wage. Federal law has no problem with this. However, the determination of whether an employee is exempt or non-exempt is made strictly by applying the definitions contained in this statute. An employer's own test or standards on the issue are absolutely irrelevant (unless, of course, the employer is correctly using the statute as its standard).

The following checklists are based directly on this act's definitions of which employees are exempt. These checklists can, therefore, be used for determining which employees are exempt from coverage under the federal wage and hour law. The applicable statute number is given with each checklist.

Checklist 10.1
Employees Who are Exempt from Wage and Hour Requirements, 29 U.S.C. 213(a)(1)

❑ Any employee employed in an actual, good faith, legitimately executive, administrative, or professional capacity.

❑ Any employee employed in the capacity of academic administrative personnel.

❑ Any employee employed as a teacher in elementary or secondary schools.

❑ Any employee employed as an outside salesman.

Checklist 10.1a
General Test to Determine if an Employee
Is Employed in an Executive Capacity,
29 U.S.C. 213(a)(1)

❑   On average, at least 50% of the employee's time is spent managing an enterprise or a department or subdivision of an enterprise.

❑   Customarily and regularly directs work of two or more other employees.

❑   Can hire and fire employees, or can at least suggest the change in the employment status of other employees.

❑   Customarily and regularly exercises discretionary powers. In other words, has the authority to make decisions.

❑   An employee who spends 80% of his or her time per week, on average, in the above activities and who receives a total compensation of at least $155 per week, is employed in an Executive capacity and is exempt. (Except, an employee in a retail or service establishment who spends 60% of his or her time per week, on average, in the above activities and who receives a total compensation of at least $155 per week, is employed in an Executive capacity and is exempt.)

Checklist 10.1b
General Test to Determine if an Employee
Is Employed in an Administrative Capacity,
29 U.S.C. 213(a)(1)

❑ On average, at least 50% of the employee's time is spent performing office or non-manual work directly relating to management policies or general business operations of the employer or of the employer's customers (clients, patients, etc.).

❑ Regularly and directly assists an owner of the business (proprietor) or an executive or an administrative employee. Or, works only under general supervision along specialized or technical lines, requiring special training, experience or knowledge. Or, executes special assignments and tasks only under general supervision.

❑ Customarily and regularly exercises discretion and independent judgment.

❑ An employee who spends 80% of his or her time per week, on average, in the above activities and who receives a total compensation of at least $155 per week, is employed in an *Administrative* capacity and is exempt. (Except, an employee in a retail or service establishment who spends 60% of his or her time per week, on average, in the above activities and who receives a total compensation of at least $155 per week, is employed in an *Administrative* capacity and is exempt.) A person employed in an academic administrative capacity is an administrative employee if they meet the above test, except that their minimum salary must be the same as the entrance salary for teachers in the school or educational institution in which they are employed.

Checklist 10.1c
General Test to Determine if an Employee Is Employed in a Professional Capacity, 29 U.S.C. 213(a)(1)

❑ On average, at least 50% of the employee's time is spent performing work requiring scientific or specialized study, or performs creative and original work in a recognized artistic endeavor, depending primarily on the invention, imagination or talent of the employee; or, who teaches, tutors, instructs, or lectures and is employed by a school system or educational establishment.

❑ Performs work predominantly intellectual and varied that cannot be standardized in point of time.

❑ Consistently exercises discretion and judgment in the performance of their work.

❑ No more than 20% of their time per week is spent on activities that cannot be described as above.

❑ Receives a minimum of $170 per week as total compensation. However, there is no minimum compensation standard for employees who are licensed legal or medical practitioners, holders of academic degrees for the practice of medicine who are engaged in internship or resident programs, or for teachers employed by schools or other institutions.

Checklist 10.2
Employees Who are Exempt from Wage and Hour Requirements, 29 U.S.C. 213(a)(3)

❑ Any employee employed by an establishment which is an amusement or recreational establishment, organized camp, or religious or non-profit educational conference center, if:

❑ The establishment does not operate for more than seven months in any *calendar* year; or,

❑ During the preceding *calendar* year, the establishment's receipts for any six months were not more than 1/3 of its average receipts for the other six months. In other words, the establishment is open for business for more than seven months in a calendar year, but it receives 2/3 of its gross income in one six-month period and not more than 1/3 of its gross income in the other six months of the year.

Checklist 10.3
Employees Who are Exempt from Wage and Hour Requirements, 29 U.S.C. 213(a)(5)

❑   Any employee employed in the catching, taking, propagating, harvesting, cultivating, or farming of any kind of fish, shellfish, crustacea, sponges, seaweeds, or other aquatic forms of animal and vegetable life.

❑   Any employee employed in the first processing, canning or packing of the marine products described above, if their work is performed at sea as an incident to, or in conjunction with fishing operations.

Checklist 10.4
Employees Who are Exempt from Wage and Hour Requirements, 29 U.S.C. 213(a)(6)

❑   Any employee employed in agriculture if:

❑   Their employer did not use more than 500 man-days of agricultural labor during the preceding *calendar* year; or,

❑   The employee is the parent, spouse, child, or other immediate family member of the employer; or,

❑   The employee is employed as a *hand harvest laborer* and is paid on a piece rate basis in an operation which has been, and is customarily and generally recognized as having been paid on a piece rate basis in the region where the employee is employed, and, the employee commutes daily from his or her own permanent residence to the farm which is the actual place of employment, and, the employee has been employed in agriculture for less than 13 weeks during the preceding *calendar* year; or,

❑   If the employee is primarily engaged in the range production of livestock.

Checklist 10.5
Employees Who are Exempt from Wage and Hour Requirements, 29 U.S.C. 213(a)(8)

❏   Employees employed in connection with the publication of any weekly, semiweekly, or daily newspaper with a circulation of less than 4000; and,

❏   The majority of the newspaper's circulation is within the county or within contiguous counties to the county where the newspaper is published.

Checklist 10.6
Employees Who are Exempt from Wage and Hour Requirements, 29 U.S.C. 213(a)(10), (12), and (15)

❏ A switchboard operator employed by an independently owned public telephone company which has no more than 750 stations.

❏ Any employee employed as a seaman on a vessel other than an American vessel.

❏ Any person employed as a babysitter on a casual basis for a family. (Does not include persons employed as babysitters in a daycare or other commercial setting).

❏ Any person employed as a personal companion to provide companionship or services to an individual who cannot care for themselves due to age or infirmity. (Does not include persons employed in this capacity on a commercial basis.)

Checklist 10.7
Employees Who are Exempt from Wage and Hour Requirements, 29 U.S.C. 213(a)(17)

❑ Any employee who is a computer systems analyst, computer programmer, software engineer, or other similarly skilled worker, whose primary duty is:

❑ The application of systems analysis techniques and procedures, including consulting with users, to determine hardware, software, or system functional specifications; or

❑ The design, development, documentation, analysis, creation, testing, or modification of computer systems or programs, including prototypes, based on and related to user or system design specifications; or,

❑ The design, documentation, testing, creation, or modification of computer programs relating to machine operations systems; or,

❑ Any combination of the above which requires the same level of skill, and who is compensated at a rate of not less than $27.63 an hour.

Some employees may be non-exempt from the minimum wage requirement, but are exempt from the overtime pay requirement of this statute. The following checklists describe which employees are exempt from overtime pay requirements only.

Checklist 10.8
Employees Who are Exempt from Overtime
Pay Requirements, 29 U.S.C. 213(b)(1)-(7)

❑ Any employee subject to the qualifications and maximum hours of service requirements as set by the Secretary of Transportation.

❑ Any employee whose employer is engaged in the operation of a rail carrier.

❑ Any employee whose employer is an air carrier.

❑ Any employee employed as an outside buyer of poultry, eggs, cream, or milk, in their raw or natural state.

❑ Any employee employed as a seaman.

Checklist 10.9
Employees Who are Exempt from Overtime Pay Requirements, 29 U.S.C. 213(b)(9)

❏ Any employee employed as an announcer, news editor, or chief engineer by a radio or television station, if the major studio of the radio or television station is located:

❏ In a city or town with an official population of 100,000 people or less, except, where this city or town is a part of a metropolitan area with a total population of more than 100,000 people; or,

❏ In a city or town with an official population of 25,000 people or less, and, this city or town is part of a metropolitan area with a total population of more than 100,000 people, and, this city or town is at least 40 airline miles from the principal city in the metropolitan area.

Checklist 10.10
Employees Who are Exempt from Overtime
Pay Requirements, 29 U.S.C. 213(b)(10)

❑ Any salesman, partsman, or mechanic primarily engaged in selling or servicing automobiles, trucks, or farm implements, IF, such employee's employer is a non-manufacturing establishment primarily engaged in the business of selling such vehicles or implements to ultimate purchasers.

❑ Any salesman primarily engaged in selling trailers, boats, or aircraft, IF, such employee's employer is a non-manufacturing establishment primarily engaged in the business of selling such vehicles to ultimate purchasers.

Checklist 10.11
Employees Who are Exempt from Overtime Pay Requirements, 29 U.S.C. 213(b)(11) - (21)

❑ Agricultural employees who are actually engaged in agricultural operations.

❑ Drivers transporting agricultural products.

❑ Taxicab drivers, if their employer is primarily engaged in the business of operating taxicabs.

❑ Firefighters and law enforcement personnel employed by public agencies, including correctional officers, if the public agency employs fewer than 5 such personnel each during the workweek.

❑ Any employee employed in domestic service in a household and who resides in the household of their employer.

Checklist 10.12
Employees Who are Exempt from Overtime
Pay Requirements, 29 U.S.C. 213(b)(24)

❑ Any employee who is employed with his or her spouse by a nonprofit educational institution to serve as the parents of children:

❑ who are orphans or one of whose natural parents is deceased; or,

❑ who are enrolled in such institution and reside in residential facilities of the institution.

❑ This exemption applies only if the employee and his or her spouse actually reside in the institution, they receive board and lodging from the institution at no cost to them, and they are together compensated less than $10,000 in cash payments per year.

Checklist 10.13
Employees Who are Exempt from Overtime Pay Requirements, 29 U.S.C. 213(b)(27)-(30)

❑   Any employee of a motion picture theater.

❑   Any employee engaged in forestry or lumbering operations whose employer has no more than 8 employees engaged in forestry or lumbering operations.

❑   Any employee of a privately owned amusement or recreational establishment which is located in a national park or national forest, or on land in the National Wildlife Refuge System. However, such an employee must receive overtime pay for working over 56 hours per week.

❑   Criminal investigators who are paid availability pay.

Finally, employees who would otherwise be non-exempt under this act are declared by this act to be exempt if they are employed in foreign countries or in specific locations that are under United States jurisdiction. The following checklist describes this exemption.

Checklist 10.14
Employees Exempt from this Act Regardless
Of the Nature of Their Work [29 U.S.C. 213(f)]

❑   Any employee whose employer is engaged in the operation of a rail carrier.

❑   Any employee, regardless of the type of work they do, whose services during the workweek are performed in any foreign country is exempt from the requirements of this act.

❑   Any employee, regardless of the type of work they do, whose services during the workweek are performed in any location within the jurisdiction of the United States, except: a State of the United States; the District of Columbia; Puerto Rico; the Virgin Islands; the outer Continental Shelf Lands defined in the Outer Continental Shelf Lands Act; American Samoa; Guam; Wake Island; Eniwetok Atoll; Kwajalein Atoll; or, Johnston Island, is exempt from this act.

10.1(b) Federal Child Labor Law

The Fair Labor Standards Act also contains the federal law on child labor. The language is fairly vague, however. At 29 U.S.C. 212(c), this statute states, "No employer shall employ any oppressive child labor in commerce or in the production of goods for commerce or in any enterprise engaged in commerce or in the production of goods for commerce."

The phrase "oppressive child labor" is defined in this act at 29 U.S.C. 203(l) to include:

(1) The employment by any employer of anyone under the age of 16 years old (unless the employer is the parent of the employee); or,

(2) The employment by any employer of anyone between the ages of 16 and 18 in any occupation which the Secretary of Labor determines to be detrimental to the child's health or well-being.

This same section of the statute also states that the following is NOT "oppressive child labor":

(1) The employment of children between the ages of 14 and 16 in occupations other than manufacturing and mining, provided that the employment does not interfere with the child's schooling or with their health and well-being; or,

(2) Any employment of any child when the Secretary of Labor has issued a certificate stating that a particular job with a particular employer is not oppressive child labor.

In addition, Section 213(c) of this act exempts certain types of employment of children from being described as "oppressive child labor." The next checklist describes these exemptions.

Checklist 10.15
Types of Child Labor Specifically Described
As <u>Not</u> Being Oppressive Child Labor
[29 U.S.C. 213(c)]

❑ Children under 12 employed in agriculture by their parents.

❑ Children 12 or 13 years old employed with their parent in agriculture.

❑ Children 14 or older who are employed in agriculture.

❑ Children 10 or 11 years old may be employed for no more than eight weeks per year as "hand harvest laborers" upon approval by the Secretary of Labor of an application for such employment.

❑ Children employed as actors or performers in motion pictures, theatrical productions, or in radio or television productions.

❑ Children 16 or 17 years old who load materials into scrap paper balers or paper box compactors, if these machines cannot be operated while being loaded, but the children cannot be employed to operate or unload these machines.

❑ Children 17 years old may drive in a job only if the driving occurs during daylight hours, the child has a proper driver's license, the child has successively completed a State approved driver education course, the vehicle has seat belts and the child uses the seat belts, the vehicle does not exceed 6,000 pounds in gross weight, the driving is only occasional and incidental to the child's employment, and, the driving does not involve: towing of another vehicle; route deliveries or sales; the transportation for hire of property, goods, or passengers; urgent, time-sensitive deliveries, more than two trips per day; transporting more than three passengers at a time; or, driving beyond a 30 mile radius from the place of employment.

10.1(c) State Wage and Hour Statutes

Each state has its own wage and hour statute. These statutes set the minimum wage requirements, when overtime pay must be paid (as well as the rate of overtime pay), and they describe the state's child labor laws (although some states may have a separate title concerning child labor).

State Minimum Wage Requirements: Each state may set any minimum wage requirement it desires, but state law cannot authorize a lower minimum wage for any employee than that employee would be entitled to receive under federal law. State law can, however, set a higher minimum wage requirement for employees than they would be entitled to receive under federal law. The result is that federal minimum wage requirements are the legal standard for determining the minimum wage of any employee, unless:

(1) State law requires a higher minimum wage than federal law, which means the state law applies and not the federal law; or,

(2) State law describes a type of employment or employee not described by federal law, which means the state law applies and not the federal law, even if such a state law allows a lower minimum wage than federal law.

State Overtime Requirements: Each state may set its own standards for when an employee must be paid an overtime wage, and how the overtime wage is to be determined. As with minimum wage requirements, however, state law cannot lessen the requirements of federal law, but state law can exceed the requirements of federal law. The result is that federal overtime requirements are the legal standard on this issue, unless:

(1) State law requires overtime to be paid beginning with hours worked that are less than 40 hours per week, which means the state law applies and not the federal law; or,

(2) State law requires the overtime wage to be 1½ times or more than the employee's regular wage, which means the state law applies and not the federal law; or,

(3) State law describes a type of employment or employee not described by federal law, which means the state law applies and not the federal law, even if such a state law allows an entirely different standard than federal law.

Child Labor Law: State child labor laws are often more restrictive, as well as more descriptive, than federal law. As with minimum wage and overtime requirements, federal law sets the minimum legal standard. If state law is more detailed, more restrictive, or more anything than federal law, the state law applies.

10.1(d) Time and Place for Paying Wages

It is the employer's decision to determine how often an employee is to be paid the wages they have earned. The common guide used by an employer in making this determination is the custom within their industry or within their community. Typically, employees are paid their wages weekly, every other week, or monthly. Some employees may also be paid on a daily basis, and other employees may be paid on a less frequent basis than monthly. These are unusual situations, but are entirely appropriate if it is the standard in that industry. Unless there is a specific agreement between the employer and the employee to the contrary (and this usually needs to be a written agreement signed by the employee), an employee must be paid their wages at the time the employer has previously determined for paying wages.

Some state laws require an employer to pay all wages due at the time they are due, no exceptions. Failure to pay wages when due can be a violation of state statute which may require a fine or other penalty to be paid by the employer. Therefore, if cash is short on pay day, pay wages first, before paying anything else. If necessary, get a loan to cover the payroll.

Terminated employees are not, generally, given any preference for receiving their wages. An employee who is terminated before the end of a pay period does not have to be paid until the next regular pay day for that employee, although the employer does have the option of paying that employee's wages at the time of termination.

The place for paying wages is the employer's place of business, unless other arrangements have been made with the employee.

10.1(e) Deductions from Wages

Wages become the property of the employee as soon as the wage has been earned. The fact that the employee is paid his or her wages on the 1st and 15th of the month, for example, is irrelevant. The date for payment of wages is simply a convenience for allowing an orderly process for keeping records and making payment. Since wages earned are the employee's property, even if still in the custody of the employer because pay day has not yet arrived, the employer must treat the wages as the employee's property. This means the employer can only make deductions from the employee's wages as required by law, or as authorized in writing by the employee.

Deductions required by law include: state and federal income tax withholding; the employee's portion of the Social Security, Medicare and Medicaid payment; and, amounts to be withheld pursuant to a court order, such as for child support or a garnishment order.

Deductions typically authorized by an employee include: contributions to retirement and benefit plans; health, life, or other insurance payments; payments due to the employer for repayment of a loan from the employer; loan payments owing to third party creditors; voluntary withdrawals for child support or alimony payments; and, any other purpose authorized by the employee.

IT IS THEFT, if the employer deducts any amount from the employee's wages for any reason that is not required by law or that has not been authorized by the employee in writing.

10.2 Benefits

A benefit is anything in addition to wages given to an employee as part of the compensation the employee receives for the work they do for their employer. Employers have no legal duty to pay any type of benefit to any employee. State and federal statutes only address the paying of a minimum wage to certain types of employees. The decision by an employer to offer and pay benefits to an employee is voluntary on the part of the employer. Once a decision to offer and pay benefits is made, however, two legal issues arise:

First, once a benefit has been offered it usually becomes a contractual obligation on the part of the employer. Even if the employment at will doctrine clearly applies to a given employee, the eligibility of that employee to receive specific benefits will generally be interpreted as being the subject of an implied, if not express, contract between the employer and that employee.

Second, while the employer can set the eligibility requirements for benefits, the factors for determining eligibility cannot be based on race, color, national origin, religion, sex, age or disability. These factors can be based, however, on length of employment, seniority, or the job held by the employee. Any employee who becomes eligible for a benefit, however, must either be paid that benefit or given the same options as other employees upon becoming eligible. See also the discussion of ERISA in Section 10.3, below.

The following checklists describe several types of benefits that are commonly offered.

Checklist 10.16
Absence, or Leave, from Work

❑ Can include either paid or unpaid absence or leave.

❑ Paid leave includes vacations, sick leave, and personal leave (leave that can be used for any reason). The employee usually receives their regular pay and benefits while absent for paid leave. Paid leave is generally limited to a maximum number of hours or days per year. It is often accumulated at the rate of a specific number of hours or days per pay period, per month, or per year. Employees may or may not be allowed to carry over unused paid leave from year to year.

❑ Unpaid leave, when allowed, is often allowed for any reason, including the extension of time away from work following a period of paid leave. The employee is not paid while absent, but they generally do not lose any eligibility they already have for benefits, nor will the employee lose their job. This is the real "benefit" of this type of benefit. There usually is, however, a maximum length of time the employee can be absent on unpaid leave without losing their job.

❑ Absence due to holidays. An employer can chose any holidays it wishes to observe during the year. These may be the federally observed holidays, holidays observed by the state, religious holidays, or any other occasion for declaring a holiday. The employer usually closes, or ceases operations, on the holidays it has decided to observe. This gives employees the day off, but whether it is a paid or unpaid absence is up to the employer. There is no inherent "right" of an employee to receive a paid holiday on these occasions.

❑ Absence due to religious observance. An employee can be given paid or unpaid leave to observe a religious practice. It is not necessary to pay employees while absent for religious reasons, unless the employer has already made a policy of doing so.

Checklist 10.17
Life, Health, and Other Insurance

❑   An employer may offer any number of insurance coverage plans as a benefit of employment. These can include life insurance, and/or health insurance, and/or disability insurance, and/or professional liability insurance, and/or any other type of insurance at the
discretion of the employer.

❑   Insurance benefits can include policies paid entirely by the employer, policies paid partly
by the employer and partly by the employee, or policies paid entirely by the employee.
This latter type of plan can be beneficial because lower premiums may be available through
the employer than if the employee purchased the same insurance on their own.

Checklist 10.18
Retirement Plans

❑ These include 401(k) plans, SIMPLE plans, IRAs, and any number of plans or annuities where the employee contributes a certain amount each pay period and the employer also contributes an amount to the employee's plan, ranging from nothing to some percentage based on the employee's contribution.

❑ Profit sharing can be included, where the employee earns the right to receive a certain percentage of the firm's profits over a specified period of time. The sums earned by the employee may be held in an account which is payable to the employee at retirement, at a certain age, or on the occurrence of other specified conditions.

❑ Stock plans, including stock options, which are similar to profit sharing plans. The employee acquires stock, or options to purchase stock, in the employer's firm according to a certain basis described in the plan.

Checklist 10.19
Educational Opportunities

❑   The employer pays some or all of the tuition or other costs of education for the employee. This can include college courses, completion of a degree program, technical training, seminars, continuing education, or any other formal education.

❑   Typically, the employee is required to continue working for a specified length of time for the employer upon completion of the education. If the employee's employment ends before the specified length of time, the employee is generally required to reimburse the employer for the costs of their education.

❑   During the education, the employee is often required to maintain a certain level of involvement in the education (such as a minimum or maximum number of credit hours per term), and to maintain a minimum level of accomplishment in the education (such as a minimum grade point average). Failure to comply with such requirements can justify the withdrawing of the benefit.

Checklist 10.20
Severance Packages

❑ Upon termination of employment, an employee may be offered an amount of money determined by some formula set by the employer. This formula generally gives the employee a certain percentage of their regular pay for a length of time based on the length of their employment. For example, 100% of their regular pay for a number of months equal to the number of years of their employment (10 years employment would result in 10 months of full pay beginning with the date of their termination). The employer can set any formula it desires.

❑ Severance packages are sometimes conditioned on the employee agreeing to waive any and all claims they have or may have against the employer for any reason. Since a severance package is merely a benefit that is not required, this can result in a valid and enforceable contract between the employer and the employee whereby the employer will pay the severance package and the employee will waive any and all claims it has or may have against the employer.

Checklist 10.21
Bonuses

❑ An amount of money, a trip, paid leave, a new car, or anything offered by the employer to an employee who meets certain criteria specified by the employer.

❑ Generally offered as an incentive for certain behavior or for the accomplishment of certain goals.

❑ Bonuses should always be paid when an eligible employee satisfies the set criteria.

10.3 The Employment Retirement Income Security Act Of 1974 (ERISA) [29 U.S.C. 1001 *et seq.*]

The purpose of this federal act is to require employers who offer benefit plans to their employees to establish firm conditions and requirements for participation in the benefit plans, to properly manage the plans, and to actually invest the money paid into the plans to insure that the benefit plans are properly funded and insured.

This act sets out minimum standards for benefit plans, as well as standards the plans must meet in order to qualify as benefit plans under the Internal Revenue Code. These minimum standards are described in the following two checklists.

Checklist 10.22
Minimum Standards for a Benefit Plan

❏   The plan must be written. The written plan must contain understandable and accurate descriptions of the plan's terms, financial status, and operations.

❏   Age and service conditions for employee eligibility must be set.

❏   The standards for how pension benefits are accrued over time must be set.

❏   There must be minimum vesting standards and limitations on "break in service" rules used to cancel the number of years an employee has counted toward vesting.

❏   Minimum standards for funding of the plan.

❏   A general requirement that pension plans must provide for the automatic payment of benefits in the form of a joint and survivor lifetime annuity, and death benefits in the form of a pre-retirement survivor annuity.

❏   Standards for the fiduciaries who administer and invest the plan's assets.

❏   Requirements that the employee must remain eligible for continuation of group health plan benefits under circumstances that would otherwise result in the loss of health coverage by an employee or by the employee's dependants.

❏   The establishment of a Pension Benefit Guaranty Corporation to insure defined benefit pension promises against under funding at the time of plan termination.

❏   A requirement that plan benefits cannot be assigned or alienated, except in the case of a court ordered Qualified Domestic Relations Order (given in divorces or legal separations).

❏   Standards for the commencement of benefit payments.

Checklist 10.23
Minimum Standards for a Plan to Qualify
Under the Internal Revenue Code

❑   The plan must be in writing. It must have clear and definite terms and conditions.

❑   The plan must be permanent and not subject to termination, except for "business necessity." The plan, however, may be modified during its life, as long as the modifications are in compliance with the plan's own terms and with applicable laws.

❑   Benefit plan assets must be segregated from the employer's assets. Once funds are deposited into the plan, they become the property of the plan and are not the property of the employer.

❑   A broad base of employees must be allowed to participate in the plan, instead of only a limited number of favored individuals.

❑   Benefits and contributions must be allocated on a broad base, instead of in a discriminatory manner.

❑   The benefits to be paid under the plan must be "definitely determinable." The plan must describe what benefits are to be provided and when.

CHAPTER 11
Employer Liability

CONTENTS

11.1 Doctrine of Respondeat Superior

Respondeat Superior is translated from Latin as, "let the master answer." It means that an employer is liable for the acts and omissions of its employees if committed within the scope of the employee's authority. Whenever an employee has caused any harm, therefore, the first issue is to determine the employee's scope of authority. The best evidence for this is the employee's written job description, provided it is current. Other evidence will include testimony as to the actual responsibilities of the employee, as well as to the actual tasks they perform. If it is determined that the employee was engaged in the performance of their job at the time they caused the harm, the employer is liable for any resulting damages. The only real exception is if the employee intentionally causes harm without the knowledge or participation of the employer. However, even in this situation, the employer may still be liable, especially if the employer knew or should have known that its employee had a propensity for engaging in the type of conduct in question. The bottom line is that an employer is responsible for its employees, period.

"Whenever the (employer) retains the right to control and direct the manner in which the details of the work are to be executed by his (employee), the doctrine of *respondeat superior* operates to make the (employer) vicariously liable for the tortious acts committed by the (employee) within the scope of his employment . . . Conversely, an (employer) is not vicariously liable for the tortious acts of an (employee) who is not subject to the control and direction of the (employer) with respect to the details of the work and is subordinate only in effecting a result in accordance with the (employer's) wishes . . . In sum, an (employer's) vicarious liability for the torts of his (employee) depends on the degree of control retained by the (employer) over the details of the work as it is being performed. The controlling principle is that vicarious liability arises from the right of supervision and control." *Vaughn v. North Carolina Department of Human Resources*, 252 S.E.2d 792 (N.C. 1979).

"Under the doctrine of *respondeat superior*, an employer is vicariously liable for the torts of his employees committed within the scope of employment, and, the employer's liability should extend beyond his actual or possible control over the employees to include risks inherent in or created by the enterprise. The mere fact that the accident occurred after working hours does not compel the conclusion that it occurred outside the scope of employment. If an employee is within the scope of employment when he inflicts injuries, the fact that the automobile that caused the injury belonged to the employee will not relieve the employer from liabilities if the employee's use of his car was with the express or implied consent of the employer. Where social or recreational pursuits are endorsed by the express or implied permission of the employer, if such activities have become an incident of the employment relationship, an employee engaged in such pursuits after working hours is still acting within the course and scope of employment." *Wank v. Richman and Garrett*, 211 Cal.Rptr. 919 (Cal.App.2d Dist. 1985).

11.2 Injuries to Employees

11.2(a) Job Related Injury or Illness

An employer is liable to its employees for job related injuries or illnesses. This issue is now addressed by state worker's compensation laws, which provide the exclusive remedy to employees for job related injury or illness. See Chapter 13 for discussion of worker's compensation.

11.2(b) Intentional Acts Against Employees

An employer is liable to its employees for intentional acts committed against the employee. It does not matter whether the intentional act is committed by the employer, by another employee, by a customer, or by any other person. As long as the intentional act is committed against the employee while the employee is working for the employer, the employer is liable. As with job related injury or illness, this is an issue largely handled by worker's compensation. However, an employee may also have a claim against the employer if it was the employer who intentionally caused the employee's injury. Such an injury includes physical as well as emotional injuries.

"An employer is immune from suit (by employees for an injury to the employee because of the workers' compensation statute) unless it acts with an actual, specific intention to harm an employee. Immunity (because of the workers' compensation statute) applies where the employer's conduct is not specifically intended or where it is only negligent, wilful, wanton or reckless." *Blake v. John Skidmore Truck Stop, Inc.,* 493 S.E.2d 887 (W.Va.1997).

"An employer may be held liable for the intentional conduct of a supervisor only where the supervisor has apparent authority to act on (the employer's) behalf." *Suarez v. Dickmont Plastics Corp.,* 698 A.2d 838 (Conn. 1997).

"In order to find an employer vicariously liable for an intentional attack upon an employee by a coworker, the attacking employee must be acting in the course and scope of employment. The employee's conduct must be so closely connected in time, place and causation to employment duties that they may be fairly attributable to the employer's business and not to personal motives." *Patterson v. Al Copeland Enterprises, Inc.,* 667 So.2d 1188 (La.App.4th Cir.1996).

"An employee may prevail in a personal injury suit against an employer only where injury is certain to occur as the result of intentional conduct. While the coworker's actions had been deliberate and wilful, he did not deliberately intend to injure the employee and the employer had no knowledge that injury was certain to occur." *Henson v. Crisp,* 946 P.2d 1252 (Wash.App. Div. 3 1997).

11.2(c) Invasion of Privacy

Invasion of privacy occurs in employment situations when an employer releases, causes to be released, or negligently (accidentally) releases privileged information about a current or former employee. This can occur by improperly maintaining employee files, by being careless in the handling of information about employees, by talking about an employee's personal matters with others, or by intentionally releasing confidential information about an employee without proper authority for any reason.

All information obtained and maintained by an employer about each of its employees must be considered to be confidential. None of this information is to be released under any circumstances without proper legal authority. Such legal authority includes a court order directing what information is to be provided about which employee, and to whom; releasing information after the employee has consented in writing to the release of the information; or, when a statute authorizes the employer to release information regardless of the employee's wishes (i.e., statute authorizing an employer to give certain information about a current or former employee in response to a request for a reference from another employer or potential employer; releasing information when it is relevant to a claim against the employer by the employee; or, when the employer has information which is the subject of mandatory reporting requirements pursuant to state statute).

An employee whose privacy has been invaded by his or her current or former employer has the basis for a lawsuit against that employer. If successful, the employee may recover actual damages, pain and suffering, and even punitive damages if the behavior of the employer was reckless or intentional.

> "The company conducted an appropriate and reasonable investigation after learning of possible sexual harassment. The company took individual employees aside without indicating what the subject matter was in an attempt to keep the inquiry confidential." Thus, there was no invasion of privacy in how the sexual harassment claim was handled. *Hines v. Arkansas Louisiana Gas Co.*, 613 So.2d 646 (La.App.2d Cir.1993).

11.2(d) Defamation

Defamation is simply telling a lie about someone. If an employer lies about a current or former employee, the employer will be liable for any damages suffered by the employee, which could very well include punitive damages. The only defense to a charge of defamation is that whatever was said is not a lie, but is the truth. In fact, truth is an absolute defense to a claim of defamation. However, while truth will be a successful defense to the claim of defamation, if there was no legal authority for giving out the information that was the subject of the claim, the employee may still have a claim against the employer for invasion of privacy.

"There was no defamatory action by the employer in using security guards to escort the former employees from the premises. There was no evidence that any statement was made to publicize the employment termination or that any false statement had been made in reckless disregard of the truth." The employer was, therefore, found not liable for defamation. *Davis v. John Crane, Inc.*, 633 N.E.2d 929 (Ill.App.1st Dist.1994).

"The state law liability standard for defamation requires the complaining party to show a false and unprivileged publication which tends directly to injure the party in his profession, trade or business by imputing general disqualification. Truthful statements, however, are not defamatory. Thus, the employer's reference which contained truthful statements about its current employee did not give rise to liability." *Guilford v. Northwestern Public Service,* 581 N.W.2d 178 (S.D.1998).

"Because freedom to express an opinion is protected by the First Amendment, a court must distinguish between statements of fact and opinion. In this case, the description of the former employee as a 'con artist' was clearly not an expression of fact, but constituted an opinion." *Quinn v. Jewel Food Stores, Inc.*, 658 N.E.2d 1225 (Ill.App.1st Dist.1995).

11.3 Injuries to Others

The doctrine of respondeat superior applies to make the employer liable for injuries to others caused by its employees. Generally, an employee injures others unintentionally or accidently, which is negligence. An employer is clearly liable for the negligent acts of its employees, provided those acts are committed while the employee is engaged in his or her work for the employer. An employer is also likely to be found liable for injuries to others which are the result of an employee's intentional behavior. Unless the employee intentionally meant to harm the person actually harmed, or to generally cause harm to someone, the employer will be responsible.

"An employer may be held vicariously liable for negligent and intentional acts committed by an employee within the scope of employment. However, an employer may not be held liable where the employee uses excessive and dangerous force, nor can it be held liable for an assault committed for personal reasons or not actuated by an intent to perform the employer's business." *Costa v. Roxborough Memorial Hosp.,* 708 A.2d 490 (Pa.Super.1998).

"An employer may only be held liable for an employee's actions where they are within the scope of employment and motivated at least in part by service to the employer. Employers are not liable for independent or intentional acts that do not serve the employer's business." *Anderson v. Toeppe*, 688 N.E.2d 538 (Ohio App. 6th Dist. 1996).

11.4 Condition of the Workplace

11.4(a) General Liability

Whether the employer owns or leases the premises that is the workplace, the employer has the primary responsibility, and liability, for the condition of that workplace. If employees are injured or become ill as a result of any condition that exists at the workplace, the employer will be liable to the injured or ill employees. The employer may have a remedy against a landlord, or against some other person who may have some responsibility for the cause of the condition that caused harm to the employee, but it is the employer who is liable. Worker's compensation laws, the federal OSHA statute (see the next section), and common law all make an employer responsible for maintaining the condition of the workplace.

"An employer is under a duty to provide his employees with a reasonably safe place to work and to furnish the necessary appliances for carrying on the work requested of the employees in a proper condition and with reasonable safety. In addition, an employer has a non-delegable duty to exercise reasonable care in maintaining the tools furnished by him and used in the furtherance of his business in such a condition as not to endanger one who uses said tools in an ordinary manner." *Harrison v. Harrison,* 597 S.W.2d 477 (Tex.App.1980)

11.4(b) Occupational Safety and Health Act (OSHA) [29 U.S.C. 651 *et seq.*]

The purpose of this act, as stated in the language of the act, is ". . . to assure so far as possible every working man and woman in the Nation safe and healthful working conditions and to preserve our human resources. . ." [29 U.S.C. 651(b)] The act accomplishes this purpose by defining at Section 654, the duties of employers and employees as follows:

"Each employer (1) shall furnish to each of his employees employment and a place of employment which are free from recognized hazards that are causing or are likely to cause death or serious physical harm to his employees; (2) shall comply with occupational safety and health standards promulgated under this chapter.

"Each employee shall comply with occupational safety and health standards and all rules, regulations, and orders issued pursuant to this chapter which are applicable to his own actions and conduct."

Pursuant to Section 654, thousands and thousands of standards have been enacted by the Occupational Safety and Health Review Commission. While the language of Section 654 looks good on paper, it is in reality impossible to comply with. This section requires a standard of absolute safety for employees and the employer is given sole liability for ensuring this unattainable standard. However, this act is the law. Chapter 15 discusses this act in more detail and offers suggestions for dealing with this act.

CHAPTER 12
Union Issues

CONTENTS

12.1 National Labor Relations Act (NLRA) [29 U.S.C. 151 *et seq.*]

12.1(a) Purpose of Act

This act is the single most important piece of legislation concerning union issues. Its stated purpose is to "encourage the practice and procedure of collective bargaining and by protecting the exercise by workers of full freedom of association, self-organization, and designation of representatives of their own choosing, for the purpose of negotiating the terms and conditions of their employment or other mutual aid or protection." [29 U.S.C. 151]

The act creates the National Labor Relations Board and gives the Board the authority to "make, amend, and rescind . . . such rules and regulations as may be necessary to carry out the provisions of this (act)." [29 U.S.C. 156] The act also declares that, "Employees shall have the right to self-organization, to form, join, or assist labor organizations, to bargain collectively through representatives of their own choosing, and to engage in other concerted activities for the purpose of collective bargaining or other mutual aid or protection, and shall also have the right to refrain from any or all of such activities except to the extent that such right may be affected by an agreement requiring membership in a labor organization as a condition of employment. . ." [29 U.S.C. 157]

Finally, the NLRA defines a number of practices as being unfair labor practices by both employers and by labor organizations (see Section 12.1(c), below). Unfair labor practices are prohibited and engaging in an unfair labor practice can result in an injunction being issued by a court to stop the practice. Failure to comply with such an injunction can result in the court issuing sanctions against the party in violation of the injunction, which include fines, imprisonment, or both. As necessary, federal law enforcement personnel can be ordered by the court to enforce an injunction.

12.1(b) National Labor Relations Board

The National Labor Relations Board is composed of five members appointed by the President and approved by the Senate. Each member of the Board serves a term of five years and may be reappointed for additional terms. Members of the Board are prohibited from engaging in any other business, vocation, or employment while they serve on the Board. The Board does have the power to delegate its authority and to establish various offices throughout the U.S. to carry out its purposes.

The main purpose of the board is "to prevent any person from engaging in any unfair labor practice affecting commerce." [29 U.S.C. 160(a)]. The following checklist sets out the statutory procedure for the Board to follow in carrying out this purpose.

Checklist 12.1
Procedure of the National Labor Relations Board to Prevent Unfair Labor Practices
[29 U.S.C. 160-161]

❑   A complaint is received by the Board accusing a person of an unfair labor practice.

❑   The Board may issue its own complaint against the person accused (respondent) of the unfair labor practice. This complaint must describe the nature of the accusation and inform the respondent of their right to a hearing before the Board.

❑   The Respondent has the right to file its answer, or response to the complaint, with the Board, as well as to appear at a hearing before the board to address the charges and offer any defenses. "So far as practicable," this hearing shall be conducted by the federal rules of evidence.

❑   At the conclusion of the hearing, the Board shall review the testimony and evidence presented and shall make a decision. The Board's decision is to state whether or not an unfair labor practice has occurred as described in the complaint.

❑   If the Board decides that an unfair labor practice has occurred, it issues an order that the person engaged in the unfair labor practice is to "cease and desist" the unfair labor practice. In addition, the Board may "take such affirmative action including reinstatement of employees with or without back pay," as is necessary to remedy the effects of the unfair labor practice. The Board's order may also require the respondent to make periodic written reports to the Board showing the extent of its compliance with the Board's orders. The Board's order cannot require the reinstatement of any employee who was terminated for cause.

❑   As necessary, the Board has authority to file a petition with the U.S. Court of Appeals (or with the U.S. District Court if the appellate court is not in session) in order to obtain enforcement of its own order through the courts. The reason for this is that the federal court system has a larger enforcement capacity for its orders than does the Board or any other federal agency. The court will then conduct its own hearing on the matter and will issue its own order describing the relief to be taken. This order becomes the final order concerning the complaint.

(continued on next page)

(Page 2 - Checklist 12.1)

❑ The final order of the Board, or of the federal court if the Board has petitioned the court as described above, can be appealed to the U.S. Court of Appeals and then to the U.S. Supreme Court. (If the Board's petition to the court was heard by a U.S. District Court, the appeal of that order is to the federal appellate court. If the petition was heard by the federal appellate court, the appeal of the court's order is to the Supreme Court.)

❑ If the Board files a petition with the court, or if either party appeals the final order (whether from the Board or from the court), the final order remains in effect and must be followed unless the court hearing the appeal issues an order staying the final order.

❑ Throughout the process, the Board has broad investigatory powers, which include the ability to summon witnesses, to compel testimony, to obtain documentary evidence, and to perform such acts as are necessary to investigate a complaint.

❑ The Board has the power to issue temporary restraining orders or injunctions until the final order has been issued.

12.1(c) Unfair Labor Practices

Sections 158(a) and (b) of the National Labor Relations Act define unfair labor practices, whether committed by an employer or by a labor organization. These practices are described below.

Checklist 12.2
Unfair Labor Practices by an Employer

❑   Interfering with, restraining, or coercing employees in the exercise of their rights to organize, to bargain collectively with the employer, and to engage in other activities for the purpose of their mutual aid and protection.

❑   Dominating or interfering with the formation or administration of any labor organization.

❑   Contributing financial or other support to any labor organization.

❑   Making employment decisions that, by design, encourage or discourage membership of employees in a labor organization.

❑   Terminating or taking any action against an employee who has filed a complaint with the Board, or who has participated in any proceedings before the Board or before a court concerning any complaint or any other matter covered by this act.

❑   Refusing to bargain collectively with the representatives of its own employees.

Checklist 12.3
Unfair Labor Practices by a Labor Organization

❑ Interfering with, restraining, or coercing employees in the exercise of their rights to organize, to bargain collectively with the employer, and to engage in other activities for the purpose of their mutual aid and protection.

❑ Causing or attempting to cause an employer to make employment decisions that, by design, encourage or discourage membership of employees in a labor organization.

❑ Discrimination against an employee who has been denied membership in the labor organization, or whose membership has been terminated, as long as the reason for the denial or termination of membership in the organization is not for the failure of the employee to pay dues or initiation fees required of all members.

❑ Refusing to bargain collectively with an employer.

❑ Engaging in, or attempting to get an employee to engage in, a strike or a refusal to carry out the normal and regular requirements of employment where the purpose of such conduct is to: a) force or require any employee or self-employed person to join any labor or employee organization; b) force or require any person to stop doing business with any other person; c) force or require any employer to recognize or bargain with a particular labor organization as the representative of its employees if another labor organization has already been certified as the representative of its employees; or, d) to force or require any employer to assign particular work to employees in a particular labor organization or in a particular trade, craft, or class, rather than to employees in another labor organization or another trade, craft, or class.

❑ Requiring the payment of excessive fees as a condition of membership.

❑ Getting or attempting to get an employer to pay a fee to the organization for services that are not performed or which are not to be performed.

❑ Picketing or threatening to picket any employer when the purpose is to force or require either the employer or the employees to recognize a particular labor organization as the representative of its employees, unless the labor organization doing this is already certified as the representative of the employees.

Specifically pointed out as not being an unfair labor practice by either an employer or a labor organization is the expression of any views, argument or opinion, or the dissemination thereof, regardless of the format or method through which the expression is made, as long as no threats or promises are included. Simply stating a position is permitted by this act. If the message is also communicated that there may be benefits to agreeing with the position expressed, or reprisals for disagreeing with the position expressed, then it becomes an unfair labor practice.

In summary, employees have a right to organize or not organize, as they wish. The employees are not to be interfered with as they make this decision, although the employer or a labor organization can express their views on the issue. Whatever decision the employees make is to be honored by all. Employees may collectively bargain with their employer for an employment contract to contain any lawful terms and conditions that are negotiated. Employees who are organized will appoint their own representatives, who will be the persons to actually negotiate and otherwise deal with the employer on behalf of the employees. Unfair labor practices are prohibited by both the employer and the labor organization. Complaints regarding unfair labor practices are to be made to the National Labor Relations Board, who has the authority to conduct a hearing and determine the issue. The ruling of the Board is final, although the courts can be brought in, as necessary, for a further determination of the issue. Final orders are enforceable by cease and desist orders, by orders to reinstate employees, or by such other action as will remedy the situation. Failure to comply with final orders can result in fines and imprisonment.

12.2 Collective Bargaining Agreements

The employer and the labor organization representing the employees have a duty under the National Labor Relations Act to bargain collectively. This means they must negotiate with each other to form a contract binding on the employer and the employees that describes wages, hours, and other terms and conditions of employment. Once negotiated and signed, the collective bargaining agreement, or union contract, controls the employment relationship. The employment at will principle does not apply between an employer and its employees when they have a collective bargaining agreement, unless the contract states that certain issues are covered by this principle. State and federal employment statutes, however, continue to apply. No parties to any contract can make an agreement to do anything in violation of the law. Any attempt to do so is unenforceable in court. Aside from this, the employer and its represented employees are generally free (and required) to make any agreement concerning their employment relationship that they wish to make.

CHAPTER 13
Workers' Compensation

CONTENTS

13.1 General Description

Workers' compensation is a state law issue, described in the statutes of each state. Pursuant to workers' compensation statutes, employers are made liable to their employees for injuries or illness caused on the job or in the course of employment. These statutes have become the exclusive remedy of injured employees against their employers. Instead of filing a personal injury lawsuit against the employer, the employee simply makes a claim as described by statute and the case is heard by a workers' compensation judge during a workers' compensation hearing. The entire process has become specialized and is largely separate from the normal legal process.

Employers are required to obtain workers' compensation insurance, or to meet the statutory requirement of being "self-insured." This is to ensure that any award for payment of wages, medical bills, or other benefits can be paid from a reliable source. The insurance company is the reliable source. These insurance policies operate in the same manner as any other insurance policy. Premium amounts are based on factors including the number of employees, the nature of the employer's business, and the number of claims that have been paid. An order from the workers' compensation judge for the employer to make payments to the injured employee is treated as the claim for payment and is made by the insurance company. As with any insurance, only claims covered by the policy will be paid and as the number of claims rises, the premium amount paid by the employer will also rise. The states also maintain a general workers' compensation fund that can pay claims made against uninsured employers. However, the state fund will go after the uninsured employer for reimbursement. The overall goal is to have a guaranteed source of money to pay any amount due to the injured employee, as determined by the judge.

An important feature of workers' compensation statutes is the schedules for payment of certain types of claims. Many types of injuries and illnesses are cataloged and given a value in dollars. If it is determined that an employee has a described injury, their award is an amount described in the schedule as the value for that injury. The employee may also, or may instead, be awarded a sum as compensation for being partially or completely disabled as a result of the injury. Such a disability is generally identified as being temporary (meaning the employee will recover), or permanent (meaning the employee will not recover). The award for a disability varies, based on whether it is partial or full, and temporary or permanent.

In *Rose v. Cadillac Fairview Shopping Center Properties Inc.,* 668 A.2d 782 (Del.Super.1995), the court ruled that the employee injured at work was limited to recovery under the workers' compensation system. "She is prohibited from bringing a personal injury suit against the employer as the injuries she suffered arose out of and in the course of her employment." Making a claim through the workers' compensation system is the exclusive remedy for employees injured on the job. This point is further clarified in *Foshee v. Shoney's Inc.,* 637 N.E.2d 1277 (Ind.1994), where the court stated that only when the complained of injury is caused by an employer's intentional act, with knowledge that injury was certain to occur, can an employee bring a personal injury claim instead of a workers' compensation claim against the employer.

13.2 Factors Affecting an Employee's Claim

Whether or not a particular injury or illness suffered by an employee is covered by workers' compensation is determined solely by the language of the applicable state statute. The general factors that determine whether or not a particular injury or illness is covered are described in the following checklist.

Checklist 13.1
General Factors Affecting an Employee's Claim

❑   The cause of the injury or illness must be accidental or unintentional.

❑   The immediate or general cause of the injury can be the action, omission, or conduct of the employer, supervisory personnel of the employer, other employees of the employer, customers, or others who have direct or indirect contact with the employee.

❑   The injury must have occurred while the employee was on the job or in the course of the employee's employment. In some situations, the employee's written job description will be an important piece of evidence for determining whether or not this factor is met.

❑   Intentional injuries to the employee by another may not be covered by workers' compensation statutes. The employee's remedy in these situations may be to file a personal injury lawsuit against the person causing the intentional injury, even if this person is the employer.

❑   Injuries resulting from the employee's own misconduct may not be covered by workers' compensation statutes. If the employee intentionally injured themselves, the injury is probably not covered. If the employee's misconduct was the result of negligence, whether the employee's or the employer's, the injury may be covered.

❑   Injury or illness resulting from an employee's pre-existing condition may not be covered. However, if the pre-existing condition was aggravated by some aspect of employment, it may be covered.

❑   Injuries occurring while the employer is going to work or coming home from work are generally not covered. In virtually all areas of employment law, going to work and leaving work are not considered to be part of the employment relationship.

❑   An employee who is injured or who becomes ill must notify their employer of the injury or illness and must make a proper claim within the statutory deadline. This is usually a very brief amount of time, such as 30 days from the date of injury or illness. Failure to timely notify the employer or to make a proper claim can prevent an injured employee from obtaining any relief under workers' compensation statutes.

❑   The employee must follow the instructions of their physician relating to the treatment of their injury or illness. Failure to do so can result in a limitation of benefits.

13.3 Employer's Responsibilities and Issues

The employer's first responsibility is to have a workers' compensation insurance policy, unless the employer has qualified to be self-insured under the applicable state law.

The key issue which triggers the applicability of workers' compensation statutes is that an *employee* must have suffered an injury or illness *on the job or in the course of their employment*. Therefore, the employer must know: (1) whether a given individual working on behalf of the employer is an employee; and, (2) what constitutes the employee acting on the job or in the course of their employment.

Whether or not an individual is an employee, an independent contractor, or a third person whom is neither an employee nor an independent contractor, should be easy to determine. It becomes difficult when an employer attempts to blur the distinction between employee and independent contractor. Since there is little liability for independent contractors, and no workers' compensation liability for independent contractors, it is tempting to use independent contractors in as many positions as possible. However, employees are legally obligated to follow the instructions and control of the employer, while independent contractors are not. Although it may be tempting to have personnel for which there is no liability (as with an independent contractor), but over which there is complete control (as with an employee), there is no type of personnel that legally fits this description. The choice must be made and the employer must have either an employee or an independent contractor, with the advantages and disadvantages of each intact, for each position. Often, the employer who attempts to mix an employee and an independent contractor into some hybrid discovers that they have an employee. This discovery is made after a claim has been made and litigated and it can be an expensive discovery. For this reason alone, an employer should clearly understand who is an employee and who is an independent contractor.

The second issue — the requirement that the injury or illness be job related — is made relatively easy by maintaining current, written job descriptions for each position. The written job description of the injured employee is *always* requested in a workers' compensation case. It is the first piece of evidence that will be used in determining what the employee's job consists of, so further determination can be made regarding whether or not the employee was on the job when they were injured or became ill. Without a written job description, testimony and any other relevant evidence must be relied upon to determine this issue. The failure of the employer to have and use written job descriptions can impact the ultimate determination of the employee's job responsibilities and how these duties relate to the injury.

Once a workers' compensation case has begun, the employer must listen to and follow the advice of its attorney (usually provided by the insurance company). Generally, this advice will be:
a) follow the orders of the workers' compensation judge; b) do not harass the injured employee; c) follow any medical restrictions placed on the injured employee when they return to work; d) do not take any action whatsoever against the employee for having made a workers' compensation claim; and, e) cooperate with your attorney in the case.

An employer should never go through any workers' compensation case without legal representation. Workers' compensation is entirely controlled and determined by state statutes and a lawyer is necessary.

The following checklist summarizes the employer's issues and responsibilities.

Checklist 13.2
Employer's Issues and Responsibilities

❏ Always maintain a workers' compensation insurance policy, unless the firm qualifies as a self-insurer under state workers' compensation law.

❏ Do not engage in any practice that intentionally or unintentionally blurs the distinction between employees and independent contractors. Know who is or is not an employee.

❏ Maintain current, written job descriptions for each position or employee.

❏ Follow any orders issued by the workers' compensation judge.

❏ Do not harass the injured employee or any other employees who may be witnesses in the case.

❏ If the injured employee returns to work with medical restrictions, follow the restrictions. In addition, make sure the employee follows the restrictions.

❏ Do not take any retaliatory action against an employee for making a workers' compensation claim, or for having been involved as a witness in another employee's claim.

❏ Do not refuse to hire a job applicant because they have made workers' compensation claims against one or more previous employers.

❏ Cooperate with your attorney and follow his advice.

13.4 Modification and Termination of Benefits

Benefits that have been awarded to an employee may be increased if the employee's condition worsens. Or, the benefits awarded may be decreased if the employee's condition improves. Benefits can even be terminated if the employee fully recovers or is able to return to work without restrictions. Benefits may also be modified or terminated if an employee unreasonably refuses to submit to medical examinations or to comply with their doctor's instructions for treatment.

13.5 Longshore And Harbor Workers' Compensation [33 U.S.C. 901 *et seq.*]

This is a federal act that supplements state workers' compensation law. This act covers employees who are injured on "the navigable waters of the United States (including any adjoining pier, wharf, dry dock, terminal, building way, marine railway, or other adjoining area customarily used by an employer in loading, unloading, repairing, dismantling, or building a vessel)." [33 U.S.C. 903(a)] Employers of such employees are liable to their employees for any injury, regardless of fault, that is covered by this act. However, "any amounts paid to an employee for the same injury, disability, or death for which benefits are claimed under this chapter pursuant to any other workers' compensation law . . . shall be credited against any liability imposed by this chapter." [33 U.S.C. 903(e)]

Employees covered by this act may be eligible for benefits under state workers' compensation laws, as well as for benefits under this act. However, the injured employee can only recover benefits once. For example, if an employee's benefit award under this act totaled $10,000, but they had already been awarded $6,000 under a state workers' compensation award, the employee could only recover $4,000 of the benefits awarded under the Longshore and Harbor Workers' Compensation statute.

CHAPTER 14
Unemployment Compensation

CONTENTS

14.1 Description

Each state has an unemployment compensation statute. These statutes establish a system through which employees who lose their job through no fault of their own can continue to receive wages for a specific period of time. The wages received by the employee are paid from a state unemployment fund, which is funded by mandatory payments from employers located in the state.

Employees who lose their jobs and wish to receive unemployment compensation must apply at an office maintained by the state. If the employee is eligible (see below), they will receive a "wage" in an amount determined by the amount of wages they were earning at the time of termination and how long they were employed. The wage they receive is rarely, if ever, equal to the wage they were being paid by their employer. In addition, they will be entitled to receive this unemployment wage only for a specified period of time, generally up to a maximum of six months, based on how long they were employed.

Unemployment compensation is not a substitute for a claim the employee may have against the employer for wrongful termination, unlawful discrimination, or any other type of claim. An employee who has such a claim may pursue it at the same time they apply for unemployment compensation.

Each employer has an account with their state's unemployment compensation authority. Employers are required to pay premiums into their account on the basis of the number of employees they have and how many claims have been charged to their account. The more employees an employer has, and the more claims that have been charged to their account, the higher the employer's payments will be. These payments are required by state statute and are not voluntary.

14.2 When Employees are Eligible To Receive Compensation

Just because an employee's job is terminated does not mean the employee is automatically eligible to receive unemployment compensation. Generally, an employee is eligible to receive unemployment compensation if:

a) they were laid off;

b) their job was eliminated;

c) they were wrongfully terminated;

d) they were coerced or induced into quitting their job by their employer;

e) the employee quit because of medical or personal reasons;

f) the employee quit because of reasons based on genuine religious beliefs; or,

g) other reasons that are determined not to be the employee's fault or in their control.

An employee may initially be granted unemployment compensation. The former employer will be notified of this decision and given the opportunity to object to the initial decision. If the employer does object, a hearing is conducted by the state agency that handles unemployment compensation. A hearing officer will conduct this hearing and will make a determination after hearing any testimony from the employer and the employee, as well as after reviewing any other evidence presented. The only issue to be considered in this hearing, however, is whether or not the employee is actually eligible to receive unemployment compensation. After hearing the testimony and reviewing any other evidence, the hearing officer will make findings of fact and, based on those findings of fact, will determine whether or not the employee lost their job through no fault of their own, as defined by state unemployment compensation statutes. If the employee is found to be ineligible, they do not receive any benefits and the employer's account is not charged. If the employee is found to be eligible, the initial award of benefits will be sustained and the employer's account will be charged.

The employee will win this hearing unless the employer proves to the hearing officer that the employee lost their job for one of the reasons described in the following section.

> "Sexual harassment in the workplace constitutes good cause for leaving employment under the state unemployment compensation law. The failure to report sexual harassment according to the employer's policy did not disqualify the employee from receiving unemployment benefits." *Marlow v. North Carolina Employment Security Commission,* 493 S.E.2d 302 (N.C.App.1997).

> "Abusive behavior by an employer that would be unacceptable to a reasonable person is sufficient good cause to quit under state law." Therefore, an employee who quits their job due to the abusive behavior of their employer may be eligible for unemployment compensation. *Streitz v. Juneau,* 940 S.W.2d 548 (Mo.App.S.D.1997).

> "An employee is not disqualified from receiving benefits where the employer announces a layoff, even where the employee volunteers to be laid off." *Goewert v. Employment Security Dept. of State of Washington,* 919 P.2d 106 (Wash.App.Div.1 1996).

There are a number of cases from many jurisdictions holding that while excessive absence from work may be a legitimate reason to terminate an employee, it is not necessarily "misconduct" pursuant to unemployment compensation laws. Therefore, an employee may be eligible for unemployment compensation even though they were terminated from their job for a legitimate reason. See, *Roberts v. B.G. Diehl,* 707 So.2d 869 (Fla.App.2d Dist.1998); and *Kelly v. Manor Grove, Inc.,* 936 S.W.2d 874 (Mo.App.E.D.1997).

14.3 When Employees are Not Eligible To Receive Compensation

An employee will generally be denied unemployment compensation if:

a) they were not really an employee (i.e., they were an independent contractor);

b) they are not really unemployed (i.e., they are on strike, they are refusing to accept work being offered by the employer); or,

c) they lost their job through their own misconduct, which usually means the employee lost their job because they were insubordinate, were refusing to do their job, violated employment policies, or were intentionally acting contrary to their employer's interests.

Losing a job through mere incompetence or an inability to do the job, however, may not make an employee ineligible for unemployment compensation. Quite often, when an employee is fired because of their job performance, regardless of how justified and correct the decision to fire the employee, the employee will be deemed eligible for unemployment compensation. The employer's objection to such a determination is understandable, and should be made, but will probably be unsuccessful. Unless the employer can prove the employee's poor performance was the result of employee misconduct, and not merely incompetence or an inability to do the job, the employee will be awarded benefits.

"Misconduct in the context of unemployment compensation is conduct that evinces a wilful or wanton disregard of an employer's interests as found in deliberate violation or disregard of employee standards of behavior of which the employer has a right to expect." *ProServe Corp. v. Rainey,* 536 N.W.2d 373 (N.D.1995).

"Unsuitability for a job position may constitute fault sufficient to support a just cause termination under the unemployment compensation act. The act was intended to provide financial assistance to unemployed workers who were temporarily without employment through no fault of their own. However, employers may justifiably fire deficient employees who cannot perform required work." Such deficient employees will not be entitled to unemployment compensation benefits. *Tzangas, Plakas & Mannos v. Administrator, Ohio Bureau of Employment Serv.,* 653 N.E.2d 1207 (Ohio 1995).

"State unemployment compensation law provides that a voluntary leaving of work because of disability shall not be deemed good cause to quit where other suitable work is available from the employer." *Phoenix Women's Health Center v. UCBR,* 695 A.2d 466 (Pa.Cmwlth.1997)

"An employee who quits must have good cause compelled by some extreme and necessitous circumstance that is objectively reasonable in order to receive unemployment compensation benefits." *Reedy v. M.H. King Co.,* 920 P.2d 915 (Idaho 1996).

"When an employee is fired for refusing or failing to follow the reasonable instructions of his or her supervisor, the employee is disqualified from unemployment compensation benefits." *Dougherty v. UCBR,* 686 A.2d 53 (Pa.Cmwlth.1996).

"State unemployment compensation law categorized theft or embezzlement from an employer as wilful misconduct which precluded the receipt of unemployment compensation benefits." *Preservation Pennsylvania v. UCBR,* 673 A.2d 1044 (Pa.Cmwlth.1996).

"An employee's sexually explicit proposition to a coworker constituted misconduct that justified the denial of unemployment benefits." *Tuttle v. Mellon Bank of Delaware,* 659 A.2d 786 (Del.Super.1995).

CHAPTER 15
Crucial Employment Law Statutes

CONTENTS

This Chapter is intended as a reference for each included statute. The discussion of each statute is organized into the same format, which is to identify:

■   The statute's name and code number, as well as whether it is federal or state;

■   Employers covered by the statute;

■   Employees covered by the statute;

■   What the statute requires or prohibits (including explanations and direct quotes);

■   Exceptions to the statute; and,

■   Suggestions for dealing with the statute.

Statutes are presented in the order of those applicable to all employers first, with those applicable to fewer employers at the end. All quotations are from the statute and only the section number of the statute will be given as the citation for the quote.

15.1 Equal Rights Under the Law [42 U.S.C. 1981-1988]

Title and Code: Known as: Civil Rights Act of 1866; Equal Rights Act; Equal Rights Under the Law; and, Section 1981. 42 U.S.C. 1981 - 1988. Federal Law.

Covered Employers: Every employer, without exception.

Covered Employees: All employees of every employer.

Requirements and Prohibitions:

■ "All persons within the jurisdiction of the United States shall have the same rights . . . as white persons" [§1981(a)] to:

■ Make and enforce contracts, "which includes the making, performance, modification, and termination of contracts, and the enjoyment of all benefits, privileges, terms, and conditions of the contractual relationship." [§1981(a)];

■ To sue and be sued, to be parties in legal actions, and to be given credibility as witnesses in legal actions based on their personal knowledge of facts and events, rather than on their race, skin color, or some other such factor. [§1981(a)];

■ To "the full and equal benefit of all laws and proceedings for the security of persons and property." [§1981(a)]

■ All non-governmental individuals, entities, and other persons, as well as any such person acting under color of State law, are specifically prohibited from interfering with any of the rights guaranteed in this statute. [§1981(c)]

■ If an employer is determined to have engaged in a discriminatory practice which violates this statute, or which violates Title VII of the Civil Rights Act of 1964, or which violates the Americans with Disabilities Act, AND, that discriminatory practice is determined to have been committed "with malice or with reckless indifference" to the protected rights of the employee, the employee may recover punitive damages against the employer. [§1981a(b)(1)]

■ If two or more persons conspire, or plan, together to deprive any person of their rights as protected under this statute, they may be held liable for conspiracy to interfere with civil rights. [§1985]

■ Anyone who knows of a conspiracy to interfere with the civil rights of another, and who has the power to prevent or to aid in preventing the actual commission of the activities conspired, but who neglects to do so, may be held liable for not preventing those activities. [§1986]

Exceptions: There are no exceptions concerning private employers or quasi-public employers. The federal government as an employer is not covered by this act, but it is already covered by other laws (including the U.S. Constitution) which contain the same requirements and prohibitions.

Dealing with this Statute: Do not make employment decisions based wholly or partially on skin color or on race. Make employment decisions based on the legitimate business needs of the firm and on the degree of an applicant's or employee's qualifications. Decisions based on an employee's qualifications, as well as on their actual ability to do the job are proper. In *Farmer v. Continental Ins. Co.,* 955 F.Supp. 970 (N.D.Ill.1997), a black woman was terminated due to her inadequate job performance. She sued, claiming that she was the victim of unlawful discrimination under §1981. The court, however, denied her claim, stating she had failed to prove race discrimination "because she was unable to show that she had performed her job satisfactorily."

15.2 The Fair Labor Standards Act of 1938 [29 U.S.C. 201 *et seq.*]

Title and Code: Known as the Fair Labor Standards Act; FLSA; Wage and Hour Law; Minimum Wage Law; and, Overtime Law. 29 U.S.C. 201 *et seq.* This act also includes the Equal Pay Act of 1963 [29 U.S.C. 206(d)], and, federal child labor law [29 U.S.C. 212]. Federal Law.

Covered Employers: All employers, without exception.

Covered Employees: All employees of all employers.

Requirements and Prohibitions: (see also the discussion and checklists concerning this act in Chapter 10, at Section 10.1(a)).

■ As of September 1, 1997, the minimum hourly wage that must be paid to an employee is $5.15. [§206(a)(1)]

■ New employees under the age of 20 years (19 years or less in age), can be paid what is referred to as a training wage of not less than $4.25 per hour, but only for the first 90 consecutive calendar days of their job, whether they work each of those days or not. No employee who is 20 years old or older can be given fewer hours to work, reassigned, terminated, or the subject of any other action where the purpose is to instead use employees who can be paid this lower hourly wage. [§206(g)]

■ Men and women who have substantially similar job responsibilities and authority, whose jobs require substantially similar qualifications, skills and abilities, and who have substantially similar qualifications, skills and abilities, must be paid on an equal basis. The precise prohibition is that employees of one sex cannot be paid less than employees of the other sex when the preceding factors apply. In addition, the wages of an employee of one sex cannot be lowered to justify paying an employee of the other sex a lower wage. [§206(d)]

■ Except when the training wage applies, children as employees must be paid at least the minimum wage. [§206(g)]

■ Employees must be paid an overtime wage of at least 1½ times their regular wage for every hour they work over an average of 40 hours per week per pay period. [§207(a)]

■ The overtime pay requirement does not apply to employees in a retail or service establishment if the regular hourly wage of an employee is at least 1½ times the minimum wage, and, at least 50% of that employee's income in any month is from commissions on goods or services. [§207(i)]

■ Employees employed in bona fide executive, administrative, or professional positions are exempt from minimum wage and overtime requirements. [§213(a)(1)]

■ Anyone hired on a casual basis as a babysitter or to do domestic work is exempt from minimum wage and overtime requirements. [§213(a)(15)]

■ Computer systems analysts, computer programmers, software engineers, or other similarly skilled workers are generally exempt from minimum wage and overtime requirements. [§213(a)(17)]

■ Persons employed in the operation of a rail carrier, an air carrier, or as drivers are generally exempt from overtime requirements. [§213(b)(1)-(4), (11), (17)]

■ Agricultural and farm employees are generally exempt from overtime requirements. [§213(b)(12) - (16)]

■ Employees engaged in forestry and lumber operations are generally exempt from overtime requirements. [§213(b)(28)]

■ Domestic service employees who reside in the household where they are employed are exempt from overtime requirements. [§213(b)(21)]

■ All employees under age 18 are restricted from working in any job that is harmful or that would interfere with their schooling. Children as employees are restricted in the number of hours per week they can work at any wage. [§213(c)]

■ Employers who violate this act can be required to pay to each affected employee all sums that should have been paid as wages had the act not been violated, plus interest. The employer may also be ordered to pay the attorney's fees incurred by employees in enforcing this act. Courts are authorized by this act to issue injunctions as necessary to insure compliance. Proof of willful violations of this act can result in fines of up to $10,000 and six months in prison, or both. [§216]

Exceptions: These are generally discussed above, with detailed discussions and checklists in Chapter 10 at Section 10.1(a).

With regard to the equal pay of men and women, there are exceptions to this requirement. Men and women who must otherwise be paid the same wage, can be paid a different wage if the reason for this difference is based on:

(1) A legitimate seniority system;

(2) A legitimate merit system;

(3) A system which actually measures earnings by quantity or quality of production; or,

(4) A legitimate differential based on any other factor other than sex.

[§206(d)(1)]

Dealing with this Statute: The first issue for an employee under this statute is to know whether each of its employees is covered — non-exempt — or not covered — exempt — by this statute. With regard to exempt employees, this statute is irrelevant. The best method for an employer to use to determine which employees are exempt or non-exempt is to maintain current, written job descriptions for each employee or position in the firm. This written description of job responsibilities, requirements, and qualifications is good evidence for determining whether an employee meets the test for being exempt from this act (see the Checklists in Section 10.1(a) of Chapter 10).

The next issue is to be able to verify that non-exempt employees are actually paid at least the minimum wage and that they are paid overtime wages when they work overtime hours. Whether an employee is actually paid by the hour or receives a salary of so much per month or year (or other time period or basis), determine the hourly wage of each non-exempt employee. To do this, divide the employee's pay in one pay period by the number of hours worked during that pay period. The result is their average hourly wage. As long as this amount is at least the statutory minimum wage, this requirement has been met. The real problem, however, usually concerns the number of hours worked. An employee is considered to be "working" when they are actually performing their job responsibilities, as well as when they are "on call" and are expected to handle at least some of their responsibilities as the need arises, whether the employee is "working" or on a break. Breaks must be paid and counted toward the number of hours worked per week unless the employee has absolutely no job responsibilities during the break. Under this act, a "break" means the employee is on their own time and has no work-related responsibilities, actual or implied, to the employer. Keep an accurate record of how many hours per week an employee works and pay the employee overtime of at least 1½ times their regular hourly wage for overtime hours. Accurate and current record keeping, therefore, is the best method for an employer to utilize in order to be sure they are in compliance with this act, with respect to non-exempt employees.

Another issue to review is the wages paid to men and women. Review job descriptions and actual work responsibilities. Men and women who have substantially the same responsibilities, substantially the same qualifications, and whose positions require substantially the same qualifications, must be paid on an equal basis. The only four exceptions to this requirement are set out above.

Regarding the Equal Pay Act [§206(d)], the method of proving whether or not an employer is paying employees differently because they are of different sexes was described in *Katz v. School District of Clayton, Missouri*, 557 F.2d 153 (8th Cir. 1977): "A *prima facie* case of violation of the Act is established where it is shown that the employer has paid workers of one sex more than workers of the opposite sex for equal work. Equal work under the Act means jobs the performance of which requires equal skill, effort and responsibility and which are performed under similar working conditions . . . Two employees are performing equal work when it is necessary to expend the same degree of skill, effort and responsibility in order to perform the substantially equal duties which they do, in fact, routinely perform with the knowledge and acquiescence of the employer. The Act cannot be avoided because the job titles of employees are not the same nor is the Act avoided if the official job descriptions of employees specify different duties. Actual job requirements and performances are controlling . . . Once a *prima facie* case of violation of the Act is established, the burden shifts to the employer to show that the wage differential is justified under (the Act)."

In another case under the Equal Pay Act, a female employee made a claim that her employer was violating this act by hiring a new, male employee at a higher hourly rate than she was then being paid for the same position. The court ruled against the female employee, because the employer proved that the effective beginning date of the male employee's job was also the same date that everyone in that position was given a raise to the new, higher rate. Therefore, all employees in the same position with the same responsibilities were receiving the same pay. *Snider v. Belvedere Township*, 216 F.3d 616 (7th Cir. 2000).

With respect to children as employees, employers are authorized by this act to verify the age of their employees if they are 19 years of age or younger. This is best handled by an instruction that states, "If you are 19 years old or younger, you must provide your date of birth. You may also be required to provide proof of your date of birth, such as your birth certificate, a passport, a valid driver's license, or other official identification that contains your date of birth." Be sure to be familiar with the types of work and the maximum hours of work per day or per week that employees of each age can work. State child labor laws are likely to be more detailed and restrictive than federal law.

15.3 Occupational Safety and Health Act [29 U.S.C. 651 *et seq.*]

Title and Code: Known as: Occupational Safety and Health Act; OSHA; and by a number of specific adjectives. 29 U.S.C. 651 *et seq.* Federal Law.

Covered Employers: All employers, except any State or the United States as an employer.

Covered Employees: All employees.

Requirements and Prohibitions: This act is the object of intense anger and frustration. It is often cited as a prime piece of evidence in support of arguments that the federal government is completely out of touch with the needs and abilities of private businesses and the market place. Nonetheless, this act is the law. It is entirely legitimate and appropriate for those who disagree with any aspect of this act to attempt to make changes through the legislative process. These efforts are sometimes successful and changes have been made. However, as long as this act remains the law, in whatever form it takes, it is also necessary to understand how it applies to your firm and to attempt to comply with its requirements. These comments have been made because there is rarely a case involving this act that an incredible amount of anger from the employer must be dealt with before the real, legal issues can be addressed. Also, it may be helpful to those few who actually like and support this act to understand that they are decidedly in the minority.

- This act applies to any work place located in any State, the District of Columbia, Puerto Rico, the Virgin Islands, American Samoa, Guam, the Trust Territory of the Pacific Islands, Wake Island, the Outer Continental Shelf lands defined in the Outer Continental Shelf Lands Act [43 U.S.C. 1331 *et seq.*], Johnston Island, and the Canal Zone. [§653(a)]

- "Each employer shall furnish to each of his employees employment and a place of employment which are free from recognized hazards that are causing or are likely to cause death or serious physical harm to his employees." [§654(a)(1)]

- "Each employer shall comply with occupational safety and health standards promulgated under this chapter." [§654(a)(2)]

- "Each employee shall comply with occupational safety and health standards and all rules, regulations, and orders issued pursuant to this chapter which are applicable to his own actions and conduct." [§654(b)]

- The Secretary of Labor is authorized by this act to make, modify, or rescind standards designed to prevent death or serious harm to employees, as well as to ensure that workplaces are free from recognized hazards. [§655]

■ The Secretary of Labor is also empowered by this act to enforce these standards through inspections and investigations of workplaces, and by the use of injunctions to correct violations of standards, as well as the use of civil and criminal penalties for violation of the standards. [§§659 - 666]

■ If, upon inspection of a workplace, a violation of a standard is found, a citation is to be issued to the employer with "reasonable promptness." Citations must be in writing and must "describe with particularity the nature of the violation, including a reference to the provision of the chapter, standard, rule, regulation, or order alleged to have been violated. In addition, the citation shall fix a reasonable time for the abatement of the violation." This period of abatement allows the employer a period of time to correct the problem before the citation will be acted upon. [§658(a)]

■ Each citation issued to an employer must be prominently posted at the workplace where the violation occurred. [§658(b)]

■ Citations cannot be issued more than six months after the occurrence of any violation. [§658(c)]

■ Civil fines of up to $7,000 can be assessed for each violation. If an employer willfully or repeatedly violates standards, that employer can be assessed a civil fine of $5,000 to $70,000 per violation. The failure to correct a violation of a standard after receipt of a citation giving notice of the violation can result in a fine of up to $7,000 per day that the violation remains uncorrected. A violation that results in death carries a fine of up to $10,000 ($20,000 for a second violation causing death) and/or six months in prison (one year in prison for a second violation causing death). Giving advance notice of an inspection by the Secretary without authority to do so carries a fine of up to $1,000 and/or six months in prison. The making of "any false statement, representation, or certification in any application, record, report, plan, or other document filed or required to be maintained" pursuant to this act can result in a fine of up to $10,000 and/or six months in prison. Any employer who fails to properly post any notices required under this act can be fined up to $7,000. [§666]

Exceptions: The only exceptions are workplaces of a state or of the federal government.

Dealing with this Statute: First, know what OSHA standards apply to your workplace. These standards are published and they are organized by industry. Also, useful information about OSHA and its standards are available through its Web Site: www.osha.gov/

Many employers will never be inspected or have to deal directly with OSHA at all, unless a complaint is made to OSHA about the employer, or unless a death or serious injury occurs at the workplace. However, employers in industries where on the job injury and even death is not an uncommon risk (such as construction or manufacturing companies), the presence of OSHA and its inspections is a part of doing business. Regardless of the likelihood of an inspection, it is always a possibility. Each firm should know what standards apply and should make a serious effort to comply with those standards.

If a notice is received that an OSHA inspection is going to be made of the workplace, the employer should immediately conduct their own inspection and do everything possible to come into compliance before the inspector arrives. During the inspection, accompany the inspector. If a violation of some standard is discovered during the inspection, and if it is a violation that can be readily corrected or at least addressed, such as by putting on safety equipment, moving an object from one location to another, clearing away debris, etc., do so immediately. This action can show an understanding of the standards and an effort to comply with the standards. Such an action can also prevent the issuance of a citation. If a citation is issued, address the problem promptly. If there is a return visit by the inspector at the end of any abatement period, corrected problems can result in no further action being taken or being required as a result of the citation (other than to stay in compliance with the standard).

The timing of an inspection can sometimes be an issue. If the inspector wants to conduct an inspection at a time of day when the firm is particularly busy with customers or otherwise, the inspection may be rescheduled to a less busy time.

Firms that deal regularly, or even occasionally, with OSHA must develop a strategy for compliance with OSHA standards and for handling OSHA inspections and citations. The only way to develop a successful strategy is to know the standards, review compliance with the standards, and develop a strategy to fit the firm's situation for dealing with inspections and citations. This is best done with the company's attorney and/or consultants. It is also helpful to maintain at least a cordial and professional relationship with the local OSHA office and the inspectors.

Any employer should read and at least consider information concerning OSHA standards for their industry that is released by industry organizations or associations. This can be a good source of this information, particularly for firms who do not expect much actual involvement with OSHA.

If the day arrives when an OSHA inspector shows up at the door of your business, and you have not previously been advised by your own attorney on how to handle such an inspection, the following checklist may be helpful. However, do not use the following information if it is different than the advice of your own attorney. This checklist provides general information. Your attorney provides specific information for the precise situation you face. Follow your attorney's advice.

Checklist 15.1
How to Handle an OSHA Inspection

❏ Have the compliance officer meet with the OSHA inspector as soon as the inspector arrives. If any other manager or official of the firm has the specific duty of handling OSHA compliance, have that person also meet the inspector upon arrival.

❏ If the OSHA Compliance Officer (inspector) is not known, a request for proper identification is appropriate.

❏ Ask the purpose of the Compliance Officer's visit. Get an answer.

❏ An inspection by the Compliance Officer can be delayed if necessary to correct any known problems, by refusing to consent to the inspection and demanding a search warrant. This may not always be a good idea, but it is an option.

❏ Never, ever, ever, volunteer any information whatsoever to the OSHA Compliance Officer or to any other person employed by OSHA (or any other government agency). Do nothing more than comply with the law. The government is not at your front door to help you. This is not cynicism, it is a fact of life in business.

❏ Do not interfere with the Compliance Officer during the investigation. Once the investigation begins, the Compliance Officer is entitled to conduct it.

❏ Take notes of everything that is said and that happens during the investigation. If possible, videotape the investigation.

❏ Request that any proprietary information revealed during the investigation be kept confidential. State that such information is a trade secret and is proprietary.

❏ Before allowing the investigation to begin, provide the OSHA Compliance Officer and all persons who will accompany the OSHA Officer on the inspection with any necessary protective clothing or equipment.

❏ When the OSHA Compliance Officer requests to inspect records, a part of the firm, equipment, or anything else, comply with the request, but do not offer or volunteer to show the Officer anything additional other than what has been requested.

(continued on next page)

(Page 2 - Checklist 15.1)

❏ If the Compliance Officer requests to speak with a non-supervisory employee, the request must be granted. However, the firm can determine whether the interview will take place during or after work hours. This interview can not be monitored by the employer.

❏ If the Compliance Officer requests to speak with a supervisory employee, ask what information the Compliance Officer needs. Advise that the information will be provided later, after a determination has been made about whether or not the requested information is the subject of a proper inquiry by OSHA. An OSHA request to speak with supervisory employees does not have to be granted.

❏ Do not lie or misrepresent anything to the OSHA Compliance Officer at any time. However, do not provide anything not specifically requested and that does not have to be provided.

❏ If, during the inspection, you notice a violation of an OSHA regulation that can be corrected (such as an employee not wearing a hard hat), correct the problem immediately. Part of the inspection may be to determine how such violations are handled when discovered.

❏ If a citation is issued, contact your attorney and rely on legal advice. The issue has become a legal matter at that point.

15.4 Employee Polygraph Protection Act [29 U.S.C. 2001 *et seq.*]

Title and Code: Known as the Polygraph Protection Act and the Lie Detector Act. 29 U.S.C. 2001 *et seq.* Federal Law

Covered Employers: All employers.

Covered Employees: All employees.

Requirements and Prohibitions:

■   This act defines "lie detector" as including "a polygraph, deceptograph, voice stress analyzer, psychological stress evaluator, or any other similar device (whether mechanical or electrical) that is used, or the results of which are used, for the purpose of rendering a diagnostic opinion regarding the honesty or dishonesty of an individual." [§2001(3)]

■   The term "polygraph" is defined as meaning "an instrument that records continuously, visually, permanently, and simultaneously changes in cardiovascular, respiratory, and electrodermal patterns as minimum instrumentation standards; and is used, or the results of which are used, for the purpose of rendering a diagnostic opinion regarding the honesty or dishonesty of an individual." [§2001(4)]

■   It is unlawful for any employer to directly or indirectly, require, request, suggest, or cause any employee or prospective employee to take or submit to any lie detector test. [§2002(1)]

■   It is unlawful for any employer to use, accept, refer to, or inquire concerning the results of any lie detector test of any employee or prospective employee. [§2002(2)]

■   It is unlawful for any employer to discharge, discipline, discriminate against in any manner, or deny employment or promotion to, or threaten to take any such action against any employee or prospective employee who refuses, declines, or fails to take or submit to any lie detector test, or any employee or prospective employee on the basis of the results of any lie detector test. [§2002(3)]

- It is unlawful for any employer to discharge, discipline, discriminate against in any manner, or deny employment or promotion to, or threaten to take any such action against, any employee or prospective employee because such employee or prospective employee has filed any complaint or instituted or caused to be instituted, any proceeding under or related to this chapter, or such employee or prospective employee has testified or is about to testify in any such proceeding, or of the exercise by such employee or prospective employee, on behalf of such employee or another person, of any right afforded by this chapter. [§2002(4)]

- Each employer is required to post a notice at the workplace which informs employees of the requirements of this act. [§2003]

- An employer who violates this act may be assessed a civil penalty of up to $10,000, an injunction may be issued to stop any employer conduct in violation of this act, and employees may recover remedies against the employer to include employment, reinstatement, promotion and the payment of lost wages, benefits, costs and attorney's fees. [§2005]

Exceptions: This act does not apply to specifically identified employers. The exempt employers are:

1) The United States Government, any State or local government, or any political subdivision of a State or local government. [§2006(a), (b), (c)]

2) Any employer whose primary business purpose consists of providing armored car personnel, personnel engaged in the design, installation, and maintenance of security alarm systems, or other uniformed or plainclothes security personnel and whose function includes the protection of facilities, materials, or operations having a significant impact on the health or safety of any State or political subdivision thereof, or the national security of the United States, or facilities engaged in the production, transmission, or distribution of electric or nuclear power, public water supply facilities, shipments or storage of radioactive or other toxic waste materials, and public transportation, or currency, negotiable securities, precious commodities or instruments, or proprietary information. [§2006(e)]

3) Any employer authorized to manufacture, distribute, or dispense a controlled substance in schedule I, II, III, or IV of 21 U.S.C. 812. [§2006(f)]

In addition, no employer is prohibited from requesting an employee to submit to a polygraph test if the test is administered as part of an actual, ongoing investigation involving "economic loss or injury to the employer's business, such as theft, embezzlement, misappropriation, or an act of unlawful industrial espionage or sabotage," and, the employee in question had access to property which is the subject of the investigation, the employee is reasonably suspected of some involvement in the matter, and the testing is conducted by qualified personnel according to currently accepted standards. [§2006(d)]

Dealing with this Statute: Unless the firm is specifically exempt from this statute, simply do not use lie detectors or polygraphs on employees. Also, all employers must display the required informative poster.

In *Mennen v. Easter Stores,* 951 F.Supp. 838 (N.D.Iowa 1997), the court discussed the purpose of this act and what it means for an employer. The court stated that this Act "prohibits an employer from using, accepting, or inquiring about the results of any lie detector test, and makes it an unlawful practice to fire, discipline, or discriminate against an employee on the basis of a polygraph test result . . . (W)hile the employer had not required the employee to take the test, it had clearly violated the (Act) by using the test results to discipline him."

15.5 Employment and Reemployment Rights of Members Of the Uniformed Services [38 U.S.C. 4301 *et seq.*]

Title and Code: Employment and Reemployment Rights of Members of the Uniformed Services. 38 U.S.C. 4301 *et seq.* Federal Law

Covered Employers: All employers.

Covered Employees: All employees.

Requirements and Prohibitions:

- Any person "who is a member of, applies to be a member of, performs, has performed, applies to perform, or has an obligation to perform service in a uniformed service shall not be denied initial employment, reemployment, retention in employment, promotion, or any benefit of employment by an employer on the basis of that membership, application for membership, performance of service, application for service, or obligation." Employers cannot discriminate in employment against employees or job applicants on the basis of service in the armed forces. However, action can be taken against such an employee on the basis of cause or on any basis that would also lead to the same action against another employee in the same circumstances, but who has no connection with the armed forces. [§4311(a)]

■ An employee who is required to leave their job because of being called to service or training in the armed forces of the United States is entitled to have their job back when they are released from training or service. The employee must reapply for their job within 90 days of release from service or training, unless the employer's circumstances have so changed as to make it impossible or unreasonable to do so. [§4312]

■ Persons reemployed pursuant to this act are to be reemployed into the position they would have had if they had continued their employment without interruption, unless they are not actually qualified for such position. [§4313]

■ Persons reemployed pursuant to this act are entitled to retain any rights of seniority they had before they left for service or training. During their first year back on the job, they can only be terminated for cause. While gone from their job in service or training, the employee may request that accrued paid leave time be used until it is exhausted during the time they are gone. However, the employer may not compel the employee to use any accrued paid leave. [§4316]

■ Employees covered by a health plan may elect to continue their coverage under the health plan for up to 18 months from the date they leave their job for training or service (or until the day after they fail to return to work as required under this act, whichever date is sooner). If the employee is gone for at least 31 days, they can be required to pay up to 102% of the full premium under the plan until they return to their job. [§4317]

■ Employees participating in a pension benefit plan shall not be considered to have had a break in service for the period of time they are away from their job in training or service. The employee is also entitled to receive accrued benefits under their plan, but only to the extent that they continue their contributions. [§4318]

■ Failure to comply with this act can result in an order to comply with the act, the awarding of liquidated damages, and the awarding of compensation to the employee. [§4323]

Exceptions: There are no exceptions.

Dealing with this Statute: Simply, do not make employment decisions based on service in the uniformed forces of the United States. Employees who are on active duty, in the reserves, or in the National Guard, must be allowed time away from work in order to report for service or training. Retaliatory action cannot be taken against such an employee because they must report for service or training. They do not, however, need to be paid while they are gone. However, the employee can request to be paid any accrued paid leave they may have had while they are gone.

15.6 Title VII, Civil Rights Act of 1964 [42 U.S.C. 2000e *et seq.*]

Title and Code: Most commonly referred to as Title VII. 42 U.S.C. 2000e *et seq.* Federal Law.

Covered Employers: All employers with a minimum average of 15 employees.

Covered Employees: All employees, whether part time, full time, temporary, or permanent, who are employed by a covered employer.

Requirements and Prohibitions:

■ It is unlawful for any employer covered by this act "to fail or refuse to hire or to discharge any individual, or otherwise to discriminate against any individual with respect to his compensation, terms, conditions, or privileges of employment, because of such individual's race, color, religion, sex, or national origin." [§2000e-2(a)(1)]

■ It is also unlawful for any employer covered by this act "to limit, segregate, or classify his employees or applicants for employment in any way which would deprive or tend to deprive any individual of employment opportunities or otherwise adversely affect his status as an employee, because of such individual's race, color, religion, sex, or national origin." [§2000e-2(a)(2)]

■ Employment agencies are prohibited from referring or refusing to refer for employment any individual on the basis of the individual's race, color, religion, sex, or national origin. [§2000e-2(b)]

■ Labor organizations are prohibited from excluding or expelling from membership any individual because of the individual's race, color, religion, sex, or national origin. [§2000e-2(c)]

■ Discrimination by an employer, an employment agency, or by a labor organization is permitted on the basis of religion, sex, or national origin (but not race or color) IF there is a bona fide occupational qualification requiring such discrimination. [§2000e-2(e)]

■ It is not a violation of this act to take "any action or measure . . . with respect to an individual who is a member of the Communist Party of the United States or of any other organization required to register as a Communist-action or Communist-front organization by final order of the Subversive Activities Control Board pursuant to the Subversive Activities Control Act of 1950 (50 U.S.C. 781 et seq.)". [§2000e-2(f)]

■ Any individual whose employment is affected for legitimate national security reasons cannot claim to be the victim of unlawful discrimination under this act. [§2000e-2(g)]

■ It is not an unlawful employment practice under this act "for an employer to apply different standards of compensation, or different terms, conditions, or privileges of employment pursuant to a bona fide seniority or merit system, or a system which measures earnings by quantity or quality of production or to employees who work in different locations, provided that such differences are not the result of an intention to discriminate because of race, color, religion, sex, or national origin." [§2000e-2(h)]

■ It is not an unlawful employment practice "for an employer to give and to act upon the results of any professionally developed ability test provided that such test, its administration or action upon the results is not designed, intended or used to discriminate because of race, color, religion, sex or national origin." [§2000e-2(h)]

■ Businesses in or near Indian reservations are not prohibited by the act from applying any publicly announced preference for employees who are an Indian living on or near a reservation. [§2000e-2(i)]

■ Nothing in this act is to be interpreted to require the granting of preferential treatment to any individual for any reason, including addressing an "imbalance which may exist with respect to the total number or percentage of persons of any race, color, religion, sex, or national origin." [§2000e-2(j)]

■ "It shall be an unlawful employment practice for (an employer), in connection with the selection or referral of applicants or candidates for employment or promotion, to adjust the scores of, use different cutoff scores for, or otherwise alter the results of, employment related tests on the basis of race, color, religion, sex, or national origin." [§2000e-2(l)]

■ Unless an exception pursuant to this act applies, "an unlawful employment practice is established when the complaining party demonstrates that race, color, religion, sex, or national origin was a motivating factor for any employment practice, even though other factors also motivated the practice." [§2000e-2(m)]

■ This act also creates the Equal Employment Opportunity Commission, referred to as the EEOC. This Commission is empowered to investigate complaints of violation of this act and to make determinations of whether or not the act has been violated. If it determines that the act has been violated, the Commission can award damages to the employee which include reinstatement, hiring (if an applicant was not hired for a discriminatory reason only), back pay, and any other relief the Commission determines to be equitable. Also, costs and attorney's fees can be awarded. In the case of an employee or applicant who was terminated or not hired for a reason not limited to a discriminatory reason, the relief awarded to that person cannot include reinstatement or hiring into the job, nor can they be awarded back pay. They can be awarded their costs and attorney's fees, however. [§§2000e-4 - 2000e-5]

Exceptions: The exceptions are noted above. The key exception is that employers may discriminate on the basis of religion, sex, or national origin if they can show a bona fide occupational qualification for such a basis for their decision. There can be no bona fide occupational qualifications on the basis of race or color.

Dealing with this Statute: This is perhaps the most significant of all federal employment law statutes. Each state has adopted its own version of this statute that applies to employers not covered by the federal act. In addition, courts have generally determined that public policy considerations apply to make the types of discrimination prohibited by this act unlawful when done by any employer, regardless of how many employees it has.

Beginning with the preparation of job descriptions, all employers must focus their efforts into making employment decisions on the basis of legitimate business necessity. This means concentrating on the actual qualifications for each position and making decisions based on an individual's own qualifications, regardless of and in complete indifference to the individual's race, color, religion, sex, or national origin.

Several significant court decisions have helped to define this act and to describe how to deal with its requirements.

"The complainant in a Title VII trial must carry the initial burden under the statute of establishing a *prima facie* case of racial discrimination. This may be done by showing (i) that he belongs to a protected class – race, color, national origin, religion, sex; (ii) that he applied and was qualified for a job for which the employer was seeking applicants; (iii) that, despite his qualifications, he was rejected; and (iv) that, after his rejection, the position remained open and the employer continued to seek applicants from persons of complainant's qualifications. The burden then must shift to the employer to articulate some legitimate, nondiscriminatory reason for the employee's rejection." *McDonnell Douglas Corporation v. Green,* 411 U.S. 792, 93 S.Ct.1817, 36 L.Ed.2d 668 (1973)

"The central focus of the inquiry in a case such as this is always whether the employer is treating some people less favorably than others because of their race, color, religion, sex, or national origin. The method suggested in *McDonnell Douglas* for pursuing this inquiry, however, was never intended to be rigid, mechanized, or ritualistic. Rather, it is merely a sensible, orderly way to evaluate the evidence in light of common experience as it bears on the critical question of discrimination. A *prima facie* case under *McDonnell Douglas* raises an inference of discrimination only because we presume these acts, if otherwise unexplained, are more likely than not based on the consideration of impermissible factors. And we are willing to presume this largely because we know from our experience that more often than not people do not act in a totally arbitrary manner, without any underlying reasons, especially in a business setting. Thus, when all legitimate reasons for rejecting an applicant have been eliminated as possible reasons for the employer's actions, it is more likely than not the employer, who we generally assume acts only with some reason, based his decision on an impermissible consideration such as race.

When the *prima facie* case is understood in the light of the opinion in *McDonnell Douglas*, it is apparent that the burden which shifts to the employer is merely that of proving that he based his employment decision on a legitimate consideration, and not an illegitimate one such as race. To prove that, he need not prove that he pursued the course which would both enable him to achieve his own business goal and allow him to consider the most employment applications. Title VII prohibits him from having as a goal a work force selected by any proscribed discriminatory practice, but it does not impose a duty to adopt a hiring procedure that maximizes hiring of minority employees. To dispel the adverse inference from a *prima facie* showing under *McDonnell Douglas*, the employer need only articulate some legitimate, nondiscriminatory reason for the employee's rejection." *Furnco Construction Corp. v. Waters, et al.,* 438 U.S.567, 98 S.Ct. 2943, 57 L.Ed.2d 957 (1978)

In *Texas Department of Community Affairs v. Burdine*, 450 U.S. 248, 101 S.Ct. 1089, 67 L.Ed.2d 207 (1981), the Supreme Court again set out the *McDonnell Douglas* test. It then described in more detail what is meant by the requirement for the employer to show that the nondiscriminatory reason it gave for its action against the employee was not pretext. "The burden that shifts to the employer, therefore, is to rebut the presumption of discrimination by producing evidence that the employee was rejected, or someone else was preferred, for a legitimate, nondiscriminatory reason . . . It is sufficient if the employer's evidence raises a genuine issue of fact as to whether it discriminated against the employee. To accomplish this, the employer must clearly set forth, through the introduction of admissible evidence, the reasons for the employee's rejection. The explanation provided must be legally sufficient to justify a judgment for the employer. If the employer carries this burden of production, the presumption raised by the *prima facie* case is rebutted, and the factual inquiry proceeds to a new level of specificity. Placing this burden of production on the employer thus serves simultaneously to meet the employee's *prima facie* case by presenting a legitimate reason for the action and to frame the factual issue with sufficient clarity so that the employee will have a full and fair opportunity to demonstrate pretext. The sufficiency of the employer's evidence should be evaluated by the extent to which it fulfills these functions . . . The employee retains the burden of persuasion. She now must have the opportunity to demonstrate that the proffered reason was not the true reason for the unemployment decision. This burden now merges with the ultimate burden of persuading the court that she has been the victim of intentional discrimination. She may succeed in this either directly by persuading the court that a discriminatory reason more likely motivated the employer or indirectly by showing that the employer's proffered explanation is unworthy of credence."

The issue of what constitutes a bona fide occupational qualification has also been addressed: ". . . the job qualifications which the employer invokes to justify his discrimination must be reasonably necessary to the essence of his business – here, the safe transportation of bus passengers from one point to another. The greater the safety factor, measured by the likelihood of harm and the probable severity of that harm in case of an accident, the more stringent may be the job qualifications designed to insure safe driving... If all or substantially all members of a class do not qualify, or if there is no practical way reliably to differentiate the qualified from the unqualified applicants in that class, it is precisely then that . . . otherwise proscribed class discrimination is permitted as a bona fide occupational qualification. This test does not mandate either the hiring of unqualified applicants or applicants whose qualifications cannot be reliably determined . . . To meet this test, an employer must have reasonable cause, that is, a factual basis, for believing that all or substantially all persons [in the protected class] would be unable to perform safely and efficiently the duties of the job involved, or whether it is impossible or impractical to deal with persons [in the protected class] on an individualized basis." *Usery v. Tamiami Trail Tours, Inc.,* 531 F.2d 224 (5th Cir. 1976)

15.6(a) Sexual and Other Types of Harassment

Sexual harassment is a type of discrimination prohibited by Title VII. It is, therefore, a form of discrimination. Harassment can also be based on the other factors prohibited as a basis for unlawful discrimination, race, color, national origin, or religion.

There are two categories of sexual harassment (both of which are equally unlawful):

(1) Quid Pro Quo Harassment, or, making sex a prerequisite for an employment decision. A claim based on quid pro quo harassment can be proven after only one incident. In addition, criminal charges are not uncommon after this type of harassment.

(2) Hostile Work Environment. This results when an employee is subjected to conduct which makes putting up with sexual harassment on the job a condition of employment. A hostile work environment is not generally proven by one incident. In fact, isolated or occasional incidents of rude behavior against an employee may not be sufficient to prove discrimination or harassment. However, when these events add up over time, a hostile environment is most definitely created.

The Equal Employment Opportunity Commission has issued regulations on sexual harassment at 29 C.F.R. 1604.11:

"Harassment on the basis of sex, race, color, religion or national origin is a violation of Title VII. Unwelcome . . . advances, requests . . . and other verbal or physical conduct . . . constitute . . . harassment when (1) submission to such conduct is made either explicitly or implicitly a term or condition of an individual's employment, (2) submission to or rejection of such conduct by an individual is used as the basis for employment decisions affecting such individual, or (3) such conduct has the purpose or effect of unreasonably interfering with an individual's work performance or creating an intimidating, hostile, or offensive working environment."

"In determining whether alleged conduct constitutes . . . harassment, the Commission (EEOC) will look at the record as a whole and at the totality of the circumstances, such as the nature of the (conduct) and the context in which the alleged incidents occurred."

"The determination of the legality of a particular action will be made from the facts, on a case by case basis."

"An employer is responsible for its acts and those of its agents and supervisory employees with respect to harassment regardless of whether the specific acts complained of were authorized or even forbidden by the employer and regardless of whether the employer knew or should have known of their occurrence."

"With respect to conduct between fellow employees, an employer is responsible for acts of harassment in the workplace where the employer (or its agents or supervisory employees) knows or should have known of the conduct, unless it can show that it took immediate and appropriate corrective action."

"An employer may also be responsible for the acts of non-employees, with respect to harassment of employees in the workplace, where the employer or its agents or supervisory employees knows or should have known of the conduct and fails to take immediate and appropriate corrective action. In reviewing these cases, the Commission will consider the extent of the employer's control and any other legal responsibility that the employer may have with respect to the conduct of such non-employees."

"Prevention is the best tool for the elimination of harassment. An employer should take all steps necessary to prevent harassment from occurring, such as affirmatively raising the subject, expressing strong disapproval, developing appropriate sanctions, informing employees of their right to raise and how to raise the issue of harassment under Title VII, and developing methods to sensitize all concerned."

The courts have provided further detail into the issue of harassment:

"Sex discrimination within the meaning of Title VII is not limited to disparate treatment founded solely or categorically on gender. Rather, discrimination is sex discrimination whenever sex is for no legitimate reason a substantial factor in the discrimination . . . An employer is liable for discriminatory acts committed by supervisory personnel . . . although the employer might be relieved of liability if the supervisor committing the harassment did so in contravention of the employer's policy and without the employer's knowledge, and if the employer moved promptly and effectively to rectify the offense . . . However, the employer could be held liable even if there were only one victim, since Congress intended Title VII to protect individuals against class-based prejudice . . ."

Where an employer created or condoned a substantially discriminatory work environment, regardless of whether the complaining employees lost any tangible job benefits as a result of the discrimination, sexual harassment of the sort Bundy suffered amounted by itself to sex discrimination with respect to the terms, conditions, or privileges of employment . . . Sexual stereotyping through discriminatory dress requirements may be benign in intent, and may offend women only in a general, atmospheric manner, yet it violates Title VII . . . How then can sexual harassment, which injects the most demeaning sexual stereotypes into the general work environment and which always represents an intentional assault on an individual's innermost privacy, not be illegal? . . . Even indirect discrimination is illegal because it may constitute a subtle scheme designed to create a working environment imbued with discrimination and directed ultimately at minority group employees.

As patently discriminatory practices become outlawed, those employers bent on pursuing a general policy declared illegal by Congressional mandate will undoubtedly devise more sophisticated methods to perpetuate discrimination among employees . . . Thus, an employer could sexually harass a female employee with impunity by carefully stopping short of firing the employee or taking any other tangible actions against her in response to her resistance, thereby creating the impression that the employer did not take the ritual of harassment and resistance seriously . . . It may even be pointless to require the employee to prove that she resisted the harassment at all. So long as the employer never literally forces sexual relations on the employee, resistance may be a meaningless alternative for her. If the employer demands no response to his verbal or physical gestures other than good-natured tolerance, the woman has no means of communicating her rejection. She neither accepts nor rejects the advances; she simply endures them. She might be able to contrive proof of rejection by objecting to the employer's advances in some very visible and dramatic way, but she would do so only at the risk of making her life on the job even more miserable . . . The employer can thus implicitly and effectively make the employee's endurance of sexual intimidation a condition of her employment." *Bundy v. Jackson*, 641 F.2d 934 (D.C.Cir. 1981)

"A plaintiff may establish a violation of Title VII by proving that discrimination based on sex has created a hostile or abusive work environment . . . Sexual harassment which creates a hostile or offensive environment for members of one sex is every bit the arbitrary barrier to sexual equality at the workplace that racial harassment is to racial equality. Surely, a requirement that a man or woman run a gauntlet of sexual abuse in return for the privilege of being allowed to work and make a living can be as demeaning and disconcerting as the harshest of racial epithets . . . Of course, not all workplace conduct that may be described as 'harassment' affects a term, condition, or privilege of employment within the meaning of Title VII . . . For sexual harassment to be actionable, it must be sufficiently severe or pervasive to alter the conditions of the victim's employment and create an abusive working environment . . . It is without question that sexual harassment of female employees in which they are asked or required to submit to sexual demands as a condition to obtain employment or to maintain employment or to obtain promotions falls within the protection of Title VII . . . But the fact that sex-related conduct was 'voluntary,' in the sense that the complainant was not forced to participate against her will, is not a defense to a sexual harassment suit brought under Title VII. The gravaman of any sexual harassment claim is that the alleged sexual advances were unwelcome . . . The trier of fact must determine the existence of sexual harassment in light of the record as a whole and the totality of circumstances, such as the nature of the sexual advances and the context in which the alleged incidents occurred." *Meritor Savings Bank v. Vinson*, 477 U.S. 57, 106 S.Ct. 2399, 91 L.Ed.2d 49 (1986)

Must the perpetrator and the victim be of different sexes in order for sexual harassment to occur? Is it possible for same-sex sexual harassment to be a violation of Title VII? The answer is that a woman as well as a man can be the victim of sexual harassment. Whatever sex the victim is, it does not matter whether the perpetrator is a man or a woman. The perpetrator and the victim can be opposite sexes or the same sex and it is still sexual harassment in violation of Title VII. The case that clarified this point is *Oncale v. Sundowner Offshore Services Inc.,* 523 U.S. 75, 118 S.Ct. 998, 140 L.Ed.2d 201 (1998): "Title VII's prohibition of discrimination 'because of . . . sex' protects men as well as women, and in the related context of racial discrimination in the workplace we have rejected any conclusive presumption that an employer will not discriminate against members of his own race. Because of the many facets of human motivation, it would be unwise to presume as a matter of law that human beings on one definable group will not discriminate against other members of that group . . . We hold today that nothing in Title VII necessarily bars a claim of discrimination because of sex merely because the plaintiff and the defendant (or the person charged with acting on behalf of the defendant) are of the same sex."

There have been many cases brought to the courts based on harassment, sexual and otherwise. The court decisions from these cases, as well as the EEOC regulations on sexual harassment, have resulted in specific information that can be used by an employer in successfully dealing with this issue. This information is set out in the following checklist.

Checklist 15.2
Steps to Include in a Sexual Harassment Policy

❏ The firm must specifically state that any type of harassment, sexual or otherwise, will not be tolerated.

❏ Inform employees that if they believe they are the victim of sexual harassment, they should report the harassment to the firm so appropriate action can be taken.

❏ Employees should be given more than one method for reporting sexual harassment. It is pointless to require an employee to report harassment to their supervisor if the supervisor is the perpetrator. There should be several methods for making this report.

❏ All reports of harassment must be taken seriously.

❏ Each report of harassment must be investigated by the firm to determine what happened. It is appropriate for the firm to conduct an internal investigation. Talk to the victim, the alleged perpetrator, and to any witness named by either the victim or the perpetrator. Caution each person talked to during the investigation that the investigation and all information obtained is confidential. Discussing the matter outside the investigation can be proper grounds for termination of employment.

❏ When the investigation is completed, make findings about what happened, all based on the investigation.

❏ If the findings are inconclusive, or it is impossible to verify that harassment occurred, notify the victim and alleged perpetrator. This, is the end of the matter unless new information is brought forward.

❏ If the findings are that harassment did not occur, notify the victim and the alleged perpetrator of this conclusion. The matter then ends for the perpetrator. Depending on what is learned during the investigation, the "victim" may be subject to discipline if it was all a lie.

❏ If the findings are that harassment did occur, notify the victim and the perpetrator immediately. Offer the victim therapy at company expense and assure them that no retaliatory action will be taken against them. Take appropriate action against the perpetrator, which could include termination of employment, reassignment to another geographic location, demotion, or loss of privileges or benefits. Do not simply look the other way when harassment has been confirmed. Also, do not treat the perpetrator lightly. People who engage in harassing behavior tend to continue doing so as long as they have the opportunity. Termination of employment may be the best option.

15.7 Americans With Disabilities Act [42 U.S.C. 12101 *et seq.*]

Title and Code: Known as: Americans with Disabilities Act of 1990; and, ADA. 42 U.S.C. 12101 *et seq.* Federal Law.

Covered Employers: All employers with a minimum average of 15 employees.

Covered Employees: All employees of a covered employer.

Requirements and Prohibitions:

- "No covered entity shall discriminate against a qualified individual with a disability because of the disability of such individual in regard to job application procedures, the hiring, advancement, or discharge of employees, employee compensation, job training, and other terms, conditions, and privileges of employment." [§12112(a)]

- "The term 'qualified individual with a disability' means an individual with a disability who, with or without reasonable accommodation, can perform the essential functions of the employment position that such individual holds or desires . . . consideration shall be given to the employer's judgment, as to what functions of a job are essential, and if an employer has prepared a written description before advertising or interviewing applicants for the job, this description shall be considered evidence of the essential functions of the job." [§12111(8)]

- "The term 'reasonable accommodation' may include — (A) making existing facilities used by employees readily accessible to and usable by individuals with disabilities; and (B) job restructuring, part-time or modified work schedules, reassignment to a vacant position, acquisition or modification of equipment or devices, appropriate adjustment or modifications of examinations, training materials or policies, the provision of qualified readers or interpreters, and other similar accommodations for individuals with disabilities." [12111(9)]

- "The term 'undue hardship' means an action requiring significant difficulty or expense, when considered in light of the (following) factors: In determining whether an accommodation would impose an undue hardship on a covered entity (employer), factors to be considered include — (i) the nature and cost of the accommodation needed; (ii) the overall financial resources of the facility or facilities involved in the provision of the reasonable accommodation; the number of persons employed at such facility; the effect on expenses and resources, or the impact otherwise of such accommodation upon the operation of the facility; (iii) the overall financial resources of the covered entity; the overall size of the business of a covered entity with respect to the number of its employees; the number, type and location of its facilities; and (iv) the type of operation or operations of the covered entity, including the composition, structure, and functions of the workforce of such entity; the geographic separateness, administrative, or fiscal relationship of the facility or facilities in question to the covered entity." [§12111(10)]

- A bona fide occupational qualification which excludes job applicants with certain disabilities may be allowed under this act if is "shown to be job-related and consistent with business necessity, and such performance cannot be accomplished by reasonable accommodation." [§12113(a)]

- Employers can require as a legitimate qualification that "an individual shall not pose a direct threat to the health or safety of other individuals in the workplace." [§12113(b)]

- Any individual "who is currently engaging in the illegal use of drugs," is not to be considered as a qualified individual with a disability. [§12114(a)]

- An employer "(1) may prohibit the illegal use of drugs and the use of alcohol at the workplace by all employees; (2) may require that employees shall not be under the influence of alcohol or be engaging in the illegal use of drugs at the workplace; . . . (4) may hold an employee who engages in the illegal use of drugs or who is an alcoholic to the same qualification standards for employment or job performance and behavior that such entity holds other employees, even if any unsatisfactory performance or behavior is related to the drug use or alcoholism of such employee." [§12114(c)(1), (2), (4)]

- This act is to be enforced by the same procedure as Title VII of the Civil Rights Act of 1964 and the remedies described in Title VII are to be applied to violations of this act. [§12117(a)]

Exceptions: A particular disability can be the subject of a bona fide occupational qualification. Anyone currently using illegal drugs is not protected by this act. However, a person who has a history of illegal drug use, but who has successfully completed treatment and is no longer using illegal drugs, could be considered as having a disability. Whether or not they are qualified for a particular position, however, depends on the qualifications required for the position in question.

Dealing with this Statute: The best thing for an employer to do is to prepare and use written job descriptions for each position. This act specifically states that such a job description, if prepared before the position was filled and that is used during the hiring process, will be considered as evidence of the essential requirements of the job. This means the qualifications and requirements contained in a written job description are evidence to be used in determining whether a particular individual with a disability can be considered as qualified for the job. Just because a person is disabled does not mean a person has to be considered for the job, or if they are already in the job, that action cannot be taken against them. The applicant or employee must be qualified, which means they are able to perform the essential requirements of the job, with or without a reasonable accommodation. Whether or not a particular accommodation is reasonable is determined by the factors set out in this act. If the accommodation necessary to allow the disabled individual to do the job causes an undue hardship on the employer, the act does not require the accommodation to be made.

The first issue in an ADA case is whether or not the employee is "disabled" as defined by the act. This issue was discussed in *Bolton v. Scrivner, Inc.*, 36 F.3d 939 (10th Cir. 1994): "The term disability means, with respect to an individual – (A) a physical or mental impairment that substantially limits one or more of the major life activities of such individual; (B) a record of such an impairment; or (C) being regarded as having such an impairment . . . The ADA regulations adopt the definition of major life activities as . . . functions such as caring for oneself, performing manual tasks, walking, seeing, hearing, speaking, breathing, learning, and working . . . To demonstrate that an impairment substantially limits the major life activity of working, an individual must show significant restriction in the ability to perform either a class of jobs or a broad range of jobs in various classes as compared to the average person having comparable training, skills and abilities. The regulations specify that the inability to perform a single, particular job does not constitute a substantial limitation in the major life activity of working . . . While (the) regulations define a major life activity to include working, this does not necessarily mean working at the job of one's choice . . . An impairment that an employer perceives as limiting an individual's ability to perform only one job is not a handicap."

A person who is disabled must be qualified for the job. The case, *Tyndall v. National Education Centers,* 31 F.3d 209 (4th Cir. 1994), deals with this issue: "To determine whether (the applicant or employee) was qualified for the position, we must decide (1) whether she could perform the essential functions of the job, i.e., functions that bear more than a marginal relationship to the job at issue, and (2) if not, whether any reasonable accommodation by the employer would enable her to perform those functions. (The employee) bears the burden of demonstrating that she could perform the essential functions of her job with reasonable accommodation."

The ADA does not require any accommodation, but only reasonable accommodations. A reasonable accommodation is one that does not cause an undue hardship to the employer. This issue was addressed in *Kimbro v. Atlantic Richfield Co.,* 889 F.2d 869 (9th Cir. 1989): "Whether a particular accommodation would have imposed an undue hardship on the employer is a question of fact . . . The cost of accommodating an able handicapped worker will be considered to be an undue hardship on the conduct of the employer's business only if it is unreasonably high in view of the size of the employer's business, the value of the employee's work, whether the cost can be included in planned remodeling or maintenance, the requirements of other laws and contracts, and other appropriate considerations . . . An employer bears the burden of establishing that a proposed accommodation would impose an undue hardship on the conduct of the business . . . As long as a reasonable accommodation available to the employer could have plausibly enabled a handicapped employee to adequately perform his job, an employer is liable for failing to attempt that accommodation." Also, in *Nolan v. Sunshine Biscuits, Inc.*, 917 F.Supp. 753 (D. Kan. 1996): "The (employee) bears the initial burden to make a . . . showing that accommodation is possible. The burden . . . then shifts to the employer to present evidence of its inability to accommodate. If the employer presents such evidence, the (employee) may not simply rest on his pleadings. He has the burden of coming forward with evidence concerning his individual capabilities and suggestions for possible accommodations to rebut the employer's evidence."

15.8 Age Discrimination in Employment Act [29 U.S.C. 621-634]

Title and Code: Known as: Age Discrimination Act; and, ADEA. 29 U.S.C. 621-634 Federal Law.

Covered Employers: All employers with an average of 20 or more employees.

Covered Employees: Employees of covered employers who are 40 years old or older.

Requirements and Prohibitions:

- No employment decision can be made based on the age of a covered employee. [§623(a)]

- An employee's age can be a bona fide occupational qualification. [§623(f)(1)]

- It is not a violation of this act if an employer's bona fide seniority system, or participation by an employee in a benefits plan, includes factors based on the age of participating employees. [§623)f)(2)]

- All employers are to post a notice at the workplace that contains information about this act. [§627]

- Violations of this act are to be handled the same as violations of Title VII. [§626]

Exceptions: Employees and job applicants under age 40 cannot be the subject of unlawful discrimination under the terms of this act. However, the states all have their own version of this act, each of which generally covers individuals 18 years of age or older. Therefore, while it may not be a violation of federal law to discriminate in employment against an employee under age 40, it could be a violation of state law. Otherwise, there are a number of bona fide occupational qualifications that can apply based on age. These BFOQ's can range from participation requirements in benefit plans, minimum retirement ages, to maximum age requirements for holding a particular position (i.e., airline pilot, firefighter, certain law enforcement positions, operation of some equipment, etc.).

Dealing with this Statute: The key issue is to avoid making employment decisions based on the age of the employee. If age is determined by the employer to be a bona fide occupational qualification, make sure it is an actual, good faith qualification. Determine why age matters based on the actual, essential requirements of the job. Also, determine if there are applicable state or federal statutes that set age limitations, or if there is case law that indicates a particular type of position can have age as a BFOQ. Review benefit plans to determine why the age of the participant is a necessary element of plan participation.

An employee is required to prove age discrimination in the same manner that discrimination in violation to Title VII must be proven. This procedure is described in *Cone v. Longmont United Hospital Association,* 14 F.3d 526 (10th Cir. 1994): "At the first stage, the (employee) must prove a *prima facie* case of discrimination. She must show that (1) she is within the protected age group; (2) she was doing satisfactory work; (3) she was discharged; and, (4) her position was filled by a younger person. If the (employee) satisfies the *prima facie* requirements under the ADEA, then the case enters the next stage. In this second stage, the burden of proof moves to the (employer). The (employer) has to present a legitimate nondiscriminatory reason for its action. If the (employer) articulates a legitimate, nondiscriminatory reason for its action, then the burden of persuasion moves back to the (employee). In this third stage of the discrimination analysis, the (employee) must show that age was a determinative factor in the (employer's) employment decision, or show that the (employer's) explanation for its action was merely pretext. Failure to come forward with evidence of pretext will entitle the (employer) to judgment . . . . The employer's burden is simply to demonstrate a legitimate, nondiscriminatory reason for its actions. The (employer) having done so, the (employee) must present enough evidence to support an inference that the employer's reason was merely pretext, by showing either that a discriminatory reason more likely motivated the employer or . . . that the employer's proffered explanation is unworthy of credence."

15.9 Consolidated Omnibus Budget Reconciliation Act Of 1986 [26 U.S.C. 4980B]

Title and Code: Known as COBRA. 26 U.S.C. 4980B. Federal Law

Covered Employers: All employers with an average of 20 or more employees and who offer a health or medical insurance plan to employees.

Covered Employees: All employees of a covered employer.

Requirements and Prohibitions:

■ An employee who is participating in a health or medical insurance plan and who loses their coverage under the plan due to a "qualifying event" must be given the option of terminating their participation in the plan or of continuing in the plan. An employee who decides to continue in the plan can do so for a maximum of 18 months from the date of the qualifying event. In addition, the employee can be required to pay the full premium required for participation in the plan (whether or not they were previously paying the full premium, a partial premium, or none of the premium).

■ Employees who choose to continue with their plan do not have to re-qualify or re-apply to the plan. They are automatically allowed to continue their coverage under the plan.

■ "Qualifying events" which trigger the application of this act include: termination of employment, except for gross misconduct; a reduction in the number of hours the employee works if this reduction in hours makes the employee ineligible for plan participation; the divorce or legal separation of an employee and spouse; a dependent child ceases to be a dependent child as defined by the health plan; the employer files for relief under the Bankruptcy Code; or, the employee becomes eligible for social security benefits.

■ Upon the occurrence of a qualifying event, the employer must give the employee the necessary information in writing for the employee to be able to make a decision under this act. Aside from providing information, the employer is not to participate in the employee's decision. Whether to continue with coverage is the employee's decision alone.

Exceptions: There are no exceptions to this act once a qualifying event occurs.

Dealing with this Statute: The employer simply needs to be aware when an employee experiences a qualifying event. The employer then needs to promptly give the necessary written information to the employee.

15.10 Family and Medical Leave Act
[29 U.S.C. 2601 *et seq.*]

Title and Code: Known as: Family and Medical Leave; and, FMLA. 29 U.S.C. 2601 *et seq.* Federal Law.

Covered Employers: Any employer who has "50 or more employees for each working day during each of 20 or more calendar workweeks in the current or preceding calendar year." [§2611(4)(A)(i)]

Covered Employees: "Eligible employees" are covered by this act. "The term 'eligible employee' means an employee who has been employed — (i) for at least 12 months by the employer . . . and (ii) for at least 1,250 hours of service with such employer during the previous 12-month period." Excluded from the definition of the term "eligible employee" is "any employee of an employer who is employed at a worksite at which such employer employs less than 50 employees if the total number of employees employed by that employer within 75 miles of that worksite is less than 50." [§2611(2)(A),(B)]

To be covered by this act, the employee must first work for a covered employer. Then, the employee must have been employed by that employer for at least one full year and have worked at least 1,250 hours during the previous 12 months of his or her employment. In addition, the employee must work at a worksite which has at least 50 employees working for the employer within a 75 mile radius of that worksite.

Requirements and Prohibitions:

■   An eligible employee of a covered employer "shall be entitled to a total of 12 work-weeks of leave during any 12-month period for one or more of the following: (A) Because of the birth of a son or daughter of the employee and in order to care for such son or daughter. (B) Because of the placement of a son or daughter with the employee for adoption or foster care. (C) In order to care for the spouse, or a son, daughter, or parent of the employee, if such spouse, son, daughter, or parent has a serious health condition. (D) Because of a serious health condition that makes the employee unable to perform the functions of the position of such employee." [§2612(a)(1)]

■   Leave taken under this act can be intermittent if the leave is for reasons C or D, above. Intermittent leave can be taken for the birth of a child or placement of a child with the employee due to adoption or foster care only if both the employee and the employer agree. [§2612(b)]

■ The employer has no obligation to pay an employee who is on leave pursuant to this act. [§2612(c)]

■ An employee may choose to apply any accrued paid leave time to the time they take leave pursuant to this act. In addition, an employer may require an employee to apply any accrued paid leave time to the leave the employee takes. [§2612(d)]

■ An employee who will be requesting leave under this act must give their employer at least 30 days written notice of such intent. However, if a reason exists where a full 30 days notice is not possible, the employee must give as much written notice as is practicable. [§2612(e)]

■ If spouses both work for the same employer, they are not each entitled to 12 weeks leave under this act. Instead, their combined leave under this act in any 12 month period cannot exceed a total of 12 weeks. [§2612(f)]

■ An employer can demand certification, or written verification of the reason for the employee's request for leave. Such a demand, if reasonable, must be complied with. [§2613]

■ While on leave pursuant to this act, an employee cannot lose seniority rights or any other benefit to which they are entitled. If, however, an employee is required to make payments into a benefit plan (whether or not matched by the employer), the employee must continue to make such payments in order to continue coverage under the plan. Employees are not entitled to receive their normal wages while they are absent for FMLA leave. [§2614]

■ Violations of this act will be investigated by the Secretary of Labor. If found to have violated this act, an employer can be ordered to pay to the employee damages equal to the employee's lost wages and benefits, as well as costs and attorney's fees. [§2617]

Exceptions: None, as long as employer is covered by the statute.

Dealing with this Statute: An employer must first determine if they are covered by this act. Next, make a determination of which employees are "eligible employees." It is then simply a matter of understanding the requirements of this act. When proper leave is requested it must be granted. Keep accurate records of employee absences due to the FMLA. An employer should readily be able to determine how much FMLA leave a particular employee has used and has remaining during any 12-month period. Also, keep in mind that the relevant time period is any 12-month period. It is not a calendar or fiscal year that is applied.

A "serious health condition" under the FMLA is defined as "requiring an overnight stay in a hospital, hospice or residential medical care facility or a period of incapacity requiring more than three calendar days' absence and continuing medical treatment." *Bauer v. Varity Dayton-Walther Corp.*, 118 F.3d 1109 (6th Cir.1997). This same standard is also described in *Price v. Marathon Cheese Corp.,* 119 F.3d 330 (5th Cir.1997): "The employee's condition was not serious, since she had not demonstrated the necessity of missing work for more than three consecutive calendar days and receiving treatment."

The notice which an employee who intends to request FMLA leave must give to her employer has also been addressed by the courts. "The FMLA requires employees to give employers sufficient notice, usually 30 days, to prevent unduly disrupting employer operations when advance notice is possible. FMLA regulations state that lesser notice is sufficient when a 30-day notice is impossible," *Hopson v. Quitman County Hospital and Nursing Home, Inc.*, 119 F.3d 363 (5th Cir.1997) The notice given must be an adequate notice of the need for leave or the employee has not properly requested FMLA leave and is not necessarily entitled to the job protections guaranteed by the FMLA, *Carter v. Ford Motor Co.,* 121 F.3d 1146 (8th Cir.1997) It is not necessary that the request for FMLA leave actually state that leave is being requested pursuant to the FMLA. "Even though the employee's letter did not cite the FMLA, it informed the employer that he was taking leave for health reasons. This should have put the employer on notice that the leave might be covered under the FMLA. It was then the employer's responsibility to inform the employee whether the leave was FMLA-qualified," *Stubl v. T.A. Systems, Inc.,* 984 F.Supp. 1075 (E.D.Mich.1997). An employee who is gone for more than 12 weeks in the 12-month period described by the FMLA, even though the employee legitimately cannot return to work due to illness, is no longer protected by the FMLA. The employer of such an employee is not required to keep the person employed, to guarantee their position if they return to work, or to do anything else otherwise required by the FMLA.

15.11 Worker Adjustment and Retraining Notification Act [29 U.S.C. 2101 *et seq.*]

Title and Code: Known as the Layoff Act or as the WARN Act. 29 U.S.C. 2101 *et seq.* Federal Law.

Covered Employers: All employers with 100 or more full time employees, or all employers with 100 or more full and part time employees who in the aggregate work at least 4,000 hours per week (not counting overtime hours).

Covered Employees: All employees who can be classified by this act as being "affected employees." An affected employee includes "employees who may reasonably be expected to experience an employment loss as a consequence of a proposed plant closing or mass layoff by their employer." [§2101(5)]

Requirements and Prohibitions:

■ "An employer shall not order a plant closing or mass layoff until the end of a 60-day period after the employer serves written notice of such an order — (1) to each representative of the affected employees as of the time of the notice or, if there is no such representative at that time, to each affected employee; and (2) to the State or entity designated by the State to carry out rapid response activities . . . and the chief elected official of the unit of local government within which such closing or layoff is to occur. If there is more than one such unit, the unit of local government which the employer pays the highest taxes for the year preceding the year for which the determination is made." [§2102(a)]

■ The term "mass layoff" means "a reduction in force which — (A) is not the result of a plant closing; and (B) results in an employment loss at the single site of employment during any 30-day period for — (i)(I) at least 33 percent of the employees (excluding any part-time employees); and (II) at least 50 employees (excluding any part-time employees); or (ii) at least 500 employees (excluding part-time employees). [§2101(3)]

■ The term "plant closing" means the "permanent or temporary shutdown of a single site of employment, or one or more facilities or operating units within a single site of employment, if the shutdown results in an employment loss at the single site of employment during any 30-day period for 50 or more employees excluding any part-time employees." [§2101(2)]

■ An employer who orders a plant closing or a mass layoff in violation of the notice requirements of this act is liable to each affected employee for lost wages and benefits for the period of time the violation lasts, up to a maximum of 60 days (which is the total notice period required). However, no affected employee can receive damages for more days worth of lost wages and benefits than one-half the total number of days the employee was employed. [§2104(a)]

Exceptions: This act does not apply to a plant closing or a mass layoff if:

(1) the closing is of a temporary facility or the closing or layoff is the result of the completion of a particular project or undertaking, and the affected employees were hired with the understanding that their employment was limited to the duration of the facility or the project or undertaking; or

(2) the closing or layoff constitutes a strike or constitutes a lockout not intended to evade the requirements of this chapter. [§2103]

In addition to the above exemptions, a layoff or plant closing required because of a sudden emergency (usually interpreted to be something out of the control of the employer), or an extension of a layoff, or a decision to turn a layoff into a plant closing is required because of business necessity, in spite of the best efforts of the employer to avoid or prevent such action.

Dealing with this Statute: For covered employers, the only way to deal with this statute is to plan ahead. In addition, any decision must be based on business necessity, which should not be a difficult basis to support or prove.

15.12 State Statutes

Of the federal acts discussed in the previous sections of this chapter, the law of any State is most likely to have its own version of the following:

■　　　Title VII of the Civil Rights Act of 1964;

■　　　Age Discrimination in Employment Act;

■　　　Americans with Disabilities Act;

■　　　Minimum Wage and Hour Law; and,

■　　　Occupational Safety and Health Act.

The common features of the employment laws of each state are:

1) Discrimination in employment is prohibited on the basis of race or color in all circumstances.

2) Discrimination in employment is prohibited on the basis of national origin, religion, sex, age, or disability, unless a good faith occupational qualification exists which applies to the job in question.

3) Generally, all employers who have at least 2 to 4 employees, whether those employees are part time, full time, temporary, or permanent, are covered by state laws outlawing discrimination in employment.

4) Generally, state laws prohibiting age discrimination apply to any individual who is 18 years of age or older.

5) State law that sets a higher minimum wage than federal law will generally control over the federal law standard. State law that sets a lower minimum wage than federal law will only control if it applies to a type of employment or employee not covered by the federal minimum wage requirement.

6) State law requires minimum standards for workplace safety. This can be through a state version of OSHA, as well as through the state's workers' compensation laws.

15.13 Public Policy

Even when there is no state or federal statute prohibiting certain conduct, or which requires certain conduct, certain conduct may be required by "public policy." Public policy is a source of law for employment law purposes. When an employer has engaged in some conduct affecting employees or the employment relationship which is not expressly prohibited or even described by statute, but the conduct of the employer causes some degree of harm, the courts will allow a remedy to resolve the harm. This remedy requires some basis in the law, but this is not usually a problem. It is fairly easy for a judge to compare employer conduct, as well as the consequences of employer conduct, to existing statutes. How to address and resolve the situation is done by determining how similar situations have been handled under current law. The judge's ultimate decision may be unique or insightful to the situation presented in the case, or it may be a variation of the remedy described in the most similar statute. In any event, the judge has used public policy as the basis for finding a remedy where none may have appeared to exist.

CHAPTER 16
Attorneys and Consultants

CONTENTS

16.1 A "Budget Hierarchy" For Using Consultants

There is no law that requires a business to hire and use a lawyer, a certified public accountant, or any other professional consultant in the preparation and implementation of its compliance plan. It is recommended, however, that a lawyer and an appropriately qualified business consultant be used at least for certain portions of the compliance planning process. (See Chapter 1, Section 1.2(c) for the discussion, "Whether to Hire Outside Help to Prepare a Compliance Program.") In addition to any other factors the firm will consider in making this decision, it is the firm's budget that will be one of the crucial factors in how much use it can make of consultants. Therefore, this section will describe a "budget hierarchy" for hiring and using professional consultants. This hierarchy will begin with a plan for the least use of consultants (for the smaller budgets) and progress through full use of consultants (larger budgets).

Checklist 16.1
Budget Hierarchy for Using Consultants

[From least use to full use of consultants.]

❑ Hire an attorney to review your legal research to make sure you have properly identified the laws that apply to your business, that you have a proper understanding of those laws, and that your plan properly deals with these laws.

❑ Hire an attorney to conduct the necessary legal research for you. Specifically, to determine which laws apply to your business and what those laws mean. The attorney may either recommend policies for dealing with these laws, or may review your policies for dealing with these laws, at your discretion.

❑ Hire an attorney to conduct the legal research, described above, and to review the results of your self-analysis, particularly on legal issues. If there are current legal problems, the attorney should notify you in the form of a letter giving legal advice that specific problems exist and what should be done about the problems. By having this information provided from an attorney in the form of legal advice, the information will be confidential between the firm and its attorney. This is crucial, as confidential attorney-client communications are generally immune from discovery in any lawsuits or other legal action that may arise.

❑ Hire an attorney to conduct the legal research and the legal portions of the self-analysis. When finished, the attorney will deliver an opinion to the firm which will detail his or her findings, conclusions, and advice. This legal advice will be confidential between the firm and the attorney.

❑ Hire an attorney for the purposes described above. In addition, hire a professional business consultant to assist in the following issues, listed in order of priority for using this consultant based on the firm's budget: a) firm's self-analysis; b) self-analysis and risk assessment; c) self-analysis, risk assessment; and creation of policies and procedures; d) self-analysis, risk assessment, creation of policies and procedures, and creation of schedule and budget; e) everything in d), and preparation of the compliance officer's job description; and, finally, f) everything in e and creation of the firm's statement of purpose.

❑ Hire the professional consultant as described above, and hire an attorney for legal research, the legal portions of the self-analysis, and to either handle or to work with the consultant on the risk assessment.

(continued on next page)

(Page 2 - Checklist 16.1)

❑ Hire the consultant and the attorney as described above, but also involve the attorney in the creation of policies and procedures.

❑ Regardless of budget or other factors the firm considers when deciding whether and how to use an attorney and consultants, the firm is always ultimately in charge. Attorneys and consultants give advice based on their expertise, but it is the firm that decides what to do with the advice.

❑ When both an attorney and a non-attorney consultant are used, consider the attorney's advice as more relevant than the non-attorney consultant's. The reason for this is that the creation and implementation of an employment law compliance plan is, largely, a legal matter. In legal matters, an attorney's advice is more qualified and, therefore, more relevant than advice obtained from someone who is not an attorney.

16.2 Necessary Qualifications of Consultants

16.2(a) Attorneys

(1) The attorney must be licensed to practice law in the state where the firm does business. If the firm has worksites with employees in more than one state, it will be necessary to use additional attorneys for each state where there is such a worksite. However, the attorney in the state where the principle place of business is located can be given the responsibility for all issues except verifying the requirements of state law outside this home state. The attorneys in the other states would only need to give advice on their respective state's issues.

(2) The attorney should have actual employment law experience. This can include: having prepared employment policies, handbooks, and contracts; representation of either employers or employees in advisory roles and in litigation; the writing of legal opinions, as well as briefs on employment law issues; and, perhaps, having spoken at seminars on employment law, as well as having written on employment law issues. Ask an attorney about their experience.

(3) The fees charged by the attorney must be of an amount and must be based on a method that is acceptable to the employer. Attorney's fees are not at all standardized, which means it is possible to find a fairly wide range of rates, as well as methods of determining fees in most areas. Ask an attorney about the fees they charge and remember, everything is negotiable.

(4) The attorney must be available for personal meetings and correspondence. Any attorney, like anyone in business, is busy, but an attorney should be reasonably available as needed for the firm. Discuss this issue with an attorney before hiring him or her. While no attorney can be available every time a client calls, the attorney and the client should understand that it is absolutely necessary to keep lines of communication open.

(5) When the decision is made to hire a particular attorney, use a written contract to spell out the fees to be charged, how they are to be paid, and what the attorney will be doing for the firm. This contract can be a formal contract, a confirmation letter, a memo, or any format that covers the necessary details.

16.2(b) Non-Attorneys

Non-attorney consultants can include anyone. Professional business consultants can be found for just about any type of matter, particularly in urban areas. A qualified consultant does not only include those who specialize in compliance planning, particularly if they specialize in health care compliance planning and you are a manufacturing firm. Look for the following qualifications:

(1) Education, training and qualifications in the same type of business as your firm. The more familiar they are with the nature of your business, and of its unique characteristics, the better. However, it should be pointed out that a good consultant can learn these things by talking with the firm and through their own research.

(2) Experience in business consultation. Successful consulting skills and abilities are different than being able to successfully run a business. Some people have both capabilities, some have one or the other. When hiring a consultant, it does not matter whether or not they could successfully operate your business; that is not what they are being hired to do. It is only important that they know how to be a good consultant.

(3) The ability to maintain independence in mental attitude as a consultant. One of the advantages of using a consultant is that they are not "burdened" with internal loyalties or conflicts resulting from being a part of the firm. A consultant must remain objective throughout the relationship.

(4) The understanding that the entire relationship and all information, correspondence, reports, and any other material is absolutely confidential.

(5) A demonstrated understanding of compliance planning issues. Ask the person how they know about compliance planning. They may have experience, special training, certification, or other qualifications.

(5) Fees and availability. As with using a lawyer, the fees charged by a consultant, as well as their availability to the firm, must be acceptable to the firm.

(6) Use a written contract with the consultant. Be sure this contract clearly describes what the consultant will be doing and how much it will cost.

16.3 Working with Attorneys and Consultants

When working with any attorney or consultant on a compliance plan, regardless of the level of involvement by the attorney or the consultant with the plan, the firm must understand the nature of this relationship. This relationship is a principal-agent relationship, with the firm being the principal (or the boss), and the attorney/consultant being the agent. Principals and agents have certain obligations to each other under the law. These include:

Principal's Obligations to the Agent:

a) The principal must compensate the agent for services rendered.

b) The principal must reimburse to the agent the costs incurred by the agent on behalf of the principal.

c) The principal must indemnify, or legally protect, the agent from liability incurred by the agent on behalf of the principal.

d) The principal must give the agent sufficient instructions so that the agent knows the scope of his or her authority to act on behalf of the principal.

e) The principal must cooperate with the agent to allow the agent to fulfill his or her obligations to the principal.

Agent's Obligations to the Principal:

a) The agent must act in good faith and with loyalty to the principal when acting on behalf of the principal.

b) The agent must follow the instructions of the principal.

c) The agent must use his or her own knowledge and expertise to carry out the instructions of the principal. When working for the principal, the agent must use whatever degree of care and skill he or she represented as possessing.

d) The agent must report timely and completely to the principal concerning the work he or she is doing for the principal.

e) The agent must preserve the confidential nature of the relationship with the principal.

f) The agent must account to the principal for all property of the principal used by the agent, or which was in the agent's possession or control. This includes cash, records, information, and any other type of property.

g) The agent must comply with the ethical standards of his or her profession.

The failure of either the principal or the agent to comply with these legal duties can result in liability for any damages that result to the other party. Such a legal claim can be based on breach of contract (either party), breach of fiduciary duty (either party, but most often the agent), or professional malpractice (either party, but most often the agent).

CHAPTER 17
Outline for the Employment Law Compliance Plan

CONTENTS

This chapter contains an outline for the employment law compliance plan. It includes sections that are necessary for any firm's compliance plan, as well as optional sections that may or may not be useful for each firm. Optional sections are printed in italics.

17.1 Statement of Purpose

A. Identify the name of the firm and include a general statement of what the firm does or stands for, such as its mission statement.

B. A statement of purpose for the compliance plan.

1. An acknowledgment of the role or importance of the employees to the firm's success;

2. To know and understand the laws, rules and regulations affecting the firm's employer-employee relationships;

3. To remain in compliance with all applicable laws, rules and regulations;

4. Any other statement specific to the firm about its purpose for the compliance plan;

C. A statement that the firm's management is committed to the compliance plan and will support the compliance plan.

D. A statement of specific goals to be accomplished through the compliance plan.

[See Chapter 2, Sections 2.1, 2.2(a), 2.2(a)(1), and Form 2.1. for a full discussion of how to prepare the Statement of Purpose, what information should be included in the Statement of Purpose, and a sample form of this statement. At the same time the Statement of Purpose is prepared, a budget and schedule for completing the compliance plan should also be prepared. See Chapter 2, Section 2.2(b) for information on preparing both the budget and the schedule.]

17.2 Compliance Officer

A. State whether this position is to be occupied by one person or by a committee. State also whether it is to be a full time or a part time position.

B. The job description of the compliance officer or compliance committee.

[See Chapter 2, Sections 2.1, 2.2(c), and Checklist 2.1 for a full discussion on how to select a compliance officer, as well as for the points to include in the compliance officer's job description.]

17.3 The Firm as an Employer — An Analysis

[Note: Chapter 3 explains how to conduct this analysis. This section of the compliance plan cannot be written until the analysis has been completed. All the information must be gathered, compiled, analyzed, and the conclusions made. Reference can be made within this section of the compliance plan to other documents that contain the data and conclusions on which this section is based. Those documents can be physically attached to the compliance plan as appendices.]

A. Current Status of Firm's Employment Practices. (Refer to Chapter 3, Section 3.1 for instructions and discussion on gathering the information necessary to complete this part of the compliance plan, each of the following points is specifically addressed in Section 3.1.)

1. Who is responsible for employment decisions and issues in the company.

2. Size and nature of the firm's work force.

3. Location(s) of the work force.

4. Listing of state and federal employment laws applicable to the firm. (Note: the discussion of these laws is set out in Part IV of this Compliance Plan.)

5. The use of written job descriptions in the firm.

6. Written employment policies of the firm.

7. Informal (unwritten) employment policies of the firm.

8. Firm's practices regarding wages, salaries, benefits and other compensation.

9. Firm's practices regarding employment records, information and statistics.

10. Discussion of all pending claims, complaints or grievances by employees.

B. Trends Which are Developing or Have Developed Concerning Employment Issues in the Firm (Refer to Chapter 3, Section 3.2 for instructions and discussion on gathering the information necessary to complete this part of the compliance plan).

   1. *If the firm is a new employer it will not have any developing trends. Therefore, such a firm would simply state that it has no trends to report.*

   2. Trends that are determined should be explained for what they are. The point is to identify and explain a trend. Then, include further discussions explaining why the trend exists. Whether good, bad or neutral the reasons for the trend are important. Policies will be developed later to encourage the continuation of good trends, and to try to eliminate bad trends.

C. How the Firm Currently Plans for Specific Employment Issues (Refer to Chapter 3, Section 3.3 for instructions and discussion on gathering the information necessary to complete this part of the compliance plan).

   1. General description of how planning is done, by whom, and who has responsibility.

   2. Discussion of specific issues (which may vary widely from firm to firm):

      a. manpower needs;

      b. new job creation;

      c. attracting qualified applicants;

      d. retaining good employees;

      e. controlling injuries and illness;

      f. *increasing productivity; and any other applicable issues.*

17.3(a) Analysis of Competitors' and Industry Standards for Employment Issues

(This section of a compliance plan is optional. The more competitive the firm's business and the more competitive it must be to attract and keep good employees, the more relevance this section will have. The firm's budget will also be an important factor.)

[Note: Chapter 4 describes how to collect and analyze this information.]

    A. Where Responsibility for Employment Issues Rests.

    B. Size and Nature of the Work Force.

    C. Location of the Work Force.

    D. State and Federal Employment Laws that Apply to Competitors and to the Industry in General.

    E. Use of Job Descriptions.

    F. Written Employment Policies.

    G. Informal Employment Policies.

    H. Compensation and Benefits.

    I. Maintaining Employment Records, Information and Statistics.

    J. Employee Claims, Complaints and Grievances.

17.3(b) Analysis of the Market Place

(This section of a compliance plan is optional. The more competitive the firm's business and the more competitive it must be to attract and keep good employees, the more relevance this section will have to the compliance plan. The firm's budget will also be an important factor.)

[Note: Chapter 5 describes how to collect and analyze this information.]

    A. Race, Color and National Origin of Employees.

    B. Sex, Age or Disability of Employees.

    C. Religion of Employees.

    D. Dress of Employees.

    E. Grooming and Cleanliness of Employees.

    F. Demeanor and Attitude of Employees.

    G. Language Ability of Employees.

    H. Hours of Work.

    I. Duties and Responsibilities of an Employee.

17.4 Employment Law Applicable to the Firm

[Note: Chapters 6 through 15 contain discussions of employment law statutes and cases. Read and study these Chapters to determine which laws apply to your firm. In addition, these chapters contain statute and case citations for further research as desired or as necessary. Conduct this research for the specific purpose of determining what law applies to the firm, the requirements of this law and any exceptions. These laws set the legal standard within which the firm must handle its employment issues. Knowing these standards will allow the firm to make appropriate policies for remaining in compliance with the law. Do not begin this part of the compliance plan until the legal research is completed. Additional information is provided in Chapter 1, Section 1.2(b) on how to conduct legal research; and, in Chapter 2, Section 2.2(e), 2.2(e)(1) and, 2.2(e)(2), and Checklists 2.2 and 2.3, more information is contained on conducting legal research and on preparing this section of the compliance plan.]

A. Federal Employment Laws that Apply to the Firm

1. List each federal law by name and by statute number. Explain why it is applicable and give a description of the portions of the law relevant to the firm (which may be a partial or a full description of the law). For example:

   1. *Title VII of the Civil Rights Act of 1964, 42 U.S.C. 2000e et seq., federal law applicable to all employers with 15 or more employees. This firm has had an average work force of 24 employees over the past twelve months; this law applies to the firm. Basically, Title VII prohibits an employer from making any employment decision on the basis of race, color, national origin, religion, or sex, unless an actual, good faith qualification of the job in question requires that an employee be a particular sex, religion or national origin. This exception does not apply to this firm for any job it now has or is contemplating. (Title VII forbids any job qualification to based on race or color, no matter what the job.)*

B. State Employment Laws that Apply to the Firm

1. List each state law by name and by statute number. Explain why it is applicable and give a description of the portions of the law relevant to the firm (which may be a partial or a full description of the law). For example:

   1. *[Name of State] Law Against Discrimination, 11-9-201 et seq., [Name of State] law applicable to all employers in this state with a minimum of 2 employees. This firm has had an average work force of 24 employees during the past twelve months; this law applies to the firm. Basically, this statute prohibits any employer from making any employment decision on the basis of race, color, national origin, state citizenship or residency, religion, sex or age. An exception is when an actual, good faith qualification of the particular job requires an employee to be a particular age, sex, religion, to have or not have a particular national origin, or state citizenship or residency, or when a disability cannot be reasonably accommodated. No exceptions are permitted by this law for qualifications based on race or color. This law is identical to the federal law, Title VII, and is similar to the federal Age Discrimination in Employment Act. However, this state law prohibits age discrimination against anyone 18 years of age or older. The courts of this state routinely consider cases concerning these federal laws when deciding cases involving this state law. (State cases are also considered and are actually given more weight, but there are simply more cases in existence that concern the federal statutes).*

C. Public Policy Issues Applicable to the Firm

1. If cases are found that state a particular public policy concerning employment law is to be applied in the state, describe that case and the relevant policy. If nothing in particular is found on this issue, make any conclusions that seem reasonable. This is especially true for firms who are not covered by federal or state statutes because they do not have the minimum number of employees. For example:

   1. *Public Policy Concerning Disabled Persons. Both federal and state law prohibit discriminating against qualified, disabled persons in employment. These laws require an employer to consider an applicant or employee equally with non-disabled applicants or employees if the disabled person is qualified for the job, and is able to perform the essential functions of the job, either with or without reasonable accommodations being made by the employer. However, the federal law only applies to employers who have a minimum of 15 employees and our state law only applies to employers who have a minimum of 10 employees. This firm has had an average of 7 employees during the past twelve months, which means neither law currently applies. This firm will conclude, however, that based on both the state and federal law, there is a general public policy applicable to all employers that prohibits discrimination in employment against qualified disabled persons. This firm will, therefore, adopt a policy that any disabled person who is qualified for a position they apply for or already have, will be considered for that position on an equal basis as non-disabled persons. When necessary, the firm will attempt to make a reasonable accommodation which may allow any such disabled person to perform the essential functions of the job which they could not other-wise perform. However, the firm will retain the sole discretion in determining whether a particular type of accommodation is reasonable. This determination will be made on a case by case basis, and will consider these factors: nature of the job in question; nature of the person's disability and its actual impact on that person's ability to perform the essential functions of the job; the nature and cost to the firm of the accommodation; likely effectiveness of the accommodation; and, level of disruption to the firm and to other employees of the accommodation.*

17.5 Risk Assessment

[Note A: Chapter 1, Section 1.1; Chapter 2, Section 2.2(f); Checklist 2.4; and, Form 2.2, discuss how to assess the risk to the firm concerning employment law issues. At the end of the firm's analysis of its risk, it should have a form, or series of forms, in which it describes activities relevant to the firm, the legal or other relevant standard for each activity, the firm's status on the activity as compared to the standard, and an assessment of the firm's current level of risk for that activity. This section of the compliance plan can simply state, *See Attached Risk Assessment Forms.* Or, it may refer to the attached risk assessment forms, but also include a summary of the risk assessment here. Or, it may reproduce the risk assessment forms into the compliance plan at this point, followed by any commentary or conclusions the firm, or its lawyer or consultant, believes to be relevant and useful.

Note B: The following is a list of activities that firms should consider for risk assessment. Not all firms will find it useful to consider all activities listed here, and there may be other activities relevant to the needs of a firm that are not listed here. This is a suggested list to be used as the firm or its attorney or consultant believes useful. The list is organized into sections, with activities listed for each section.]

Activities to Consider for Risk Assessment

Job Descriptions:

- How job descriptions are created.

- How job descriptions are reviewed.

- How job descriptions are modified.

- How job descriptions are used.

Advertising for Applicants:

- Use of job description in preparing advertising.

- Types of advertising used by the firm. (List each type separately).

Application and Interview Process:

- Use of prepared application forms.

- Use of resumes prepared by applicant.

- How applications and resumes are received (in person, mail, electronically, etc.).

- How the determination is made regarding which applicants to interview.

- How interviews are conducted. (Be detailed; break this into several activities as appropriate).

- How an applicant is evaluated. (Be detailed; break this into several activities as appropriate).

- How the job description is used during this process.

Testing During the Application Process:

- Types of tests used. (List each type of test separately).

- How each type of test was prepared.

- How each type of test is administered.

- How each type of test is analyzed.

- Use of the job description in determining whether a given test is relevant to a job.

- How the determination is made that a given test is relevant to a particular job.

Deciding Who to Hire:

- Who makes the decision.

- How the decision is made, which factors are considered and the relevance of the factors as compared to each other. Be detailed and break this into several activities as appropriate.

- How unsuccessful candidates are notified.

- How the successful candidates are notified.

Wages and Benefits:

■ Factors used to determine how wages and benefits are set for each position. Be detailed and break this into several activities, based on the factors, as appropriate.

■ Method for determining whether an employee is exempt or non-exempt from state and federal wage and hour statutes.

■ Types of benefits offered. (List each type of benefit separately).

■ Determining what amount to withhold from an employee's pay and why.

Employee Files and Information:

■ Types of information collected and maintained. (List each type separately).

■ How information is collected (i.e., from applications, resumes, credentials, interviews, from forms filled out by employee, etc.)

■ How information is maintained (i.e., in paper or electronic files, both or other methods).

■ Control of access to information.

■ Security measures used with information.

■ How privacy and accuracy of information is ensured.

■ When information is disclosed, and to whom.

Employee Evaluations:

■ Use of the job description during evaluations.

■ How evaluations are conducted and by whom.

■ Frequency of evaluations.

■ Actual purpose(s) of evaluations.

■ How results from evaluations are evaluated.

■ How information obtained during evaluations is maintained.

Employment Policies:

■ How policies are created.

■ How policies are reviewed.

■ How policies are modified and/or rescinded.

■ How employees are informed about the policies, including any changes to policies.

■ Topics covered by written policies. (Identify each topic).

■ How well actual practices compare to written policies. (This should be broken out into a different listing for each policy that differs from actual practices).

■ Topics covered by informal policies. (Identify each topic; some or all of these may or may not be included in the previous item).

Employee Discipline:

■ How warnings are used. (List this as a different activity for each method of warning used in the firm).

■ Other types of discipline used. (List each method separately).

■ Use of progressive discipline.

■ How the job description is used during the discipline of any employee.

Termination of Employment:

■ Handling of employee resignation.

■ Factors determining whether or not an employee who resigned is eligible for rehire.

■ Handling of lay offs.

■ Factors determining whether or not a laid off employee is eligible for rehire.

■ How the decision is made to terminate an employee.

■ How the termination of an employee is handled. (Describe as appropriate).

■ Who is involved in the process of terminating an employee.

■ How the job description is used in the termination process.

■ Factors determining whether or not a terminated employee is eligible for rehire.

■ Ability of a terminated employee to challenge their termination. If this option exists, state the source (i.e., contract, firm policy, etc.), how the process works, when an employee is eligible to challenge their termination, and the factors that may result in the employee not being terminated.

■ How an employee who resigns, is laid off, or is terminated can recover their personal property from the workplace.

■ How an employee who resigns, is laid off, or is terminated returns company property.

■ How insurance and other information or paperwork is presented to an employee who resigns, is laid off, or is terminated.

References:

■   How requests for references about current or former employees are handled.

■   How and when the firm requests references about applicants or employees.

Unemployment Compensation:

■   How the decision is made on whether or not to challenge a claim for unemployment compensation by a former employee.

■   Who makes the decision to challenge a claim for unemployment compensation.

Workers' Compensation:

■   How workers' compensation claims are handled.

■   How the decision is made on whether to challenge a particular claim.

■   How continued employment of an employee during their workers' compensation claim is handled.

■   How the re-employment, or return to work, of an employee who has been unable to work due to injury or illness is handled.

■   How the firm handles an employee who remains employed after the conclusion of their workers' compensation claim, regardless of the outcome of the claim.

Workplace Safety:

■   How the firm generally handles workplace safety.

■   How the firm handles specific workplace safety issues. (List each issue separately).

■   How the firm deals with OSHA.

■   How the firm deals with state agencies who regulate workplace safety.

■   How the firm corrects safety problems.

Internal Employee Complaints and Grievances:

■   Is there is a formal procedure for this issue?

■   If there is a formal procedure, describe it. (Separate into several items as appropriate).

■   If there is not a formal procedure, describe how employee complaints would be handled. If this informal procedure has never been used, describe how it is known that this procedure would be followed. Explain why this informal procedure has not been made into a formal procedure.

■   How employees are notified about the grievance procedure, about how it works, and how they can use it.

■   Who is involved in the handling of grievances.

■   How complaints and grievances are investigated.

■   How the results of the investigation are handled.

Anti-Harassment Policy:

■   Same as in the previous section, *Internal Employee Complaints and Grievances*.

Employee Lawsuits:

■   When a current employee files a lawsuit against the firm, describe how the firm responds, including how the firm determines what, if any, retaliation can legally be taken against the employee (such as firing them).

■   When a former employee files a lawsuit against the firm, describe how the firm responds.

■   How information about the lawsuit is given out within the work place.

■   How the firm handles current employees who are identified as witnesses in the lawsuit, whether as witnesses for the firm or for the plaintiff-employee or former employee.

■   How decisions are made concerning what to do when the lawsuit is resolved (whether through settlement or trial) with or to the plaintiff-employee and any employees who were witnesses or otherwise involved in the lawsuit.

Audits, Surveys, and Investigations by Outside Agencies:

■   How the firm prepares its work force.

■   Consequences to an employee who fails or refuses to participate in the preparation.

■   The role of employees during an audit, survey or investigation.

■   Consequences to an employee who fails or refuses to participate in the actual audit, survey or investigation as they have been prepared by the employer.

■   Follow-up procedures by the firm that involve the employees after completion of the audit, survey or investigation.

■   Consequences to an employee who fails or refuses to participate in any follow-up procedures.

How the Firm Keeps Informed of Employment Law Issues:

■   The firm's attorney.

■   Books, newsletters, and other publications.

■   Meetings and seminars, whether in-house or out.

■   List any other methods.

The final portion of the Risk Assessment section of the compliance plan is a summary in narrative format describing the overall risk of the firm with regard to employment issues. Areas of high risk may be identified together, common themes as causes of moderate or high risk may be described, and the strengths of the firm may be listed, along with recognized reasons for these strengths. The purpose of this last part of the Risk Assessment is to describe what all the charts and information collected during this process mean. It is important that the summary be a summary, not a detailed restatement of all the data in a narrative format. A good summary is useful, but too much information is cumbersome.

17.6 Policies and Procedures

Note 1: See Chapter 2, Section 2.2(g), and Checklist 2.5, Creating and Writing Compliance Plan Policies.

Note 2: There is a difference between the policies of a firm's employment law compliance plan and its regular employment policies. While it is true that there is much overlap between the policies that make up the employment handbook or manual and those that are a part of the compliance plan, the differences between these two sources are their different purposes. A compliance plan is primarily concerned with keeping the firm in compliance with applicable law. An employment manual is primarily a reference for employees (as well as for the employer) that describes how issues of the firm's employment relationships will be handled. The perspective of the employment manual is to set out and describe each issue important to employment with the firm. Therefore, it will include more information, as well as additional policies than are likely to be found in the compliance policies. An employment manual usually includes these subjects: (a) A general introduction or welcome from the firm's CEO to the employees; (b) A brief history of the firm; (c) A description of the firm's management and organizational structure; (d) Names and titles of key personnel and departments, with addresses, telephone and fax numbers, e-mail addresses and Web sites; (e) The firm's mission statement, ethical standards, and philosophy behind doing whatever the firm does; (f) Statement of employment at will; (g) Policies against discrimination, harassment and violence; (h) Procedure for dealing with any claims of discrimination, harassment or violence; (i) Categories or classifications of employees or of employment in the firm; (j) Description of any introductory or training period for new employees; (k) An explanation of what information is required of employees, as well as why this information is required; (l) A description of the contents of and how to obtain access to an employee's own file; (m) Disciplinary and termination policies and procedures; (n) The firm's policy about personal use of firm property, including telephone/fax lines, e-mail accounts, Internet accounts, Intranet accounts, computer and electronic equipment and systems, vehicles, credit cards, postage, petty cash, and so on; (o) How employees are to dress while on the job; (p) How employees are to conduct themselves on the job; (q) Pay schedules; and, (r) Detailed descriptions of all benefits offered by the firm. The purposes of the compliance plan policies, as well as what those policies are and will include, are set out below.

A. Purpose of Compliance Plan Policies and Procedures (This is an introductory section to the actual compliance policies and procedures of the firm. Sections 1 - 5, below, are topics to include in this introduction to the firm's policies and procedures.)

1. To describe how the firm will comply with applicable employment law. *The firm and its management are committed to complying with all employment statutes and policies that apply to the firm. It is our intent to create an environment free of problems and issues that should be avoided. If some issue does arise, however, we will be in a good position to effectively resolve the matter.* This language is the central message to communicate, although it can be expressed in a number of ways.

2. To describe how the firm will handle its employer-employee relationships. This is the "natural" purpose of employment policies and procedures.

3. To make it possible for employees to understand how the firm views its responsibilities as an employer. By reading any firm's employment policies, it is possible to make conclusions about what the firm considers important. Mission statements and general statements that a firm is "committed to its employees" or is "creating a good environment" or that it "wants its personnel to excel in their careers as they help the firm excel" or other such statements are either verified or not by the actual policies of the firm. While not all employees pay attention to things like this, many do, especially those employees who are really determined to excel in their careers (either with the firm or with a competitor). It is necessary that the picture of the firm as an employer created by its policies and procedures matches the firm's own self-image as an employer. This is the issue to address under this topic.

4. To make it possible for employees to understand their obligations to the firm. The employment relationship, as with any relationship, has mutual obligations.

5. To describe how special problems or issues will be handled. This includes grievances, harassment, dealing with specific government regulations that apply to the firm, dealing with specific contract issues between the firm and other companies (including the government), investigations of the firm by government agencies (whether as a routine part of business or as a special matter), and any other matter that is considered by the firm to be more than a "normal" employment issue.

B. The Actual Policies and Procedures. The policies created and adopted by the firm to comply with the law are set out in full at this part of the compliance plan. All but the smallest firms (less than 10 employees, although this number is arbitrary), should prepare comprehensive policies. This means to have policies for all issues relevant to the firm, not just for those issues that the Risk Assessment has determined to be the likeliest source of problems. Use the information from the Risk Assessment to develop policies in such detail, or to develop special policies that may not otherwise have been considered, to deal with areas of risk. If appropriate, base policies for issues of high risk on elements or strategies that have succeeded in creating low risk issues. It is like preparing instructions for driving a car. It is important to have instructions for each thing necessary to successfully drive a car, not just for those things that present the most trouble. For example, if turning left across a divided highway has been identified as a high-risk issue, a set of policies that only covers how to make this turn safely is not of much use for determining how to start the car. Instead, create an issue for everything relevant to the firm, but provide more detail or attention (as appropriate) to the higher risk issues.

Listed below are forms for tables of contents for these policies (they are not presented in any particular order of preference). Following these forms is a detailed analysis of Form 17.1 and how information from the firm's self-analysis, analysis of competition and of the industry, from the market place analysis, from the analysis of applicable employment law, and from the firm's risk assessment are considered in the preparation of the policies. As for the actual wording of each policy, refer to Checklist 2.5: Creating and Writing Compliance Plan Policies; or follow the advice of the firm's attorney or other consultant.

Form 17.1
Table of Contents of Compliance Plan Policies
(Option 1)

❑ Purpose of the Compliance Plan (including statement of management's commitment)

❑ Use of Written Job Descriptions (in general and specific uses such as evaluations)

❑ Hiring Employees (looking for, applications and resumes, interviewing and testing)

❑ Evaluating Employee Performance

❑ Discipline and Termination

❑ Resignations and Lay-Offs

❑ Wages and Benefits (determining wages and addressing each benefit offered)

❑ Employee Files and Information (how and why collected, maintenance and access)

❑ Employment Policies (how they are set, reviewed, changed)

❑ Discrimination and Harassment (a description of what this is and what the firm does about it)

❑ Use of Employer Property by Employees

❑ Property of Employees at the Work Place

❑ Investigations and Searches by the Employer (when and why these may occur)

❑ Employee Grievance Policy

❑ Workplace Safety (how it is monitored and ensured)

❑ Special Issues (this section would include how the firm handles specific rules and regulations of government agencies, terms and conditions of contracts, demands of competition and the market place, etc.)

❑ Staying Informed About Employment Law (how the firm keeps itself knowledgeable)

Form 17.2
Table of Contents of Compliance Plan Policies
(Option 2)

❑ Why We have a Compliance Plan

❑ Our Commitment to our Compliance Plan

❑ Why and How We Use Written Job Descriptions

❑ How We Find Employees

❑ How We Determine Whom to Hire

❑ How We Determine How Well an Employee Performs

❑ How We Handle Discipline

❑ How We Handle Employee Resignations, Lay-Offs, and Termination

❑ How We Determine Wages

❑ How We Handle Issues Involved in Benefits (i.e., eligibility and record keeping)

❑ How We Attempt to Eliminate Discrimination and Harassment from the Work Place

❑ How We Attempt to Ensure Work Place Safety

❑ How and Why We Control Use of Firm Property

❑ How We Respect Employee's Property at the Work Place

❑ How We Handle Specific Rules and Regulations that Apply to Our Industry/Firm

❑ How Employees Can Participate in the Compliance Process (suggestions, complaints)

❑ How We Stay Informed about Relevant Employment Law Issues

Form 17.3
Table of Contents of Compliance Plan Policies
(Option 3)

(This option might be better for smaller firms.)

❑   Purpose of and Commitment to the Compliance Plan

❑   Job Descriptions

❑   Hiring Employees

❑   Performance Evaluations

❑   Resignation and Termination

❑   Wages and Benefits

❑   Discrimination and Harassment

❑   Workplace Safety

❑   Suggestions and Grievances

❑   Special Issues (any that apply to the firm)

❑   Staying Informed About Employment Law

Form 17.4
Table of Contents of Compliance Plan Policies
(Option 4)

(This option is best for a very small employer.)

❑   Purpose of the Compliance Plan

❑   Written Job Descriptions: Why and How they are Used

❑   Specific Issues Addressed (include only those issues that the Risk Assessment
    determined were at any level of risk besides low)

Form 17.5
Detailed Analysis of Table of Contents of Compliance Plan Policies (Option 1)

[Showing how information from the firm's Self-Analysis, Analysis of its Competition and its Industry, from the Market Place Analysis, from the Analysis of Applicable Employment Law, and from the Firm's Risk Assessment, are all considered in the preparation of the policies.]

❑ **Purpose of the Compliance Plan.** This is not merely a restatement of the *Statement of Purpose* from the first part of the compliance plan. It should be as described in paragraph A of this section.

❑ **Use of Written Job Descriptions.** Can include a description of how job descriptions are being used in the firm's industry as a method of setting a non-legal standard for use of job descriptions. The point would be that an analysis of the firm's own policies would result in the conclusion that the firm either meets or exceeds industry standards. The same approach could also be taken for standards among the firm's competitors. The legal standard for what a written job description is can also be given (with legal citations as appropriate, but not necessary), so an analysis of the firm's job descriptions will show a compliance with the legal standard. The key issue is that the firm uses written job descriptions that meet the legal criteria for a job description (to describe the essential functions of a particular job or position). Additional policies in this section would demonstrate how the firm uses its job descriptions: a) when creating advertisements to attract applicants; b) during the hiring process; c) during employee evaluations; d) when considering any action about a particular employee such as modifying responsibilities, promotion, discipline, or termination. When writing each policy on this or on the other issues described below, setting out the standard on which the policy is based is appropriate and even advisable. It demonstrates that the firm is aware of what it is attempting to comply with through each policy.

❑ **Hiring Employees.** A common area of risk to employers is how they handle the hiring of employees. Yes, it is difficult to find good, qualified employees who will stay with the firm for a long time. And, yes, having to worry about legal issues when hiring an employee just seems to make it more difficult. This is why these policies must be carefully prepared, so the firm is allowed to concentrate on finding qualified applicants instead of becoming mired in legalities. Fortunately, the general legal standard for every step in the hiring process is to actually focus on matching the qualifications of applicants to the legitimate, essential requirements of the job. The policies for hiring employees should include techniques for determining the qualifications of each applicant. The firm may already have good techniques for doing this, as may one or more competitors. Industry standards may also describe how to determine qualifications. Market place standards cannot be a justification for unlawful discrimination, but they may help in establishing exactly what the legitimate qualifications are. Use of a proper, written job description throughout the hiring process is a

(continued on next page)

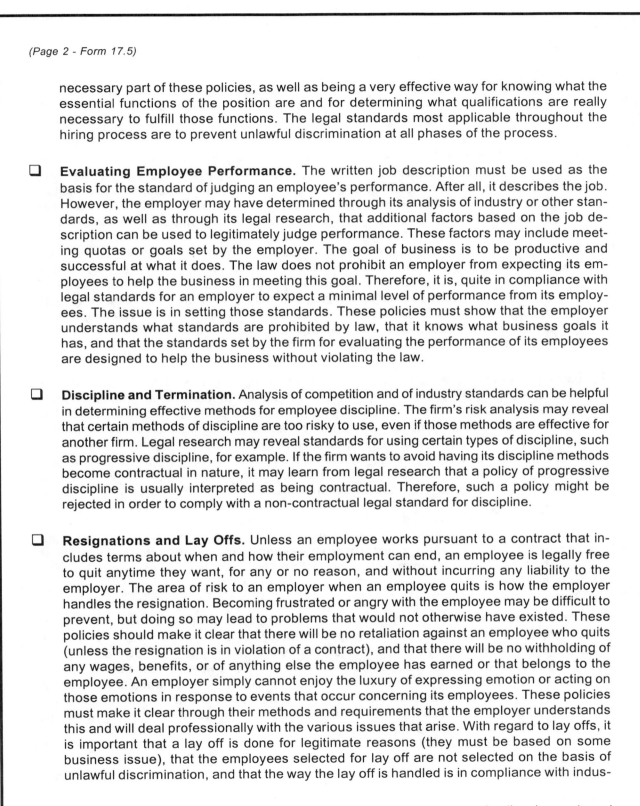

(Page 2 - Form 17.5)

necessary part of these policies, as well as being a very effective way for knowing what the essential functions of the position are and for determining what qualifications are really necessary to fulfill those functions. The legal standards most applicable throughout the hiring process are to prevent unlawful discrimination at all phases of the process.

❑ **Evaluating Employee Performance.** The written job description must be used as the basis for the standard of judging an employee's performance. After all, it describes the job. However, the employer may have determined through its analysis of industry or other standards, as well as through its legal research, that additional factors based on the job description can be used to legitimately judge performance. These factors may include meeting quotas or goals set by the employer. The goal of business is to be productive and successful at what it does. The law does not prohibit an employer from expecting its employees to help the business in meeting this goal. Therefore, it is, quite in compliance with legal standards for an employer to expect a minimal level of performance from its employees. The issue is in setting those standards. These policies must show that the employer understands what standards are prohibited by law, that it knows what business goals it has, and that the standards set by the firm for evaluating the performance of its employees are designed to help the business without violating the law.

❑ **Discipline and Termination.** Analysis of competition and of industry standards can be helpful in determining effective methods for employee discipline. The firm's risk analysis may reveal that certain methods of discipline are too risky to use, even if those methods are effective for another firm. Legal research may reveal standards for using certain types of discipline, such as progressive discipline, for example. If the firm wants to avoid having its discipline methods become contractual in nature, it may learn from legal research that a policy of progressive discipline is usually interpreted as being contractual. Therefore, such a policy might be rejected in order to comply with a non-contractual legal standard for discipline.

❑ **Resignations and Lay Offs.** Unless an employee works pursuant to a contract that includes terms about when and how their employment can end, an employee is legally free to quit anytime they want, for any or no reason, and without incurring any liability to the employer. The area of risk to an employer when an employee quits is how the employer handles the resignation. Becoming frustrated or angry with the employee may be difficult to prevent, but doing so may lead to problems that would not otherwise have existed. These policies should make it clear that there will be no retaliation against an employee who quits (unless the resignation is in violation of a contract), and that there will be no withholding of any wages, benefits, or of anything else the employee has earned or that belongs to the employee. An employer simply cannot enjoy the luxury of expressing emotion or acting on those emotions in response to events that occur concerning its employees. These policies must make it clear through their methods and requirements that the employer understands this and will deal professionally with the various issues that arise. With regard to lay offs, it is important that a lay off is done for legitimate reasons (they must be based on some business issue), that the employees selected for lay off are not selected on the basis of unlawful discrimination, and that the way the lay off is handled is in compliance with indus-

(continued on next page)

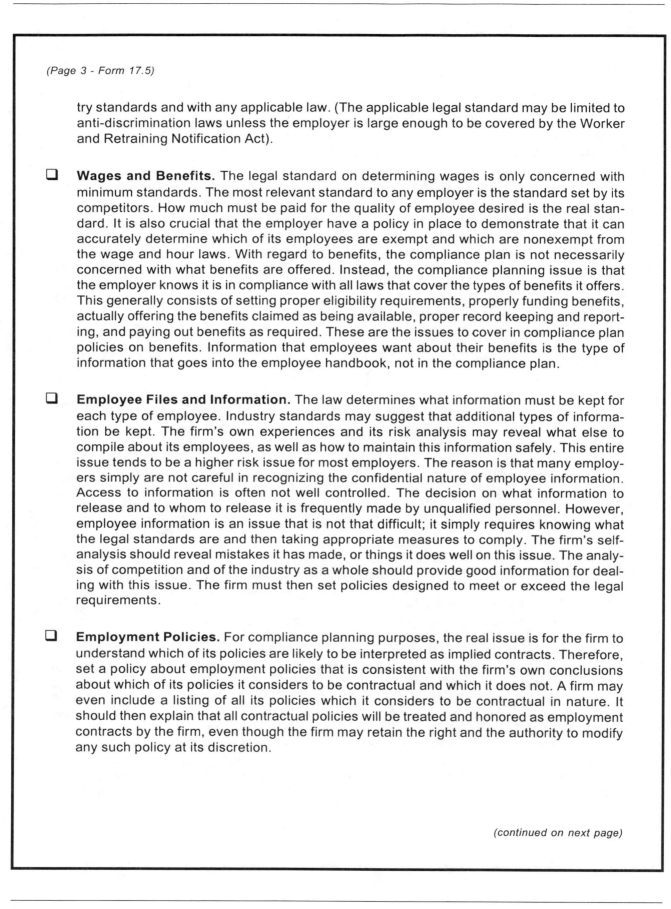

(Page 3 - Form 17.5)

try standards and with any applicable law. (The applicable legal standard may be limited to anti-discrimination laws unless the employer is large enough to be covered by the Worker and Retraining Notification Act).

❑ **Wages and Benefits.** The legal standard on determining wages is only concerned with minimum standards. The most relevant standard to any employer is the standard set by its competitors. How much must be paid for the quality of employee desired is the real standard. It is also crucial that the employer have a policy in place to demonstrate that it can accurately determine which of its employees are exempt and which are nonexempt from the wage and hour laws. With regard to benefits, the compliance plan is not necessarily concerned with what benefits are offered. Instead, the compliance planning issue is that the employer knows it is in compliance with all laws that cover the types of benefits it offers. This generally consists of setting proper eligibility requirements, properly funding benefits, actually offering the benefits claimed as being available, proper record keeping and reporting, and paying out benefits as required. These are the issues to cover in compliance plan policies on benefits. Information that employees want about their benefits is the type of information that goes into the employee handbook, not in the compliance plan.

❑ **Employee Files and Information.** The law determines what information must be kept for each type of employee. Industry standards may suggest that additional types of information be kept. The firm's own experiences and its risk analysis may reveal what else to compile about its employees, as well as how to maintain this information safely. This entire issue tends to be a higher risk issue for most employers. The reason is that many employers simply are not careful in recognizing the confidential nature of employee information. Access to information is often not well controlled. The decision on what information to release and to whom to release it is frequently made by unqualified personnel. However, employee information is an issue that is not that difficult; it simply requires knowing what the legal standards are and then taking appropriate measures to comply. The firm's self-analysis should reveal mistakes it has made, or things it does well on this issue. The analysis of competition and of the industry as a whole should provide good information for dealing with this issue. The firm must then set policies designed to meet or exceed the legal requirements.

❑ **Employment Policies.** For compliance planning purposes, the real issue is for the firm to understand which of its policies are likely to be interpreted as implied contracts. Therefore, set a policy about employment policies that is consistent with the firm's own conclusions about which of its policies it considers to be contractual and which it does not. A firm may even include a listing of all its policies which it considers to be contractual in nature. It should then explain that all contractual policies will be treated and honored as employment contracts by the firm, even though the firm may retain the right and the authority to modify any such policy at its discretion.

(continued on next page)

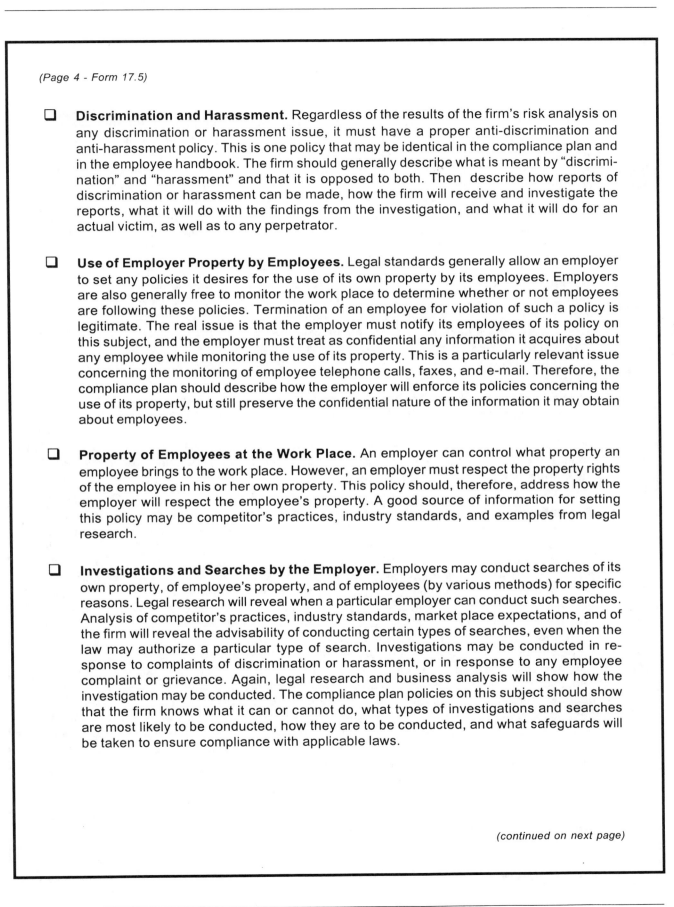

(Page 4 - Form 17.5)

☐ **Discrimination and Harassment.** Regardless of the results of the firm's risk analysis on any discrimination or harassment issue, it must have a proper anti-discrimination and anti-harassment policy. This is one policy that may be identical in the compliance plan and in the employee handbook. The firm should generally describe what is meant by "discrimination" and "harassment" and that it is opposed to both. Then describe how reports of discrimination or harassment can be made, how the firm will receive and investigate the reports, what it will do with the findings from the investigation, and what it will do for an actual victim, as well as to any perpetrator.

☐ **Use of Employer Property by Employees.** Legal standards generally allow an employer to set any policies it desires for the use of its own property by its employees. Employers are also generally free to monitor the work place to determine whether or not employees are following these policies. Termination of an employee for violation of such a policy is legitimate. The real issue is that the employer must notify its employees of its policy on this subject, and the employer must treat as confidential any information it acquires about any employee while monitoring the use of its property. This is a particularly relevant issue concerning the monitoring of employee telephone calls, faxes, and e-mail. Therefore, the compliance plan should describe how the employer will enforce its policies concerning the use of its property, but still preserve the confidential nature of the information it may obtain about employees.

☐ **Property of Employees at the Work Place.** An employer can control what property an employee brings to the work place. However, an employer must respect the property rights of the employee in his or her own property. This policy should, therefore, address how the employer will respect the employee's property. A good source of information for setting this policy may be competitor's practices, industry standards, and examples from legal research.

☐ **Investigations and Searches by the Employer.** Employers may conduct searches of its own property, of employee's property, and of employees (by various methods) for specific reasons. Legal research will reveal when a particular employer can conduct such searches. Analysis of competitor's practices, industry standards, market place expectations, and of the firm will reveal the advisability of conducting certain types of searches, even when the law may authorize a particular type of search. Investigations may be conducted in response to complaints of discrimination or harassment, or in response to any employee complaint or grievance. Again, legal research and business analysis will show how the investigation may be conducted. The compliance plan policies on this subject should show that the firm knows what it can or cannot do, what types of investigations and searches are most likely to be conducted, how they are to be conducted, and what safeguards will be taken to ensure compliance with applicable laws.

(continued on next page)

(Page 5 - Form 17.5)

☐ **Employee Grievance Policy.** Employees have grievances, whether or not those griev-ances are acknowledged by the employer. While no employer wishes to listen to mere whining, it can be beneficial to solicit employee grievances, or comments, on certain is-sues. When a firm has made a commitment to a compliance plan, it should also make a commitment to encouraging employees to give feedback about the effectiveness of the compliance plan. This policy should identify the types of grievances or comments the firm wishes to encourage from employees. In addition, the policy should describe how the firm intends to evaluate and investigate each grievance. Then, when findings and conclusions are made, the policy should state that the firm will take appropriate action.

☐ **Workplace Safety.** The firm's analysis of itself, of this issue with competitors and in the industry, and of concerns from the market place may identify specific safety issues. If so, the firm should determine the appropriate legal standard for those issues and then de-scribe in this policy how it will comply with that standard. If the firm is regularly inspected by OSHA or other workplace safety agencies or organizations, the standards by which those investigations are conducted will be the standards of safety the firm must meet or exceed.

☐ **Responsibility of Employees in the Compliance Plan.** Either as a separate policy, or included in all policies as appropriate, the obligations and responsibilities of employees in ensuring the firm complies with the law must be described. It is impossible to have a compliance plan without requiring employees to take a share of the responsibility for making the plan work. In addition, consequences for failing or refusing to participate in the compliance plan may be described.

☐ **Special Issues.** Any special rule, regulation, local ordinance, policy, or other issue that applies to the firm should be identified and described in separate policies. Each such policy should then describe how the firm will comply with the requirements of each special issue included in its compliance plan. These issues may also include "pet peeves" of the firm's owner or management (as long as it is a legal "pet peeve"). For example, an employer who is enthusiastic about physical fitness may adopt a policy describing how employees who participate in specific fitness programs and achieve certain goals as a result, will become eligible for special benefits like additional vacation days. Such a policy is probably legal, especially if it accommodates employees who are disabled, but it should be described and any legal issues should be addressed. An employer who has specific religious beliefs and who wishes to encourage certain behavior or conduct by employees because of the employer's own religious beliefs must be careful not to create any policy based on religion. It will be necessary, instead, to create a policy that may encourage the desired behavior (such as making charitable donations) for the behavior's own sake, or for public relations purposes, or for some non-discriminatory reason. It may take imagination and effort, but most special policies not required by a formal rule or regulation can be prepared and implemented lawfully.

☐ **Staying Informed About Employment Law.** The purpose of this policy is to state how the firm knows what laws apply to it and how it stays current in its knowledge of the law. It is a policy designed to give validity to the firm's statements of what the legal standards are for its compliance plan policies.

Form 17.6
Sample Format for a Compliance Plan Policy

TITLE OF POLICY: Content of a Job Description

LEGAL STANDARD: A job description is in writing and describes the essential functions required to perform the job.

POLICY: The firm will create and use written job descriptions for each position in the firm. A position that is filled by a number of employees all having essentially the same responsibilities will have one written job description that applies to each employee in that position. Employees who have a unique job or who have unique responsibilities will have their own written job description. Each job description will reasonably describe the essential responsibilities of the job, including the extent of any authority over other employees, any special qualifications required, and whether any bona fide occupational qualifications (as defined by state or federal law) apply to the position.

[Note: This is not necessarily how to write a policy describing the content of a job description. The language in this sample policy is presented as an illustration of a policy format. The key points of this illustration are that the policy has a title (perhaps as well as a number or code for organization purposes), that the relevant legal standard (if any) is given, and that the policy is described and its description complies with the legal standard.]

17.7 Enforcement

A. A statement that, as part of its commitment to its compliance plan, the firm will enforce the policies which make up its compliance plan. This statement may include an acknowledgment that a compliance plan that is not actually used creates a worse situation than not having a compliance plan at all.

B. Description of how the compliance plan will be enforced. This could consist simply of the statement that, "Violations of the compliance plan by any employee or other personnel of this firm will be handled promptly and by such methods as are appropriate for the circumstances." This type of statement is not meaningless, as it simply states the firm is reserving the sole discretion to handle each violation on a case-by-case basis. There is nothing wrong with this approach, as long as the firm is consistent in how it actually deals with violations.

C. Records concerning enforcement measures taken. It is necessary to keep a record of reports or complaints that the compliance plan has been violated, as well as of the response of the firm. These records will demonstrate how the firm handles violations of its compliance plan. If it is apparent that the firm does not take its compliance plan seriously enough to enforce it properly, a court reviewing a dispute will likely conclude that the firm might just as well not even have a compliance plan. The intent of keeping these records is to demonstrate to a court that the firm does, indeed, take its compliance plan seriously and that it enforces it appropriately.

17.8 Training and Education

See Chapter 19, Implementing the Compliance Plan, for a full discussion of this part of the compliance plan.

17.9 Auditing Compliance

See Chapter 20, Maintenance and Modification of the Compliance Plan, for a full discussion of this part of the compliance plan.

CHAPTER 18
Analyzing the Completed Compliance Plan

CONTENTS

18.1 Analysis of the Compliance Plan

When there is a written compliance plan in existence, it means the firm has completed a great deal of work. It has learned a great deal about itself, about its industry and competition, and the market place where it conducts business. It has engaged in legal research, conducted a risk analysis, and has used the information obtained from these efforts to prepare a plan that should keep it out of trouble. Before implementing the compliance plan, however, it is advisable to analyze the completed plan against a checklist to make sure it is ready. It is really no different than a pilot completing a pre-flight checklist before taking off. If there are problems, or if there is a need for some adjustment, it is best to discover and address these issues while it is still relatively easy to do so.

The actual checklist a firm uses to conduct this analysis depends on the nature and extent of its compliance plan. The checklist presented here is based on a fairly extensive compliance plan.

The answer to all questions in the checklist should be "yes."

Checklist 18.1
Analysis of the Compliance Plan

❑ Has the plan been prepared specifically for the firm, as opposed to being a generic plan designed for use by a number of firms?

❑ Has the firm's management actually been involved in the preparation of the plan?

❑ Is there a statement of purpose?

❑ Does the statement of purpose include a statement that the firm's management is committed to the plan? Is this statement of commitment believable?

❑ Has a compliance officer or a compliance committee been chosen?

❑ Is there a clear job description for the compliance officer/committee?

❑ Is the compliance officer/committee ready to begin implementation of the plan?

❑ Regarding the firm's self analysis: Has each issue been investigated? Is all the data available? Has all the data compiled been analyzed? Have all findings and conclusions been made? Does the firm have a clear picture of itself as an employer? Has the firm used the information from this analysis in preparing the compliance plan policies?

❑ Regarding the Analysis of the Firms Competitors (if done): Are the competitors that were analyzed direct competitors? Is the analysis complete? Has all the data been compiled and analyzed? Have all findings and conclusions been made? Does the firm have as clear a picture as possible of its competitors as employers? Has this information been used in preparation of the compliance plan policies?

❑ Regarding the Analysis of Industry Standards (if done). Are there at least some industry standards on employment issues? Have these standards been correctly identified? Have these standards been examined? Have all necessary findings and conclusions been made from this examination? Does the firm have a clear understanding of industry standards that concern employment issues? Has this information been used in preparation of the compliance plan policies?

(continued on next page)

(Page 2 - Checklist 18.1)

❑ Regarding the Analysis of the Market Place (if done): Is this analysis complete? Has all the data been compiled and analyzed? Have all necessary findings and conclusions been made from this examination? Does the firm have a clear understanding of industry standards that concern employment issues? Has this information been used in preparation of the compliance plan policies?

❑ Has the legal research necessary to prepare the plan been completed?

❑ Have all applicable federal employment laws been identified and described for the firm?

❑ Have all applicable state employment laws been identified and described for the firm?

❑ Has public policy on employment law been determined as it applies to the firm?

❑ Does the firm know what it must do to comply with the law? Have the legal standards for the compliance plan policies been determined?

❑ Has the firm's attorney completed his or her review of the plan (whatever the extent of this review may be)?

❑ Is it the opinion of the firm's attorney that the plan is ready to be implemented?

❑ Is the risk assessment complete?

❑ Does the risk assessment make sense?

❑ Does the firm understand its strengths and weaknesses, as well as the reasons for these strengths and weaknesses?

❑ Have the findings and conclusions from the risk analysis been used in the preparation of the compliance plan policies?

❑ Are all the compliance plan policies completed?

❑ Are all necessary issues covered by the policies?

(continued on next page)

(Page 3 - Checklist 18.1)

❑   Are the policies clear and easy to understand? Do they make sense?

❑   Is each policy relevant for the issue it is designed to address?

❑   Does the firm understand the reasoning behind each policy?

❑   Does the firm understand the legal standard applicable to each policy?

❑   Does the firm understand how its self-analysis, the analysis of competition and of industry standards, the analysis of the market place, the legal research, and the risk assessment were all used to prepare the policies?

❑   Does each policy contribute to ensuring that the firm will be in compliance with the law and with any other relevant standard?

❑   Is the firm ready to be judged by these policies?

❑   Does the firm believe itself ready to begin implementation of the policies?

If all the answers to this checklist are "yes," the firm is ready to implement the plan. If there are any "no" answers, or any answer other than an unqualified "yes," the firm should address those particular points from the checklist. If there is an unfinished analysis, incomplete legal research, or a lack of willingness to commit to any policy, or any other issue that is not ready, the firm must resolve the matter before implementing the plan.

CHAPTER 19
Implementing the Compliance Plan

CONTENTS

19.1 Implementation of the Plan

19.1(a) When to Implement the Plan

When the compliance plan is completed, has been analyzed, and is declared to be ready for implementation by the compliance officer and the firm's management, it is time to do so.

19.1(b) The Steps in Implementing the Plan

(1) **Set an Effective Date.** Review the steps presented in this section, determine how long it will take to accomplish them, then pick the date on which the firm's compliance plan will become operational. Each step in this section must be completed before actually implementing the plan with its full force and effect. If the firm desires to phase in the plan through its various work sites, or to phase in the plan by section, or on any other phased-in basis, determine the schedule for accomplishing the phase-in.

(2) **Train and Educate the Firm's Personnel.** Everyone in the firm must know the basics of the compliance plan. Each person should also know the sections of the plan that affect them well. "Everyone in the firm" means everyone, from top to bottom and all parts in-between. No one is to be left out. How to train and educate personnel is described in the Section 19.2.

(3) **Test Personnel.** A test of some sort should be included as part of the training process. This is necessary to demonstrate that the training has been effective. Everyone in the firm should be able to demonstrate that they know their role in the compliance plan. Section 19.3 describes how to conduct this testing.

(4) **Develop a System for On-Going Training.** The initial training given to all personnel prior to the implementation of a compliance plan will become the training program given to all new personnel. There also needs to be a review program administered to all personnel on a regular basis, such as annually. Finally, whenever changes are made to the compliance plan, personnel need to be trained in the changes. Section 19.4 discusses on-going training.

(5) **Do It.** Once the firm's personnel are trained and know what to do, it is time to implement the plan.

19.2 Training Personnel

19.2(a) The Instructor

The instructor or instructors used for training must have the same characteristics as any good teacher. The instructor must know and understand the compliance plan, they must know how to communicate the necessary information to the personnel they are instructing, they must have patience, and they must be willing to encourage and answer as many questions as necessary. Ideally, the firm's compliance officer or committee will be the instructor. If this is simply not possible for some reason, the next choice would be someone else who is a part of the firm. If an attorney or a consultant has been involved throughout the creation of the compliance plan, that person may also be a good choice for the instructor. Only as a last resort should the firm hire someone who is not a part of the firm and who was not involved in the creation of the compliance plan as its instructor.

19.2(b) Facilities and Resources

A small firm (i.e., a couple of owners and 5 employees) may simply go to lunch together, pass out a copy of the compliance plan to everyone, and then explain how the plan works. In fact, some variation of this approach could be very effective for firms of various sizes. The instruction could take place in a conference room, in the biggest office available, in the store before or after hours, or in any other space at the work site large enough to hold everyone in relative comfort. The elements which the facility for instruction should possess are: a) It is large enough to seat the size of group to be instructed; b) Everyone receiving instruction must be able to see and hear the instructor; c) Each person should have a desk, part of a table, or some surface on which to review materials and to write or take notes; d) The facility should be free of distractions, quiet, and well lighted; and, e) The facility must be available for as long as the instruction is to last. Most businesses will have (or can create) such a location at the workplace. However, if a firm has the budget, it may desire to lease conference facilities for conducting instruction.

The basic resources and materials necessary for instruction are a copy of the compliance plan policies for each person, paper for notes, and writing instruments. The need for additional materials will be largely determined by the instructor, by how many people are being instructed at once, and by what is available (i.e., what we have and what we can afford to get). Any additional materials usually include things the instructor needs, such as a projector of some type, a computer terminal, a screen, a blackboard with chalk or markers, a tripod, posters, tape, clips or other types of fasteners, and a pointer.

It may not be necessary for every person to have a copy of the entire compliance plan. All should receive a copy of the Statement of Policy and of the Policies, but the other sections can be made available only for limited distribution. These other sections include a great deal of information that the firm may legitimately decide is to be available on a "need to know" basis only.

Different personnel in the firm may receive their instruction in different facilities. For example, owners and upper management may have the instructor meet with them by appointment in their own office. Key personnel may be taken to a special facility for a somewhat personalized instruction, while rank and file employees will meet in the company cafeteria. It all depends on what works best for the firm as long as the facility is effective for instruction.

If any personnel have a disability that must be accommodated before they can receive their training (including the test at the end of the training), work with that person to arrange the necessary accommodation. This is required by the Americans with Disabilities Act.

19.2(c) When to Schedule Instruction

The first issue is to determine how long the training will take. For most firms, the period of time necessary will be in the range of one to four hours.

If at all possible, it is best to schedule compliance plan training during the regular hours of work of those being trained. This does mean, however, that personnel would not be able to do their regular work during the time taken for instruction. A firm deciding to schedule its training during regular business hours may have to conduct the training on a staggered schedule in order to have personnel on the job while others are being trained.

Another option is to close the business for a part of the day and to conduct training at that time. This could be done by opening late, closing early, or taking a long lunch.

A final option is to schedule the compliance plan training at some time that is not during regular working hours. This could include during lunch, before or after hours, or on a weekend (not recommended unless employees are used to working on weekends at least occasionally).

Employees who are non-exempt from wage and hour laws must be paid their regular wage during any training session, whether it occurs during normal work hours or at another time. In addition, the time spent in training counts towards the determination of a 40-hour week for overtime purposes. Exempt employees do not have to be paid for participating in training.

19.2(d) What to Include in the Instruction

The purpose of the training is for employees to each know what is expected of them from the compliance plan. It is not necessary to include anything about compliance planning in general, or about the firm's own compliance plan that does not go directly to fulfilling this purpose. In fact, the more direct and to-the-point the instruction, the better by far.

As an example for the curriculum a firm may use for its compliance plan training, consider the following:

A) Explain briefly what a compliance plan is, that the firm now has one, and that the purpose of this training is for each person in the firm to learn their role in the compliance plan. (This is to explain why there is a training session and why it matters to the employee.)

B) Make the point that the firm and its owners/management are absolutely committed to the compliance plan. This point must be made in some manner that conveys its significance to the employees. (This is to explain that the compliance plan is serious and will be treated seriously at all times.)

C) Explain the policies in the compliance plan that affect or concern the personnel at the training session. (This is to explain how the plan works and what is expected from the employee.)

D) Throughout the training, encourage questions and answer them all. The whole point is for employees to learn. They must know they can actually ask any question and get a real answer, even if the question is asked several times.

19.3 Testing Personnel

The final part of the training session is a test. This test serves two important purposes: First, it provides feedback about how well a given employee has learned what they should have learned. Second, it provides verification of the effectiveness of the training. Employees who do not pass the test should receive retraining until they are able to pass the test. The employee's test results should also be placed in their employee file. A failure to pass the test could be a basis for termination of employment.

Records of the testing should be maintained with all the compliance planning documentation. It is evidence of how effective the firm has trained its employees in its compliance plan.

The test itself should be a written test that asks several questions to be answered by the employee. The number of questions should not be excessive and should be limited to a range of 10 to 25 questions. The format of the questions may be multiple choice, true-false, short answer, or a combination of these types. Each question should have a clear and precise correct answer. Since someone will inevitably dispute whether their answer is really incorrect and whether the "correct" answer is really correct, it should be possible to show anyone who requests the actual source of the correct answer. Do not set a grading scale, such as A, B, C, D, F. Instead, grade on a Pass/Fail basis. A passing score should be a *minimum* of 70% correct answers, with a higher minimum preferable, such as 85%. The instructor should grade each test and grading should take place immediately after the tests are taken. Results should be made available as soon as possible, with any necessary retesting (or retraining and then retesting) also being scheduled as soon as possible.

The questions on the test should be written by the instructor. The topics to be covered by the questions should be those that are most relevant to the personnel who are being tested. Therefore, ask direct questions about their role in the compliance plan. Examples of test questions (regardless of format) include:

- Who do you talk to if you have questions about the compliance plan?

- How is a violation of the compliance plan reported?

- If you observe one employee harassing another, what are you to do?

- If you believe you are the victim of discrimination, what do you do?

- What is your role during a (government agency) investigation?

- What is the procedure if someone is injured or becomes ill?

The test may require that employees answer from memory or from their notes and any materials that were passed out during the training. If employees are allowed to refer to their notes and to written materials while taking the test, the score required to pass the test should be 95% to 100% correct answers.

19.4 A System of Ongoing Training

19.4(a) New Personnel

Personnel who are new to the firm must be trained. If new personnel come to the firm on a fairly regular basis, regularly scheduled training sessions might be the most useful. If this is not the case, each new employee can receive their compliance plan training as part of the orientation process. The compliance officer can determine whether the training must take place before the person starts work, or within a specific amount of time after they begin working with the firm.

The training received by new personnel, including the test, can be the exact same training conducted when the compliance plan is first implemented. Naturally, training designed to be given to a number of people at once will be modified if it is to be given to new people one at a time. However, the content of the training should be the same. Training of new personnel will be the most extensive system of training in the compliance program.

19.4(b) Regular Reviews of the Compliance Plan

Just because you learn something once does not mean you know it forever. Therefore, on some regular basis, such as once a year, all personnel should be required to participate in a review of their role in the compliance plan. This does not need to be as extensive as the initial training, although it may be. For most firms and employees, however, a one to four hour review each year will be sufficient. The same test that is given to new personnel should be included as a part of this review training. (One option that may be appropriate, at least for some personnel, is to give the test before the review. Those personnel who pass the test with a high percentage of correct answers, such as a 95% minimum, would not be required to participate in the review.)

19.4(c) Training for Changes in the Compliance Plan

Change is inevitable. Over time, some changes will be made to a firm's compliance plan. When these changes affect the role of personnel in the compliance plan, the affected personnel need to be trained in the changes. It may be appropriate to simply add the necessary training to the annual review of the compliance plan. If not, special training sessions should be scheduled to handle the changes.

CHAPTER 20
Maintenance and Modification
Of the Compliance Plan

CONTENTS

20.1 The Necessity of Maintenance

Maintenance of the plan consists of making sure it works. This is the compliance officer's responsibility.

Maintenance includes evaluating the plan's effectiveness. The compliance officer must determine if the compliance plan is actually lowering the firm's risk with regard to employment issues. Problems that may have developed in the past should be prevented, avoided, or lessened because the plan is working. If these types of results are not being realized, the plan may not be working, either because there is a flaw in the plan or it is not being carried out as designed. The compliance officer must determine the answer.

Maintenance also includes: responding to questions about the plan from employees, management, and whoever has a question; making sure that training is occurring as required; preparing reports as required by the firm's management; and recognizing changes in the market place or in legal requirements that may require a change in the plan.

20.2 How to Maintain and Evaluate the Plan

20.2(a) Is the Plan Reducing Risk?

The firm's original risk analysis created a benchmark against which to measure the next risk analysis. Each new analysis of risk creates a new benchmark that can then be compared to the most recent analysis, as well as to previous analyses. By measuring change, or lack of change, between various benchmarks, the firm will be able to determine if the risks being measured are being reduced. As new or different risks are identified, they should be added to the risk analysis, just as risks that are no longer relevant should be removed. A risk does not lose relevance because it is consistently a low risk issue. Instead, a risk loses relevance because the issue no longer matters. For example, risks caused by doing business in a particular state become irrelevant if the firm stops doing business in that state.

The initial risk analysis is based on information gathered by the firm's self-analysis, by its analysis of competitors, of its industry, its market place, as well as through legal research. Each new risk analysis should also be based on an updated analysis of the same factors. It is, however, the firm's self-analysis that is the most important. The compliance officer may even determine that analyzing competitors, the industry, and the market place need only be done every two years or on some other infrequent basis. Self-analysis, by the same methods described in Chapters 2 and 3, should be conducted on a fairly regular, or ongoing basis (based on the size of the firm and its budget). From the results of the self-analysis, the compliance officer can prepare a new risk assessment. After analyzing the new risk assessment, the compliance officer should be able to determine what changes in risk have occurred since the previous assessment. Then the question of whether the plan is reducing risk can be answered.

20.2(b) How is the Plan Being Received by Employees?

What do the employees think of the compliance plan? While it is not necessary for all employees to like a plan in order for it to be effective, if there is actual resistance or distaste for the plan, the reason(s) must be determined.

One method for determining employee acceptance of a plan is to consider the questions they ask. Requests for instructions and how to do certain things described in the plan should be expected, as well as encouraged. These questions usually indicate that employees are attempting to carry out their roles properly. However, if the questions convey a message of, "why do we have to do this?" there could be a problem. Some questions like this would not be unusual, as there is often an initial resistance to something new. A sign of a problem would be that this type of question persists.

Another method for determining employee acceptance is if employees are carrying out their responsibilities under the compliance plan. While not everyone will always do everything exactly as they should, most employees should be fulfilling their obligations. A passive form of rebellion is when people do not do what they are required to do. If this is the situation, there may be a problem. This method will not be effective in all compliance plans, as not every plan will require affirmative conduct on the part of employees.

Consider also any suggestions or comments received from employees about the compliance plan. Are these comments mostly constructive? If so, it shows an acceptance by the employees of the plan. A number of comments about the same issue would indicate a widely recognized need for some attention to the issue. A complete lack of comments may, but does not necessarily, indicate a lack of interest or of caring by the employees. If there are a number of comments that are clearly not constructive, or that send the message that the compliance plan is not working, there might be a problem.

Such observations as described above are helpful, but will not fully answer the question of how the compliance plan is being received by employees. It is necessary to ask questions. Different methods of asking questions and of allowing answers to be given should be used. Most people will not give a useful answer when asked face-to-face. It can be intimidating and the person asked may be concerned about giving an answer that makes them appear a certain way. Therefore, requests should be made fairly often for employees to write out their opinions about the compliance plan as a whole and about certain portions of the plan. They should then be able to submit their opinions in some manner that preserves anonymity, if so desired. While not everyone with an opinion will respond, those with the strongest opinions generally do, as do those who have an interest in or a concern about the firm.

Simply listening is an effective method for determining what people think. Walk around and listen. Ask one person what others are saying. Pay attention to the conversations taking place. Observation, asking questions, and listening carefully are all effective methods of learning.

Make a note of what is learned. Do not be concerned with who has provided the information. The goal is not to find out who likes or does not like the plan. The goal is to determine if there are actual or potential problems with the plan because of the way it is being received.

When reviewing this information, look for patterns and recurring themes. This is the best method for determining exactly what problems might exist. Then determine how the problems should be addressed. A change in a policy may resolve the matter, or a change in training methods may be required to more effectively instruct employees on the real issue behind the problem.

20.2(c) What is Management's Opinion?

Do the owners and/or management like the compliance plan? Do they believe it is worthwhile? The questions and comments of personnel in management should be collected and analyzed in a similar manner as the comments of employees are analyzed. The advantage with management, however, is that members of management (especially if they are also an owner) will more freely tell you exactly what they think. Some may be skeptical or cynical, some may be reluctant to admit a compliance plan could work, or some may be slow to admit there are problems with the plan. Whatever the opinions are, the compliance officer must find out and must determine if there are problems with the plan, with some part of the plan, or merely with an attitude of someone in management.

20.2(d) Are the Demands of Business Changing?

This is an issue always being asked for many reasons. The same methods already in place to find answers to this question should work for compliance planning purposes. If changes occur that effect the compliance plan, the compliance officer must determine if a change in the plan is necessary.

20.2(e) Has the Law Changed?

The law does change, but there is always much more talk about change than actual change. This is especially true of federal law. Any change in federal law requires that a bill be proposed, debated, and passed by Congress, then signed into law by the President. If there is a veto of the bill by the President, the bill dies unless Congress can override the veto. It can take a long time for a bill to successfully make it through this process and actually become a law. Many bills proposed and debated in Congress never become law. Many bills are introduced into the House or the Senate as a political ploy, with the sponsors knowing they will never be approved and sent on to the President. However, news reports may appear, along with much discussion in the media, about such a bill. While it is good to pay attention to such things, unless the bill has a real chance of becoming law, it will have no effect on your firms compliance plan. Information about bills pending in either branch of Congress can be obtained by contacting your Representative or your Senator, or by reading the status of the bill on the Web site of either the House of Representatives [www.house.gov] or of the Senate [www.senate.gov].

One of the best methods for a non-lawyer, as well as for a lawyer, to stay informed of changes in employment law is to subscribe to an employment law newsletter. These newsletters are usually published monthly and contain a great deal of information about new case decisions, potential statutory changes, and actual changes in statutes. While most are written for use by practicing attorneys, they are also very useful to non-lawyers who are trying to stay informed about employment law.

The best method of staying informed about any changes in the law that affect the firm is to talk to a lawyer. Have the firm's lawyer review the compliance plan each year to determine if anything should be changed due to changes in statutes or, more likely, as a result of case decisions. Discuss any such changes with the attorney so the change is understood. Request an opinion letter from the attorney explaining what the change is and what it means for the firm and its compliance plan.

20.3 Modifying the Plan

20.3(a) Making Changes

Based on the compliance officer's maintenance and evaluation of the plan, the decision will be made about whether to make changes and what changes to make. Any such changes should be clearly written and supported.

20.3(b) Implementing Changes

Changes are implemented by actually making them a part of the written compliance plan, and by training personnel in any changes who are affected by the change.

CHAPTER 21
Self-Disclosure and Other Problems

CONTENTS

21.1 Self-Disclosure

A common result of a firm's self-analysis is the discovery of past mistakes or violations of the law in how it prepares and submits billing statements or requests for compensation, as well as in reports prepared and filed pursuant to contracts or government regulations. When such a discovery is made, the firm is faced with two options: keep the discovery to itself; or notify the appropriate party of the past problem. If the firm asks its attorney for a legal opinion on what to do in this situation, the attorney is ethically bound to advise his or her client to follow the law. This usually means the firm must notify its customer, the government agency, or any other party it has done business with who has received an erroneous statement or report that there has been an error. A corrected statement or report would then have to be prepared and submitted. This could result in a reimbursement of funds to the customer, a statement for additional funds, or the termination of a contract. However, this situation is vastly different when the other party is a private business or an individual, or when it is the state or federal government.

There are two federal statutes that apply to this situation, the False Statements Accountability Act [18 U.S.C. 1001 *et seq*.] and the False Claims Act [31 U.S.C. 3729]. The text of each federal statute is set out below:

False Statements Accountability Act [18 U.S.C. 1001 *et seq*.]

Section 1001. Statements or entries generally. (a) Except as otherwise provided in this section, whoever, in any manner within the jurisdiction of the executive, legislative, or judicial branch of the Government of the United States, knowingly and willfully –

- falsifies, conceals, or covers up by any trick, scheme, or device a material fact;

- makes any materially false, fictitious, or fraudulent statement or representation; or

- makes or uses any false writing or document knowing the same to contain any materially false, fictitious, or fraudulent statement or entry; shall be fined under this title or imprisoned not more than 5 years, or both.

(b) Subsection (a) does not apply to a party to a judicial proceeding, or that party's counsel, for statements, representations, writings or documents submitted by such party or counsel to a judge or magistrate in that proceeding.

(c) With respect to any matter within the jurisdiction of the legislative branch, subsection (a) shall apply only to –

(1) administrative matters, including a claim for payment, a matter related to the procurement of property or services, personnel or employment practices, or support services, or a document required by law, rule, or regulation to be submitted to the Congress or any office or officer within the legislative branch; or

(2) any investigation or review, conducted pursuant to the authority of any committee, subcommittee, commission or office of the Congress, consistent with applicable rules of the House or Senate.

False Claims Act [31 U.S.C. 3729]

Section 3729. False claims. **(a) Liability for certain acts.** Any person who –

(1) knowingly presents, or causes to be presented, to an officer or employee of the United States Government or a member of the Armed Forces of the United States a false or fraudulent claim for payment or approval;

(2) knowingly makes, uses, or causes to be made or used, a false record or statement to get a false or fraudulent claim paid or approved by the Government;

(3) conspires to defraud the Government by getting a false or fraudulent claim allowed or paid;

(4) has possession, custody, or control of property or money used, or to be used, by the Government and, intending to defraud the Government or willfully to conceal the property, delivers, or causes to be delivered, less property than the amount for which the person receives a certificate or receipt;

(5) authorized to make or deliver a document certifying receipt of property used, or to be used, by the Government and, intending to defraud the Government, makes or delivers the receipt without completely knowing that the information on the receipt is true;

(6) knowingly buys, or receives as a pledge of an obligation or debt, public property from an officer or employee of the Government, or a member of the Armed Forces, who lawfully may not sell or pledge the property; or

(7) knowingly makes, uses, or causes to be made or used, a false record or statement to conceal, avoid, or decrease an obligation to pay or transmit money or property to the government, is liable to the United States Government for a civil penalty of not less than $5,000 and not more than $10,000, plus 3 times the amount of damages which the Government sustains because of the act of that person, except that if the court finds that –

(A) the person committing the violation of this subsection furnished officials of the United States responsible for investigating false claims violations with all information known to such person about the violation within 30 days after the date on which the defendant first obtained the information;

(B) such person fully cooperated with any Government investigation of such violation; and

(C) at the time such person furnished the United States with the information about the violation, no criminal prosecution, civil action, or administrative action had commenced under this title with respect to such violation, and the person did not have actual knowledge of the existence of an investigation into such violation;

the court may assess not less than 2 times the amount of damages which the Government sustains because of the act of the person. A person violating this subsection shall also be liable to the United States Government for the costs of a civil action brought to recover any such penalty or damages.

(b) Knowing and knowingly defined. For purposes of this section, the terms "knowing" and "knowingly" mean that a person, with respect to information –

(1) has actual knowledge of the information;

(2) acts in deliberate ignorance of the truth or falsity of the information; or

(3) acts in reckless disregard of the truth or falsity of the information, and no proof of specific intent to defraud is required.

(c) Claim defined. For purposes of this section, "claim" includes any request or demand, whether under a contract or otherwise, for money or property which is made to a contractor, grantee, or other recipient if the United States Government provides any portion of the money or property which is requested or demanded, or if the Government will reimburse such contractor, grantee, or other recipient for any portion of the money or property which is requested or demanded.

(d) Exemption from disclosure. Any information furnished pursuant to subparagraphs (A) through (C) of subsection (a) shall be exempt from disclosure under section 552 of title 5.

(e) Exclusion. This section does not apply to claims, records, or statements made under the Internal Revenue Code of 1986.

[Note: 5 U.S.C. 552 (mentioned in subsection (d), above) is the Freedom of Information Act, which calls for the broad disclosure of federal government records. This act requires that federal agencies must disclose agency records unless the specific records requested could be withheld pursuant to one of the enumerated exceptions listed in the statute. Although Congress created these exemptions in recognition of legitimate government and private interests that could be harmed by the release of certain types of information, these exemptions are to be narrowly construed. *U.S. Dept. of Justice v. Julian*, 486 U.S. 1, 108 S.Ct.1606, 100 L.Ed.2d 1 (1988)]

In addition to these two federal statutes, there may also be similar state laws, state licensing laws, and ethical requirements to report such errors and violations. No firm wants to conduct a self-analysis only to discover a need to turn itself in and, therefore, become subjected to the need to reimburse money and, perhaps, pay fines, penalties, or even be subject to a prison sentence. However, discovery of such a problem and then deciding not to report it will undoubtedly amount to a willful and intentional act in violation of any applicable state or federal law. That decision, if discovered, prosecuted, and proven in court, will result in a harsher penalty than would have been the result had the firm turned itself in voluntarily. The best advice this or any book can give on this issue is this: Be aware that a self-analysis can discover problems. Some of these problems are the firm's business alone and can be dealt with internally without violating any law. Other problems, however, may require a self-disclosure to a government agency or to a customer or other contracting party. This self-disclosure will often require money to be reimbursed and even fines and penalties to be paid. However, exactly how to self-disclose this type of information should be done only on the specific advise of the firm's attorney. The disclosure should be made, but the method and timing of the disclosure is a matter to be discussed and decided upon with the firm's attorney.

21.2 Personnel Unwilling to Participate In the Compliance Program

21.2(a) Owners and Management

It is not unusual that a business decides to do something without the unanimous consent of its owners. Whether to invest the time and resources necessary for a compliance program is a decision to be made by the firm's owners. All that is necessary is that the decision be approved in the same manner as other such decisions are approved. If it is not approved, the firm will not prepare and implement a compliance program. If it is approved, even if the approval has dissenters, the firm will prepare and implement a compliance program.

Members of management, from the top on down, are employees of the firm. If the owners of the firm have decided to create and implement a compliance program, management must comply. If they do not, whether it is the CEO, the owners or someone else must deal with the situation as appropriate, either directly or through the appropriate governing body. This can include dismissing the manager or any other action that achieves the desired result.

In companies where there are a small number of owners who are actively involved in business operations, disagreement on any major issue is difficult. There are, unfortunately, no easy solutions. If the ownership is unable to resolve the issue, they may have to table the issue for a period of time. Those who favor a compliance program will simply have to build a case in support of implementing a compliance program in order to convince the other owner(s) that it is necessary.

21.2(b) Employees

Participation in the compliance program can be made a condition of employment for any employee. Inform employees that a compliance program is being implemented and that each employee must participate as required. If they fail or refuse to participate as required, the employee can be disciplined or terminated from employment.

21.3 Gathering Information for Analysis

Conducting research and investigation is not a simple process. It is always a process that takes time, persistence, care and patience. This is true whether conducting a self-analysis, an analysis of competitors, of industry standards, of the market place, or of anything else. If one or more people in the firm have decided to conduct the analysis themselves, they must be prepared for the work. An important aspect of conducting any analysis, however, is recognizing when it is time to get help. Not every person can analyze everything. In addition, an analysis is more difficult when it is done for your own benefit instead of for someone else or for some purpose in which you have no real commitment. This is why a professional consultant is sometimes a better choice for conducting the analyses necessary for preparing a compliance program. While a firm can certainly conduct their own effective analysis, if those conducting the analysis continue to have difficulty in gathering information, in analyzing the information, or in having their analysis and conclusions accepted, they should consider getting outside help. They should at least consider having a good source to consult about their questions and problems.

21.4 Conducting Legal Research

Legal research can be conducted by anyone who is willing to take the time and care necessary. This has been discussed in previous chapters in this book. However, the best person to use for legal research continues to be a lawyer. If the legal research necessary for the compliance plan is a problem, consult with a lawyer. This is one part of the compliance plan that cannot be prepared solely on the basis of watching expenses. After all, this is an *employment law* compliance plan. A legal expert, a lawyer, should have some role in the process.

21.5 Finding a Compliance Officer

There are two parts to this issue: determining whether to have a compliance officer or a compliance committee; and, finding the qualified person(s) for this position.

For the first issue, having a single compliance officer instead of a committee is recommended. While a committee is appropriate for some firms, committees tend to have a difficult time making decisions quickly. Sometimes, the position of compliance officer requires that decisions be made immediately, without the luxury of time to form a consensus for action. This is more easily done by one person than several.

The compliance officer needs, above all, the self-confidence to be able to make decisions and to defend those decisions. Everybody makes mistakes occasionally, but persons in executive positions are there because they have faith in themselves. They know that they will either make the right decision or, if they did not make the best decision, they know they will be able to handle the situation anyway. This is the kind of person who makes a good compliance officer.

Finding a good compliance officer is like finding any other good employee. It is necessary to look hard and carefully, to be willing to pay for the skills needed, and to be tenacious. The best person may already be in the firm, it may be a person who can handle the position along with other responsibilities (especially in a smaller firm where hiring a full time compliance officer is just not an option), or it may be someone who is not yet a part of the firm. The compliance officer is a crucial part of an effective compliance program. It is, therefore, necessary to: a) determine who in the firm has the best skills to handle the compliance officer responsibilities; or, b) who in the firm can work together and share these responsibilities effectively; or c) advertise to find someone outside the firm to handle this position.

Table of Statutes

Table of Cases

Index

[Each topic is referenced to its location by Chapter and Section number.]